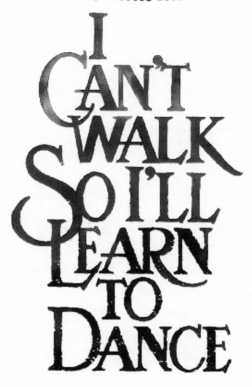

I Can't Walk So I'll Learn To Dance

For over 30 years
doctors thought she should be institutionalized...
then she proved them wrong

Carolyn Martin

With **Gregg Lewis**
Foreword by Philip Yancey

ZondervanPublishingHouse
Grand Rapids, Michigan

A Division of HarperCollins*Publishers*

I Can't Walk—So I'll Learn to Dance
Copyright© 1994 by Carolyn Martin
All rights reserved

Published by Zondervan Publishing House
Grand Rapids, Michigan 49530

Library of Congress Cataloging-in-Publication Data

Martin, Carolyn, 1946-
  I can't walk—so I'll learn to dance / Carolyn Martin with Gregg Lewis.
    p. cm.
  ISBN 0-310-57600-8 (hardcover)
  1. Martin, Carolyn, 1946—Health. 2. Cerebral palsied–United
States–Biography. I. Lewis, Gregg A. II. Title.
RC388.M28   1994
362.1'96836'0092–dc20
[B]   93-49580
                                                                          CIP

In the interests of privacy, some of the names in this story have been changed.

All Scripture quotations, unless otherwise indicated, are taken from the Holy
Bible, New International Version®. NIV®. Copyright© 1973, 1978, 1984 by
International Bible Society. Used by permission of Zondervan Publishing
House. All rights reserved.

Printed in the United States of America

Edited by Dan Runyon and John Sloan
Jacket Design by the Comark Group
Jacket Illustration by Don McClean

94 95 96 97 98 /❖ BP/ 10 9 8 7 6 5 4 3 2 1

This edition is printed on acid-free paper and meets the American National
Standards Institute Z39.48 standard.

CONTENTS

Foreword

by Philip Yancey

It is a peculiarity of cerebral palsy that the outward signs of the condition—floppy arm movements, drooling, inarticulate speech, a bobbing head—make the person appear retarded. Cerebral palsy patients get used to people's discussing "that poor retarded person" within their hearing. In reality, the mind is often the one part of their body that works perfectly; muscular control is what they lack.

Carolyn Martin, who struggles with cerebral palsy, has poor control over her hands and her voice and cannot easily communicate because too often her words come out unformed and muddled. She cannot walk without assistance and spends most days in a wheelchair. As far as is known, she was damaged when doctors used instruments to assist her birth. Left for dead, she managed to survive after a nurse revived her. The thinking part of her brain remained undamaged, although it took several years for anyone in her family to notice that fact.

After she got an education and learned to write, a remarkable story in itself—Carolyn spent years recording her life story in a manuscript that filled many boxes. Writing is hard work for Carolyn. With her hands flopping around, crumpling the paper and knocking the typewriter's guide bar up and down, she spends several minutes positioning a sheet of paper in the proper tracks. As she types, metal key guards help guide her fingers to the right keys, but even so, her fingers often land wrong. To type a single page takes her at least forty-five minutes. Like every good writer, she goes through draft after draft, each time repeating the laborious process.

When I first read Carolyn's manuscript—the original totaled almost fifteen hundred pages!—I felt that I had just gained new eyes that granted me the ability to see into a world I had never before known. Like Helen Keller's autobiography, or *My Left Foot* by Christy Brown, or *The Elephant Man* by John Merrick, Carolyn's book expresses a unique angle of vision that shows life in a startlingly different light. "In my dreams I was always normal," Carolyn says, but this book tells of her reality, not her dreams.

Carolyn was branded an imbecile from birth. Mainly, she lay in a crib and cried all day. Her maturity was stunted in every way, and for that reason she can now remember what has long eluded most of us: the cruel comments other people made about her as an infant, the endless tantrums, the first words she ever spoke, the painstaking process of learning to read. In effect, she is rendering the viewpoint of a two- or three-year-old child.

Like the "Wild Child" in François Truffaut's movie, Carolyn was virtually impossible to civilize. She "walked" by humping along the floor like an upside-down lizard. Fear was a constant companion; she bawled at every stranger, at every new sensation. Feeling helpless and guilt-ridden, she watched as the strain caused by her disability drove her family apart. Isolated inside a body that would not cooperate, unable to communicate outside her own private sphere, she was utterly alone.

"You're not worth the money it would take to educate you," a school counselor informed her. "You're just lazy," said her exasperated father. A doctor hooked her up to an electric shock machine to try to "cure" her. A minister told her that she was "chosen by God" to be disabled. Then, in a scene that defies all comprehension, he sexually abused her.

I found it excruciating just to read some of Carolyn's struggles; I could not imagine living them. Yet the beauty of Carolyn's writing is that she renders these scenes with an unadorned matter-of-factness. She is unafraid to look the fool. This is her life, the only life she has ever known, and she has written this book, she says, in an attempt to fit together the broken pieces. She writes with such compelling honesty that I seldom found myself pitying Carolyn: Pity would be a wholly inappropriate reaction to an account so full of humor, vulnerability, and simple human courage.

For twelve years Carolyn lived in a home populated mainly by mentally retarded patients, which changed everything about her experience of growing up. Looking back on my own life, I think of high school friends like Tom, the captain of the tennis team, and Gary, who played chess on 3 x 5 cards in every class. Carolyn spent her teenage years with friends like Barry, who tore off all his clothes and ate plants and dirt, and Arlene, who only knew three sentences and called everyone "Mama."

I have visited institutions for the mentally retarded, but the residents all tended to blur together into categories: IQ range, type of brain damage, educability. I had never before seen beyond those labels to encounter real, individual people. For that, it took Carolyn Martin, who lived on the other side of the glass windows, incarnate among them as it were, a perceptive mind trapped inside a broken body.

Most of Carolyn's best friends from those formative years are people who would today, due to amniocentesis, likely be aborted. One of the many gifts of Carolyn's manuscript is that she gives us an entirely new view of what it means to be a human being, to contain the image of God inside a body shriveled and deformed and kept alive by feeding tubes. Carolyn herself is the "marginal" kind of person that most modern Americans would abort in the first trimester of pregnancy.

This is no Pollyanna story: Carolyn knows despair, a despair so deep that she looked for ways to kill herself—only to realize that she lacked even the physical ability to accomplish that one act of finality. But she also knows humor and passion; and gradually, over time, she has learned to love and trust as well.

Carolyn has the ability to transform simple acts of life, which we all take for granted, into moments of high drama. Whe she left her wheelchair and wobbled down the aisle to receive her college diploma (she had earned her high school diploma at age twenty-seven), other students and parents stood and cheered and cried for fifteen minutes. When she served me a cup of tea in her living room, I felt like standing and cheering, for I had heard every detail of the three-month process she went through in learning to brew and serve a proper cup of tea without scalding herself or destroying her kitchen.

This book itself is a miracle of grace. In the act of writing, Carolyn has achieved a kind of normality. Held in your hands, this book resembles any other book; it is not deformed and twisted and damaged. Carolyn Martin—aided by the wonderfully selfless talents of Gregg Lewis—has, out of all the pain and struggle, produced something whole and marvelous and good. Carolyn has come to believe, truly believe, that even with her drool and her flailing arms, she experiences and displays the image of God (in view of Isaiah 52–53, perhaps she does so better than most of us). This book stands as proof. In these pages indeed, Carolyn Martin—the woman who can barely walk—has learned to dance.

Acknowledgments

There are numerous people I ought to thank, people without whose help and encouragement this book would never have been written. The contributions many people have made to my life are part of the story, but I'd like to acknowledge a few special people here.

Philip Yancey—a great fellow writer and my good friend. Without the risk he took in meeting me, the personal investment he made in me and my story, the encouraging way he affirmed and believed in me, his prodding and midwifery, my words may have stayed stored away forever in my cardboard box.

Gregg Lewis—a man of integrity. I trusted him with my life's work and he proved to be an exceedingly trustworthy editor and friend.

Nancy Iremonger—Philip gave her the nearly impossible task of organizing twenty-five years of writing that had outgrown three overflowing Washington apple boxes. My work would not have come to birthing without her organizational skills, personal commitment, insights, and creative assistance to Gregg and me through each stage of this project. She is a treasure.

Rose Reynoldson—A woman never afraid of the truth.

Pastor Jim Rismiller—He put the "tools" into my hands and had the faith to believe that with God's help I would do the work.

Karen Mains—She saw a book in my eyes even when I didn't want to write it for fear of the pain it would require. Now I'm free because I released that pain onto hundreds of manuscript pages.

Zondervan Publishing House—I'm grateful to publisher Scott Bolinder, my editors John Sloan and Dan Runyon, and everyone on their publishing team who believed my story deserves to be told.

And finally,

The Lutheran Bible Institute—Its faculty and my fellow students have always been a great encouragement to me.

Introduction

Leftover Funny Bones

You really ought to meet Carolyn Martin. Only when you see the staggering physical challenges she faces every day can you truly appreciate the lifelong journey she has written about here. Only when you encounter the person Carolyn has become can you begin to imagine the emotional and psychological hurdles she has overcome. Only after you struggle to communicate with Carolyn in the most casual and simple conversation can you comprehend the enormity of her task in recounting and writing her life story.

As her coauthor, editor, and friend, I would like to introduce you to Carolyn with a quick snapshot-in-words to provide a clearer picture than you could get looking at any two-dimensional photo.

Carolyn says, "When God created me, he must have used leftover funny bones. Because of my cerebral palsy, I look like a collection of spare parts. Much of the time I forget what my outside looks like. Inside I'm just me. And to me, that's normal."

Most of the people Carolyn encounters see her as anything but "normal." Her obvious physical limitations cause them to assume she's mentally limited as well. They turn away to avoid an awkward personal interaction.

"I suppose I am their worst nightmare," Carolyn continues. "None of my limbs works properly. I leak at both ends. My voice sounds like I have a mouth and throat full of gravel. And when I sing, which I love to do, I sound subhuman. My scarecrow body lists to one side of my wheelchair and

11

my rubber-band neck sends my head bobbing wildly with every movement I make.

"Perhaps some people shy away because they're afraid of becoming like me. (They are only a car wreck away.)"

Carolyn's profound physical limitations turn mundane daily activities into major challenges requiring an exhausting supply of physical energy and emotional fortitude. Preparing and eating meals can be a dreaded adventure fraught with so many spills and thrills that she often seems to burn more calories while cooking than she manages to consume while eating. Factor in the time and energy required to clean up the residue, and you can't blame Carolyn for often feeling eating just isn't worth the effort.

A lifetime of coping with cerebral palsy has taught her to plan carefully and think analytically. There is little that Carolyn can do without first dividing the process into segments, thinking through the large and small motor movements required by each step, and then devoting her full concentration in the attempt to get her maverick muscles to carry out her mind's instruction.

Her limitations have forced Carolyn to become an expert in creative problem solving. Rather than spend ten or fifteen minutes struggling to remove a twist-tie from a new loaf of bread, Carolyn uses a pair of large-handled scissors to snip off the end—twist and all; a simple clothespin then seals the wrapper and keeps the bread fresh. To crack an egg, she puts it in a tea strainer, raps it against the side of the sink, and then fishes out the pieces of shell. To pour something hot, she first places the cup or the bowl in the sink so what she spills runs down the drain without scalding her.

Throughout her apartment are further testaments to Carolyn's ingenuity. On the side of her refrigerator hangs a magnet on a stick—a tool for retrieving can lids that fall on the floor or slide into the sink. In the bathroom she keeps her soap inside an old sock because the all-or-nothing grip of her left hand would send a slippery bar sailing. The front door wears a short leash, the kind you'd use for a big dog, so that Carolyn can easily pull it closed. Beside her phone with huge numbers is an answering machine using a friend's clear voice. The machine asks callers to leave a message so that Carolyn can return their call later when a friend can be there to help translate what she wants to say. Long, wide ribbons hang from lamp-pull chains.

To turn pages when she reads, she uses an eight-inch chunk of broomstick with an old-fashioned rubber thumb-cover stretched over one end.

Daily routines present such difficult challenges, it's amazing Carolyn has the energy or creativity to write. Feeding a sheet of paper into her specially adapted word-processor can take as much as ten minutes. Pecking away in her one-finger style at an estimated typing speed of one page per hour, you have to marvel at the thousands of pages she has written and rewritten for the multiple drafts of this book.

I've trimmed and tightened this story, rearranged some elements, and filled in a few spots, but the ideas and even the words are as much Carolyn's as are her incredible life experiences. For in her writing, Carolyn Martin has finally found a clear voice. You will hear it as you read the rest of this book—her story, her words.

—Gregg Lewis

Chapter 1

Mosaic of My Childhood

I thought that retelling my life story would be like putting a familiar puzzle together. I soon discovered that some of the pieces have been lost and quite a few of the ones I still have are warped or have the images marred. I find it is now impossible to put the puzzle back exactly as it once was. However, I am not the kind of person who ever throws something away just because it is less than perfect.

Over the years I have accumulated bulging boxes in which I store things that seem worthless, in the hope that one day I will look there and find just the right something or other from which I can mend or invent something useful. My junk boxes are very apt metaphors for my life. I, too, am a collection of odd and broken pieces. In writing this book I have pieced them all together to create a mosaic of my life.

———————— • ————————

Some months before I was born in June 1946, my parents were looking at a photo magazine. The cover story showed some children with cerebral palsy. My mom casually commented to my dad, "When we get a little money ahead, we ought to send some to children like these. They need all the help they can get." As it turned out, my parents ended up giving far more than they ever could have imagined to the CP cause.

My mother's labor proved long and difficult. The doctors used forceps to assist my birth. By the time I entered the world, my little body was blue, limp, and lifeless. Seeing neither movement, nor hope for the baby, the doctor turned his attention to my mother, leaving me for dead on a nearby table. A nurse, against the doctor's better judgment, insisted they try to revive me. Someone administered oxygen, and I was granted the privilege of life—with cerebral palsy.

Whether the damage was due to the difficult labor, the use of forceps, or the failure to resuscitate me immediately after birth, the doctor must have suspected problems from the outset. He warned Mom not to expect me to develop at the same pace as her other seven children. But when almost a year passed without my being able to hold my head up, let alone roll over, sit up, or begin to crawl, Mom grew more and more concerned.

As a result of her continued worry and questions, our doctor finally referred me to a neurologist. After examining me, running me through a few basic tests and questioning my mother, this specialist quickly noted the obvious. Not only had I failed to develop any mobility at all, but I showed absolutely no deliberate motor movement whatsoever. While all infants jerk their limbs in uncontrolled random movements, within weeks they normally begin to reach out and touch things. Soon they learn to grasp grownup fingers and favorite toys. At one year of age, I neither reached nor grasped.

I had learned no simple words such as "mama" or "dada," and exhibited no recognizable patterns of vocalized sounds. I cried. I screamed. That was it. Because I couldn't move my head to look at anything that caught my attention and my eyesight was poor, I showed little response to visual stimuli.

At the same time, I overreacted to auditory stimuli. Any new or unexpected noise—it didn't even have to be loud—seemed to trigger mini-explosions through every synapse in my body. My arms and legs would jerk in a violent and uncontrollable startle reflex that invariably surprised me so that I'd cry and often scream in fright.

His initial examination complete, the neurologist gave Mom his diagnosis. He said I was an "imbecile." There was no hope that I would ever be more than a vegetable. He told Mom that the best thing to do was to put me in an institution, try to forget I existed, and "Get on with life."

To fully appreciate my mother's refusal to take that neurologist's advice, you need a quick introduction to my family.

———— • ————

When I made my appearance into the world, my family lived on a small hog ranch in rural San Jose, California. My father, whom everyone in the family called Pappy, worked at the Kaiser Gypsum Plant. In the evenings and every weekend, he and my older brothers and sisters worked the ranch. Pappy's extra vocation always demanded more of him than he wanted to put into it, but the ranch helped feed us. And with eight children to support, it was important to have a steady second income.

Pappy's first loves were hunting, fishing, and tinkering with his guns. Even though the demands of his dual work routines limited his time in the wilds, he always looked like the man he was—a rugged outdoorsman entirely at peace with nature. By the time I came along as the family caboose, Pappy was already gray. What hair he had left seemed to have crept down and fringed around his head. Hair found more fertile ground on his face, where he boasted a soup-strainer mustache, long sideburns, and day-old whiskers as prickly as porcupine quills. He was a tall, large man. But not fat. His dark, serious eyes would gain a certain impish gleam when he felt in a playful mood.

Pappy was bedridden for a year after undergoing stomach and back surgeries. He suffered chronic back problems for years, his condition constantly aggravated by heavy farm work and the daily chore of shoveling tons of food for the hogs.

Mom, with her creamy pink-and-white complexion and her baby-fine hair that refused to stay in place unless she braided it into a bun and shellacked it down with hair spray, had to work the ranch. Her responsibilities included daily garbage runs to get feed for the hogs and regularly driving the animals to market. All this was on top of her regular duties as cook, housekeeper, mother to her large brood of children, and full-time nurse to her invalid husband. That was the year Mom had me.

Most of the time Mom maintained a calm and accepting nature, but she was sometimes frustrated with the overwhelming workload required by a family of our size. She often had to get along with the most minimal of household necessities and never had money for anything that could be termed "luxuries."

Adding to the challenge was Mom's own lack of organizational skills. To keep from misplacing her money and small items of value, she put them in her antique sugar bowls and vases. But Pappy took fiendish delight in letting her know that he knew all her hiding places. Then Mom would get furious and move all her treasures.

Mom and Pappy had a tinderbox relationship that often erupted into fireworks. They always seemed to be extreme opposites who seldom managed to meet each other halfway. Yet they stayed together through their storms even while marching to different drummers and pursuing very different goals.

Mom's dream was to provide a life for her children that was very different from the one she had experienced as a child. After her mother divorced her father for being an unfit husband and parent, her mother supported the small family (Mom had one brother) with her dressmaking skills. But Mom hated growing up on a financial shoestring. Even more, she disliked the feeling of loneliness and promised herself she would one day have a big family and lots of money. She achieved her first goal and continued dreaming of ways to achieve the second.

Pappy was a cautious saver, not a spender. He worked hard. Whenever he worked with his hands or invented something, he was happy. Pappy always seemed reluctant to spend money—especially on anything he considered luxuries (including things like indoor plumbing and heating). He seldom bought anything new. If he could repair something from the junkyard to use on the ranch or in the house, he did.

It took a lot of time and effort for Mom and Pappy to learn the most rudimentary art of cooperation—which they seldom practiced.

The times they did get along, they managed somehow to be a less-than-average team.

———— • ————

During the years our family lived on the ranch, Mom's mother helped with the children. Gaga, which is what we all called my grandmother, lived in a small white stucco house just across our driveway. Gaga was tall, with silver-gray hair she always wore in a hair net. Her wrinkled skin was fun to touch. But she so detested the brown age spots that speckled her hands that she never went anywhere without her gloves—not even to the grocery store. It was her considered opinion that "proper ladies" should never go around gloveless or hatless.

I can't remember Gaga's wearing anything but paisley dresses and her green jade pin. She used Cashmere Bouquet bath powder every day, and on special occasions she smelled of White Shoulders perfume.

———— • ————

Mom appreciated and probably needed all the help she could get raising her big, triple-decker family. On the top deck were my half-brother Don (who belonged to Mom before she met Pappy), Robert, and Maxine. In the middle were Ken and Shirley. And down in the hull were Rosemary, Elizabeth, and me.

Don was nearing twenty when I was born. He seemed more like a good uncle than a brother to us younger kids. He had his own life established as early as I can remember.

Robert was dark and quite stout. He always hated being the shortest among giants, because his sisters used to tease him unmercifully. Fortunately for him, I turned out to be the family runt; though I look taller than my 5'2" because I'm not as rounded and fully packed as other members of my family.

I remember seeing Maxine only once when I was small. She sat in a rattan chair on the porch holding her son, who wasn't much younger than I was. He was terminally ill and died a short time later. After his death, Maxine headed off for Chicago where she worked as a model and an entertainer for many years.

Ken, an eleven-year-old at the time of my birth, was the oldest sibling who actually lived at home for most of my growing up years. Though constantly in trouble with his four younger sisters, his patented (but false) look of innocence often fooled Gaga and Mom and got him out of many deserved spankings. In what may have been a foreshadowing of his career as a fireman, Ken liked to start fires and blame them on one of us.

Shirley, just a year younger than Ken, played the role of big sister. She wore her long brown hair in braids to avoid Gaga's lethal curling irons—the primitive kind that got hot on the stove and seemed the most hideous kind of torture. In the midst of our chaotic family, Shirley set her own pace with a mild, peaceful nature. She was always much more interested in nursing sick animals back to health than she was in high fashion, or even high school.

Rosemary and Elizabeth were two and one year older than I was. They may as well have been twins, for despite being very different personalities, I almost always saw and thought of them together. Those two actually created their own language. Early in life, anyone who wanted to understand Elizabeth would have to ask Rosemary to interpret.

Chubby and shy as a child, Rosemary took her cues from her younger sister. Sober as a miniature judge, Rosemary learned to take Elizabeth's antics in stride.

Elizabeth was the spark, the live wire who made things happen—things that frequently got her in deep trouble with Gaga. She enjoyed being mischievous even when she knew she'd have to bear the consequences. Or maybe I should say "bare" the consequences. I remember the day she called our grandmother an "old battle axe" and then streaked across the pasture buck naked to escape punishment. Whenever Elizabeth got angry, she'd strip and run. And there seemed to be no way Gaga or anyone else could tame her.

———————•———————

I clearly belonged to the Martin family, inheriting the same brown hair and brown eyes as my siblings, but from the beginning everyone realized I was different. Before long I realized it, too.

I lived my first four years in the restrictive but protective confines of my baby buggy. Even at an age when most children are in preschool or dreaming of kindergarten, I couldn't sit up, crawl, or roll over. I couldn't use a spoon or hold a bottle. I couldn't pick up a toy. I had absolutely no voluntary control over any part of my body. My neck muscles remained so weak that my head had to be carefully propped on a pillow all the time to keep me from smothering myself or choking on my own drool.

I don't remember being particularly frustrated by my limitations at that age. I suspect I just accepted the narrow confines of my existence because that was all I'd known. If I felt trapped at all, it probably had less to do with my immobility than my inability to communicate. Without words, I could never tell anyone what I wanted or even let them know I actually wanted something. Unable to do anything but scream and cry, I indeed looked to be the vegetable the doctors predicted I would be.

Chapter 2

A Sassy Little Tomato

Any unexpected noise or unfamiliar voice triggered my hypersensitive startle reflex. I panicked, jerked, and began to scream in terror with each new sound. So my baby buggy always had to be pushed out of a room before a guest or stranger could enter.

My fear of strangers proved a serious obstacle when Mom enrolled me in a special preschool program. No way would I cooperate with any therapist or teacher. I threw toys, screamed, bit, and purposely urinated on those who were so patiently trying to help me. The therapists concluded they could do nothing for me until I settled down and trusted them.

Mom and Gaga were dumbfounded as to how I always knew when they were taking me to the clinic preschool. I was only three years old, so tiny, and always propped between the two of them in the front seat of the car. They knew I couldn't see over the dash or out of the window. I remember thinking how silly they were not to know that trees, telephone poles, and wild smells belong in the country, while tall buildings, automobile horns, and traffic lights belong in the city. I kept track of the smells, the sounds, and the skyline. No matter what route Mom chose to drive to the clinic, I kicked and screamed until she turned the car around and we headed back home.

My tantrums sorely embarrassed Mom and Gaga, but the therapists and teachers were reassuring. They told Mom my behavior could mean I was a survivor who might just make something of myself some-day.

One day when I was three or four, something happened that changed my attitude about strangers. A man I'd never seen before walked into our kitchen. I was about to cry when one of my sisters grabbed the buggy and headed for the bedroom. Just as suddenly, this brave and friendly stranger stopped the buggy, swooped me up in his arms and exclaimed in a fascinating Danish accent, "Hey, aren't you yust a tiny one to be making so much noise?"

He responded to my continuing tantrum of fear in a calm and loving manner. Without trying to shut me up, he just held me while I squirmed and screamed. He was clearly in control. Nothing I could do upset him.

His strategy worked. I eventually quieted and began to study him. We stared each other down. I spotted a candy bar in his shirt pocket and tried to get it. "Oh! You want that? Here try again." He laughed as he slid the candy bar up from the bottom of his pocket and steadied it within my reach. When I squished it with my viselike grasp, he grinned, tore open the wrapper, and fed it to me piece by piece.

Mom and Gaga watched in shocked silence. For the first time in my life I was being civilized enough to let a stranger pick me up and hold me. From that time on, my family let me stay out among people when we had company. And they made a new habit of keeping my buggy close by so I could watch as Gaga and Mom worked around the house. One day when Gaga made a sarcastic comment about Maxine's boyfriend, I laughed out loud. I didn't understand exactly what my grandmother said, but I sensed from her tone of voice that whatever she said was funny and not very nice.

Gaga and Mom turned and stared at me in amazement. Doctors had told them I would be nothing more than a vegetable. Now it seemed I was turning out to be quite a sassy little tomato. Did I really understand what people said to me? How much did I understand? Right then and there Gaga and Mom decided to quiz me on things they thought a four-year-old might know.

"Where is Ken?" was the first question.

I rolled my eyes toward the open kitchen screen door because he and Pappy were outside working. As the questions became more and more precise, I continued to roll my eyes toward the answer. Where were the hinges on the cupboard? Was the potato masher used to stir coffee or mash potatoes?

Mother and grandmother were amazed to discover that I knew the names and uses of all their kitchen utensils as well as the names and whereabouts of each family member. They made such a fuss over me that I remember thinking, *What silly grownups!*

But I also thought, *What a wonderful game!* I was expected to repeat my performance throughout the day for anyone who missed the earlier shows, and I became an instant show-off. But I remained an emotionally explosive child—especially whenever the tension or noise level in the house rose above the usual level of chaos.

Since my two shining moments had come when the house was relatively quiet, Gaga and Mom began to wonder if I might do better in a more stable and calm environment. They decided to move me into my grandmother's little cottage across the drive.

Gaga's house was surrounded by patches of wildflowers, pampas grass, and flower and vegetable gardens. She played music to help me relax and dutifully looked after my every daily need—from feeding me to carefully propping me up in a wooden box and carrying me outside where I could sit in the warm sun and play. This new life with Gaga gave me a sense of security I'd never known before.

We shared our little home with Gaga's black-and-white terrier named Britchy. One look at him explained his name. White in front, with black hindquarters, he looked like he was wearing a pair of dark woolly britches. Britchy wagged his tail almost constantly—especially after a bath. And he got a lot of those because cleanliness was a basic requirement of living with Gaga.

I enjoyed watching Britchy bounce around in play, envying his energy and his mobility. When the afternoons grew hot, he would sleep beside me in the shade. It seemed almost incomprehensible that just across the driveway was a world of anxiety and noise.

The positive effects of the move soon became obvious. Gaga and I had hardly settled into our new routine when I began gaining some coordination. Pappy, using blueprints my therapists gave us, built me a little standing table with a hole cut out of it and a gate to safely enclose me. This table supported me in an upright position and allowed me to play by myself for many enjoyable hours. Pappy painted the table fire-engine red and adapted the plans with adjustable legs so it could "grow" with me.

I was provided a variety of educational toys to help develop dexterity skills. When frustrated with them, I angrily threw them off my standing table. And Gaga would scold me. After many repeated offenses I discovered that if I really concentrated, I could indeed pound the pegs through my toy workbench by gripping the bench with my right hand and using my more coordinated left hand to swing the hammer. With Gaga's constant prompting to "Slow down and think about what you want to do" I learned to do more and more things.

Whenever I tried to hurry or rush through something, I couldn't. Then my frustration would get the best of me, and I'd cry uncontrollably for hours. I cried not only because I was angry about my inability to do what I wanted to do but also because I thought I was such a bad girl for crying so and upsetting Gaga. I desperately wanted to please her.

When calm, I especially enjoyed playing with put-together toys. I quickly grew bored with those framed preschool puzzles with the individual cut-to-fit pieces. They were too easy. I much preferred larger picture puzzles because I felt a sense of accomplishment when I finished one.

I did a lot of trial-and-error learning, so thinking paid off. I worked out a way to stack blocks against the wall to make tables and beds for my dolls. I liked using big blocks with letters and numbers and took great pleasure in learning to recognize the letters of the alphabet.

With all her good common sense about raising children, I think Gaga did have her blind spots with me. She remained overly protective, feeling that she always knew best and had to defend me even from my own brothers and sisters. And she could be terribly indulgent, so much so that I learned to be very manipulative. Once we were shopping in a store when I saw a doll with its own trunk. I simply had to have that doll, so I threw a tantrum. Gaga and Mom were sorely embarrassed and bought the doll just to shut me up. Despite mistakes she might have made, without the love and care Gaga gave me, I might never have calmed down enough to go to school.

———————•———————

One day Mom announced that she wanted to take Gaga and me for a ride. She had found a lovely flower garden some children had planted in a schoolyard and thought I would enjoy seeing it. She assured me that we wouldn't go in the school; she just wanted to show us the garden.

This garden was under the window of a special-education classroom in which I could see children doing interesting things. I wanted to go in right then—especially after Gaga told me the children in that class got to work in the garden and plant pansies. I loved to be down on the ground getting dirty—something Gaga never let me do enough of.

Mom said it would be rude to go in the school that day and disrupt the classroom. But she promised I would be able to go to school very soon if I really wanted to, if I was a good girl, and if I promised to do what the teacher told me to do. I promised. And the momentous day soon arrived.

The thing that impressed me the most my very first day at school was how well all the other children behaved. No screaming. No crying. No tantrums. Each one was sat quietly or stood in stand-up tables that had places for four children each. The kids played quietly together, everyone appeared happy, nothing out of order. I remember thinking how wonderful it would be if I could only be as good as those kids.

The first big test of my resolve to be good came soon after I began school. I was staring out the window, daydreaming, when the teacher warned me to start listening or she would draw the drapes. But I was in a standing table right next to the window. Soon something outside caught my attention again. Without another warning the teacher marched over and pulled the drapes. How surprised I was! Gaga usually threatened me a thousand times before taking any such action. It amazed me that the teacher never got angry. She just walked over and closed the drapes. I immediately understood that she expected me to obey her, and I obeyed without throwing my usual tantrum.

By this time in my life I had some vague awareness that I was somehow "different"—at least in the eyes of some people Gaga and I encountered when she took me shopping. They noticed me riding in a stroller-cart intended for toddler-age children and asked Gaga, "What's wrong with your child?"

But I never felt out of place or "different" at school. My class was part of a special-education program, and my classmates had a variety of handicaps. I think we all had to be tied in our seats, or buckled into a stand-up table to prevent falls. I felt especially sorry for one boy who not only had to be strapped into his seat, but his head had to be tied to the back of his chair to keep him from hurting himself.

At school I enjoyed playing house and doing art. A teacher's aide would carry me over to the housekeeping center, strap me upright in a little chair, and put dress-up clothes on me. Then I would play house with two little boys about my age who wore body braces but could walk. I always played the mother. One of them would be the father and the other, our little boy. For the art activities such as painting, an aide would wrap my fingers around a brush and then move my wrist back and forth to create big, colorful, splashing strokes.

I enjoyed this new kind of playing with friends, but what I loved best of all were the times when aides left me alone to get my hands dirty—fingerpainting, playing with wet clay, or digging up garden dirt. Getting dirty was my idea of true fun. It would have saved Gaga many hours of washing, ironing, and sewing up the seams of my nice frilly dresses had she let me wear my favorite purple overalls more often—especially when I went to physical therapy.

I now cooperated with the therapists, allowing them to strap me to a trike with a high-backed seat and fasten my feet to blocks on the pedals. Just like my new friends, I was soon riding all around the schoolyard wearing a small football helmet, which both protected my head and gave me unprecedented confidence. What fun!

I tried to learn to crawl using a creeper, a canvas sling on a frame with wheels that held me in a crawling position. All I had to do was move my arms and legs in a symmetrical manner—difficult to learn and remember. Frustrating as that was, I wouldn't quit trying. If my classmates could do it, I knew I had to try, too.

Some of the other children at my school rode a school bus—actually a shiny new station wagon with wood-trim doors. I would point and stomp every time I saw it—until Mom and Gaga understood I wanted to ride with the others. Mom and Gaga weren't too sure about the idea at first. After all, I still wasn't able to sit up by myself. But they agreed to let me try.

The young bus driver, Mike, knew just how to reassure my mother and grandmother. He positioned me carefully in the very back seat with two high school girls who attended my school. I sat propped between them while they showed me their books and talked about what the pictures meant. They were so good to me that I hoped to grow up to be just like them.

Each day on the way to school, mothers helping their children onto the bus would often peek into the back and try to coax a response out of me by saying, "Aren't you a sweety! Come on, give me a smile."

They didn't know me very well because I wasn't a sweety at all. I was really a bad little girl for causing my family so much trouble at home.

I had no way to talk about my emotions. When these intense feelings swept over me, they seemed to erupt in uncontrollable giggles, or in violent bursts of anger that resulted in tears, then terrible guilt. And whenever I cried, someone in my family would blame someone else for upsetting me. Then I cried even harder because I was causing so much tension and anger and fighting among the people I loved most.

No one ever told me I was a bad girl. I just knew I was.

Chapter 3

Growing with Gaga

For a long time my family pushed me around in a blue-painted stroller contraption called a Taylor-Tot. I discovered that by hooking my feet under the detachable footrest, I could lift the piece off, stand on the floor, and wheel around in what then amounted to a unique walker. Mom and Gaga exclaimed over my ingenuity.

I soon grew out of the thing, so one of my therapists gave Pappy instructions for building a large baby walker. Gaga made a seat out of heavy muslin, and Pappy constructed the frame and mounted huge casters on it. I wasn't used to such big wheels. On my first test drive it took off so fast that I lost control. Afraid I would fall, I screamed and wanted out.

Gaga held me and scolded Pappy for putting such big casters on a walker. Pappy told her if she knew so much, she could fix it. He stomped out. The walker disappeared, and I never learned what happened to it. I just knew that the problem was my fault. All I seemed to do at home was cause trouble.

Not long after that Pappy took a temporary assignment for Kaiser up in Alaska. No one explained to me why he had to go, but I knew that he was having a lot of arguments with Mom and Gaga. So on some level, if only subconsciously, I thought his leaving was probably my fault as well.

With Pappy in Alaska, we moved off the hog ranch and into what Mom called her "dream house." It had once been a hunting lodge with twelve huge guest rooms and a private wing with its own private entrance. Mom thought all that room would enable her to take in more foster children (something she had done for years) and start a special camp for kids who could stay the summer, enjoy the country setting, and take day trips to points of interest in that part of California.

The grounds surrounding the lodge were wooded like a huge park. Mom had a nice swimming pool built. Though I was terrified of the water at first, I soon enjoyed playing in the pool with the older kids so much that I cried when I had to get out. I particularly loved walking in the water because it helped hold me up and keep my balance.

The bedroom I shared with Gaga had a huge window overlooking a field where migrant workers picked string beans. Later in the day, when the laborers were finished, Gaga rounded up the other kids to go down the rows and pick the leftovers. We then had fresh beans with bacon for supper. I couldn't pick beans, but I could snap the ends off the beans for Gaga, and I loved to help. I never understood why Shirley, Rosemary, and Elizabeth weren't more enthusiastic about it.

———————————•———————————

As a baby I made a few sounds. And from watching my older sisters getting their hair combed, I learned my first real word: "Ow!" But at age six, I still didn't talk. I didn't even try. I had no real need for speech. Gaga anticipated most of my needs and desires. When I wanted to communicate, I pointed, cried, or screamed.

One day when Gaga and I were enjoying the quiet refuge of our big bedroom, she sat me at the table in the middle of the room and cut me a slice of fresh-baked cake to snack on. I had a mouthful of cake and crumbs all over my face when Mom walked in. I looked up and said, "Have a piece of cake."

The words came out thick, muddy, and distorted, but I knew that Mom understood because I saw the surprise on her face. She looked from me to Gaga and asked, "Did you hear that?" Without waiting for a reply, she looked at me again. "What did you say, Posie?" ("Posie" was my family nickname because Mom thought I looked like a fragile little flower.)

When I made my offer again, Mom and Gaga hugged me, repeated my words over and over, and generally acted as if I'd performed the most amazing trick they'd ever seen. I didn't understand why this was such a big deal. I always figured I would talk someday if I really needed to.

Once Mom and Gaga knew I could say some words, however distorted my speech, they forced me to talk. They refused to let me point. In fact, when I pointed, they actually turned their backs and refused to acknowledge me until I tried to say what I wanted. Sometimes I had to repeat myself several times. Often they failed to understand my words even then. But they insisted that I *try* to talk. Gradually my speech began to improve, or else my family learned to interpret my mishmash of sounds. Maybe both.

I couldn't stand to have a new storybook in the house and not know the story. And it never took much pestering to get Gaga to read to me. She was an excellent reader with the natural ability to bring characters alive with the inflections of her voice.

I quickly memorized, word for word, many of the stories my grandmother read to me. Later I recited those stories in my scrambled, distorted speech for my dolls who sat propped against the wall. Once Gaga interrupted a story to ask what I was doing. When I told her I was reading to my dolls, she smiled. I don't think she really understood. At least not like my dolls, who never asked me to repeat myself, talk more slowly, or try a different word. That's why I liked talking and "reading" to them so much.

———————•———————

The size of our new house, plus the fact that Mom and Gaga had more to do than watch me all day, spurred my physical development. In order to explore every corner of that lodge, and to get from one room to another without waiting for someone to move me, I invented my own method of mobility. I'd roll over on my back, bounce on my bottom, and at the same time stiffen and shove my legs out straight, inching my body in the direction my head was pointing. I did this again. And again. Bounce, shove. Bounce, shove. Moving like an upside-down lizard squirming down the hall and into the front room to watch afternoon television with the other kids.

My favorite thing to watch was children dancing.

But I wanted to be a doer, not just a watcher. If I saw children on TV doing somersaults, I saw no reason why I couldn't try them, too. Off I went on my bouncing bottom, down the hall, taking shortcuts through all the dustiest places, to the exercise mattress in a back room. There I diligently practiced my own off-balance gymnastics until I thought they resembled a somersault.

At school and at home I found a growing sense of pride and accomplishment in learning. I was happiest when left alone to learn on my own. Gaga's words: "Think what you are doing! What if I wasn't here to help; what would you do then?" became a challenge. I often refused help and only called Mom or Gaga to come and witness my completed effort.

My newfound confidence and adventurous nature took a serious blow when I tipped my trike over at school and was hospitalized with internal injuries. Mom and Gaga were so upset with the school that when I returned to class they insisted that my teachers encourage me to play quietly. To protect me from recess roughhousing, the teachers entertained me by building a house around me, using huge building blocks as I sat strapped safely in my chair. So I continued to enjoy school even though I was no longer allowed to ride my trike.

———————— • ————————

When school let out for the summer, Mom went to visit Pappy, who had been in Alaska over a year. He didn't like the job Kaiser had sent him to do, but he loved Alaska. He had quit his first job and found construction work, building a dam outside of Anchorage.

He especially liked the big bucks—both the big money on payday, and the big game he could hunt on days off. He had convinced my older brothers Robert and Ken to follow him to Alaska. Now he wanted Mom and us girls to join them. He saw Alaska in the 1950s as a promised land of unlimited adventure and opportunity.

Mom wasn't so sure. She was hesitant enough about taking my older sisters to an uncivilized construction camp. She and Gaga decided it would be unwise to subject me to Alaskan winters. I remained painfully thin and was always cold when the weather turned chilly. On cool, California winter nights I slept with a hot-water bottle. Even then it took my hands and feet two or three hours to warm up in the morning. Alaska was just too big a risk for me.

My family reached this decision: Mom and my sisters would go, but Gaga and I would stay behind. Hard as it was for a seven-year-old girl to be separated from her family, it was probably best. As things turned out, my family's living quarters at the Alaskan construction camp were little more than a tarpapered shack, landscaped with gravel, without indoor plumbing, or even running water.

Alaska may have been Pappy's dream, but it was never Mom's. While she and my sisters had to adjust, Mom never accepted the barbarian lifestyle. She was the talk of the construction camp because she vowed never to serve a meal without a tablecloth, a sugar bowl, and a little cream pitcher on her table. Living in the wilderness didn't mean she had to be so uncivilized as to set plates on a bare table, or doctor her coffee by pouring evaporated milk directly out of the can.

Since there was no school near the job site, the plan was for my sisters to continue their education by correspondence. The Calvert course of study offered academics through the mail in conjunction with the *Book of Knowledge* and *Lands and Peoples*. The books and courses were purchased, but my sisters never completed the work and missed a year of schooling.

For a few months, Gaga and I remained in the old hunting lodge by ourselves. But Mom soon found it impossible to keep up payments on the lodge, and there was no way for her to work out business details, living thirty miles from the nearest town and without a telephone. So Mom's dream house was sold, and Gaga and I moved to Santa Cruz. Gaga thought the ocean and salt air would do me good, and she had many friends along the beach where she had lived and worked in a big hotel years before.

We moved into a rundown beachfront motel owned by Gaga's longtime friends. The units were free-standing cabins, each with its own outhouse in the back. Although Gaga kept our tiny two-room cottage spotless, the musty scent of the sea permeated the walls. I loved the smell, so ageless, lonely, and mysterious—like an old trunk filled with treasures.

Life there was simple. The kitchenette contained a small stove and an ice box for which we had ice delivered twice a week. Gaga kept a red-and-white checkered oilcloth on the little table, where she served meals on mismatched plates and tableware. We drank out of a collection of Cheeze Whiz glasses with a tulip pattern on them. Almost every day we had a fresh bouquet of wildflowers in a carnival glass, peanut-butter jar sitting on the table.

In the bedroom, the only other room, Gaga set up her treadle sewing machine and made most of what we wore. I suppose we couldn't afford new clothes, but Gaga said that "store-bought" clothes never suited her. While she worked, I spent long hours on our bed watching her and using the high-runged footboard as a jungle gym for playing "Tarzan" with my hand-me-down stuffed monkey named Jasper. Jasper slept in an ancient tin trunk along with Gaga's big old family Bible, yellowed newspaper clippings about the 1906 earthquake, and such other personal treasures as an antique mantel clock and a naked porcelain doll Gaga always planned to dress if she ever got around to sewing clothes for it.

On rainy winter days Gaga would open her old trunk carefully, lovingly, go through its contents, and make great plans for a time when we would have "a little house of our own." But some months later, when she was out of money, she sold the trunk and all its contents for fifty dollars. Even though Mom regularly sent money for my expenses, Gaga wanted to feel that she could buy what we needed without asking for help.

Most days Gaga took me up and down the beach and kept up on community gossip by talking to old friends who ran concessions along the boardwalk. Mr. Weaver, the popcorn man, and Nick, who owned a beachfront store, liked to chat with Gaga and remember "the good old days" when she was a regular part of the beach's work force. Several times Gaga pawned her watch to Mr. Weaver and then bought it back when we got a letter and more money from Mom.

Nearly every day we stopped to visit Joe, a disabled vet who lived alone in a house behind the grocery store and always wore a crazy beach hat with a donkey on it. Joe owned a wooden wheelchair with big wheels in front. His chair fascinated me. I wondered if I would have one like it when I got older. I still used a contraption that looked like a big baby stroller that we called my "cart" but was fast outgrowing it.

Sometimes I played alone in the motel courtyard while Gaga sewed, did housework, or worked on the tiny strip of dirt outside our door, which she'd turned into a flower garden. No piece of bare ground remained flowerless if Gaga had her way. But most of my time was spent with people. In addition to Gaga's friends, I often played with two little neighbor girls who loved to pretend school and tried to teach me to spell with my blocks. We also had some college students staying in the big house on our court. Sometimes they played school with us.

Gaga didn't want me going to a real school. Maybe she couldn't see any point in it, or perhaps she remembered the trike accident and worried about my getting hurt again. But Mom remained convinced that I needed an education. She threatened to take me to Alaska to live with her if Gaga didn't arrange to get me back into a formal educational program.

So I was enrolled in a special kindergarten class in Salinas, riding each day with a woman who picked up several other kids along the way. I felt glad to be in a classroom with other children once more. And I enjoyed going to speech therapy and learning how to blow eggshells through a maze because the therapist believed proper breath control was a crucial step to better speech.

I talked a lot at that point. The trick was getting people to understand me. Even though I became an expert at repeating myself, most words came out as clear as mud. I often butted heads with my therapist when he wanted me to say a word I couldn't pronounce and I used another word instead. The frustrated therapist insisted I say it his way. But I could be just as stubborn as he. And he didn't know Gaga and Mom had taught me to think of another way to say the same thing when I couldn't say a particular word, or when they couldn't understand something I said. That made perfect sense to me.

So I didn't think too highly of my new school, and not just because of the speech therapist. I could never figure out why my teacher wanted me to learn to open an envelope with a letter opener. As I struggled to hold the letter still enough to insert the plastic blade, I could feel the teacher's eyes watching me. And I thought, *It's a grown-up's job to open mail. I'm just a kid. Why aren't they teaching me to read?* I didn't understand teachers. And they certainly didn't understand me.

Frustrated as I was with school, I never got bored with learning in my day-to-day world. Billboards had lots of words on them. I knew basic phonics and never considered sounding out a word to hear myself say it. I began to read long before anyone suspected I could. I assumed that all children learned on their own in the same way and that grown-ups just could not figure children out. I got that idea from school.

Perhaps because I had difficulty speaking, I developed a fascination with words. I was especially intrigued by words that sounded the same but had different meanings. On rainy days when no one came out to play, I entertained myself by playing a game in my head, trying to think of all the homonyms I knew—though it was years before I knew they were called "homonyms."

It was also during these wet days on the forlorn and deserted beach that Gaga made me practice the words "Please" and "Thank you." When I forgot or refused to use those words, I would not get what I wanted. Time and again, Gaga would tell me, "Just because it is hard for you to talk doesn't give you the right to be rude to anyone. A young lady always needs to be polite."

On warm winter days after school Gaga took me for walks, pushing my cart along the barren, empty boardwalk. Without another soul in sight, I played alone in the sand while Gaga sat on the wooden steps and watched the churning winter waves. Every so often I noticed a faraway look in my grandmother's eyes. I wondered if the sea was doing what she hoped it would do for me.

My own love of the mighty and wild ocean was passed on to me from Gaga on those lonely afternoons. I came to love the sea's timeless surging and its giant stormy roar.

Chapter 4

Ugly Duckling in Alaska

After Pappy's construction job ended, my parents bought a house in Anchorage near a school that my sisters could attend. It was supposed to be just a temporary place until Mom and Pappy decided what to do next.

In the meantime, Pappy signed on for "bush" jobs at sites so remote they could be reached only by small plane. Such work paid well to compensate for the inconvenience and for the understanding that in bad weather, workers might be stuck out in the bush for as long as three to six months.

With the prospect of Pappy's being gone for months, Mom invited Gaga and me to join the family for an extended visit. I squealed with excitement the day Gaga told me the plans. After more than a year I'd get to see my family again.

Mom and my sisters had traveled to Alaska by ship through the Inland Passage. According to Mom's letters, it was a spectacular trip that Gaga and I just had to take.

I was eight and the only child on board our ship. The stewards appointed me to ring the bell for all meals—they placed my hand on the rope, I clenched my fist around it and yanked with all my might! They never allowed Gaga to so much as lift my cart over a threshold. A crew member was always there with a smile to assist us.

Unlike some passengers, I had no problem getting my "sea legs." The motion of the ship seemed little different from my wobbly gait as I stood in my cart and clutched the ship's rail for balance. Once I lost my shoe, and it nearly tumbled into the water. Gaga scolded me for that because I'd been playfully dangling the shoe on my toes when I dropped it.

We spent most of each day up on deck, watching the ship slice through the icy waves and feeling the sea mist in our faces. When the ship navigated through the silent and glorious Inland Passage itself, I was awestruck by the closeness of so many millions of trees bordering the blue sea with their live green elegance. At the narrowest points in our passage, the forest seemed almost to reach out over the water to shove our ship on its way north.

Mom met us when we docked at Seward. From there we drove through the wilderness to Anchorage. We saw towering forests, mighty rushing rivers, snowcapped mountains, and the rugged, rocky coastline of Cook Inlet. Just as we spotted a road sign announcing *MOOSE PASS*, Mom began to explain that moose frequently crossed the highway. Just then, a mother moose bounded out of the woods and onto the road. Behind her followed twin calves, teetering on long spindly legs and looking terribly awkward and shy.

I squealed with delight over those first wild animals I'd seen in the wilderness. The sight of those moose calves and the scent of that forest were etched in my mind forever. In a single moment, on my very first day in Alaska, I felt forever enchanted by the essence and silent splendor of that uncivilized land.

During the final leg of our trip, Mom apologized and tried to prepare us for the house. She reassured Gaga that it was just a "stopgap." With so many newcomers from the "lower 48," she explained, "There was just nothing else to buy." To hear her talk, it was barely livable, but she kept saying, "At least it's shelter."

The moment we pulled into the driveway, I was fascinated. The place reminded me of a junkyard set on a hill. Weeds, wildflowers, toppled trees, and parts of torn-down cars landscaped the front yard. So much to explore. Steps hewn right out of a steep dirt embankment led up to a homely, wood-framed structure with two front doors. The haunting little box windows could never let in enough sunlight or keep out enough cold to be cheerful or cozy in any of its four rooms.

Pappy had agreed to buy the house after seeing it just once, and that—under the cover of winter darkness. The previous owners explained that they'd built the house using discarded materials, but that never bothered Pappy, especially when they assured him it was well built. He never inspected the house and took the owners at their word because he learned they were "church people." While Pappy himself didn't go to church, he expected anyone who did to be trustworthy. But this time he was disappointed. The previous owners skipped town long before the mask of winter melted off to reveal the flawed truth.

Before moving in, Pappy decided to take up all the rugs because they stank with mildew. It was then he discovered that the house had no real floor—only gunnysacks and cardboard laid over weak, rotted studding without any subfloor to nail to. The front room was one small step from being a junkyard itself. Cold, gray, brick-patterned wallpaper was brightened only by yellow and brown stains marking where water had leaked through the flat roof and down the inside walls.

A good carpenter who took pride in his skill at building everything plumb, Pappy very quickly realized that nothing in that house was level or straight, but he had already bought it, his family had to have shelter, and there was nothing to do but curse the former owners while he tried to tackle the worst of the problems.

Pappy planned to dig a well on our property, but first he would have to put a real foundation under the house so it could withstand the vibrations of well drilling. In the meantime, Gaga and I had to get used to not having running water. Gaga goodnaturedly pitched in to help haul water from a neighbor's well. We heated it on the wood stove in the bedroom.

When it rained, which it seemed to do constantly for weeks after we arrived, we also had to hang laundry in the bedroom to dry. How hilarious it looked to see Pappy's stiff-frozen long johns thawing in front of the stove. My sisters would bring in a stick, and we whacked those long johns to soften them up, laughing and feeling naughty for doing such violence to Pappy's clothes—even if he wasn't in them. Pappy would never have thought it as funny as we did.

One extremely cold morning I awakened to a strange and heavy quiet. I didn't hear the usual dripping of rain on the plastic strung above my bed to divert the water. And when Mom opened the door, I saw that everything outside was blanketed with snow—fresh, quiet, and beautiful.

Our old dog Britchy became a puppy again, bounding out the door and then barking in shock as he hit the fluffy white ground. Though I woke up frozen to the bone, I begged to go out to play and help build my first snowman. Mom talked me into eating breakfast first, then she wrestled me into a snowsuit and boots, carried me outside, and tossed me into a snowbank.

Gaga worried about my getting cold, sitting in the snow for so long, but Mom was enjoying my first snow almost as much as I was. Big fluffy flakes fell from the sky like magic, landing on my upturned face, melting in my open mouth as I laughed out loud. By mid-morning all the trees were finely dressed in white lace, and by mid-afternoon our ugly junkyard had been transformed into a pure white fairyland—a paradise in the cold.

That was also the day we discovered a new wrinkle in my type of cerebral palsy. In playing outside for so long, I got more chilled than I'd ever been in my life. I developed an acute case of what might best be described as "pre–rigor mortis." My usual rag-doll body turned as stiff as Pappy's frozen underwear, and I had to share space in front of the stove with them.

Having grown up in sunny California, Gaga, too, loved watching the snow pile up in the yard. She didn't even seem to mind having to carry a snow shovel with her to the outhouse. Our outdoor toilet back in balmy Santa Cruz had been spotless and came complete with an actual, standard toilet seat. Yet Gaga never complained about our primitive Alaskan backyard outhouse, a no-frills "standard Martin version" with no seat—just a gaping hole where a very wide board had been pried off.

In fact, the hole in our one-hole outhouse was so wide that it seemed a death-defying feat just to perform an act of nature. I was so terrified of falling in and never being found that Mom allowed me to use the chemical toilet in the house that she normally reserved only for civilized company. Allowing this also saved her from having to carry me outside every time I needed to go.

Despite the hazards and hardships of Alaskan life in the mid-fifties, Gaga caught the same vision of opportunity that drew Pappy to this last American frontier. At the age of seventy-six, she decided that she wanted to homestead. During an afternoon drive, she spotted the land she wanted and asked Mom to file on it for her. The site wasn't large, but Gaga envisioned a small log cabin and a little garden clearing nestled in her own birch woods. Though she and my father had never had a very good relationship, he agreed to clear the land and build her a cabin. He told her that it was the least he could do, since she had practically raised me.

Alaska-sized dreams and homesteading always seemed to be important topics of conversation whenever grown-ups got together. But when we kids got bored with eavesdropping, we had our own dreams to pursue, our own plans to make. When adults gathered in our kitchen to talk, kids were usually left to their own devices in the front room. I guess my parents figured the room was past destroying, so nothing short of a noisy, knockdown riot would bring any grown-ups' wrath. No one seemed to keep count of how many friends and neighbor kids were in the front room playing, and I longed to blend into the crowd.

Back in California I'd spent much of my time sitting and playing on the floor. Our Anchorage house was so cold that I had to be confined to a chair for hours and stay wrapped in a blanket. My sisters and their friends often brought their activities to me, handing me toys, letting me hold their dolls, and even moving game pieces for me around a board. But I still wanted to get down and play with them. Gaga forbade me, saying, "Posey, if your mother's mop freezes to that floor, so would you!"

My three sisters understood my frustration. Shirley said she had some baby-sitting money saved up; they could take me to the store and supplement my California-style wardrobe with warmer clothes. We did not ask Gaga or Mom for fear they'd say no. Shirley lifted me into my cart, snuck me out of the house, and pushed me, bouncing and jiggling along the dirt roads to the nearest store—the first time in my life I remembered going anywhere without Mom or Gaga. At the store Shirley let me pick out a pair of green flannel-lined jeans and a yellow-and-green long-sleeved sweatshirt.

After she paid for them, Shirley took me into a dressing room and put the jeans and shirt on me to make sure we couldn't take them back if the grown-ups made a fuss. It made me feel so good, so mischievous to sneak off just as if I was one of the other kids.

Gaga happened to be standing at the kitchen door when we walked up the driveway. You should have seen the shock on her face when she realized I had escaped her watchful eye and gone off with the others as if I'd been doing it all my life. I think when she saw my new pants and shirt, she resigned herself to what she already knew: I was determined to do whatever it took to be like all the other kids.

Gaga reminded me to say *thank you* to Shirley for the warm clothes. And since I was so obviously thrilled and proud of myself for sneaking off, she and Mom forgot to be angry and laughingly told us to go play.

———————— • ————————

Once I was finally given freedom to scoot around and explore the house, nothing escaped my eye. One afternoon I discovered an unfamiliar storybook and tried to sound out the title. The words were too hard, so I took the book to Shirley to read to me.

She had a better idea. "Let's play school, and I'll teach you to read for yourself." We decided it would be a surprise to everyone else. I got really excited because I'd been wanting to read for a long time.

Shirley tucked an old army blanket into the plastic-covered gray-and-red couch in the front room because there was no way for me to stay upright if I had to sit on bare, slippery plastic. She pulled a small, green child's desk over in front of me. Then she proceeded to make my first "reader" out of pieces of cardboard, bound together with heavy string so I could grasp it and turn the pages without tearing them.

Shirley worked magic with scissors, crayons, and cardboard, making Dick and Jane do all the same things they did in real first-grade readers. We shooed Gaga and Mom from the living room, Shirley telling them if they came back or even peeked in the door, we wouldn't let them see our surprise. They left us alone because we were being so quiet and good.

Shirley reviewed what I already knew about basic phonics, and I relied on common sense to figure out some words, but some of the words she showed me seemed to be exceptions to the rules. So I decided to open the book and just read. A few of the words I recognized from billboards in California or newspaper headlines. Shirley had always been pretty good at deciphering my attempts at speech, but I think I surprised her and even myself. Reading was much easier than I thought it would be!

Before long, Shirley decided I was ready and called Gaga and Mom in for our surprise. They were indeed amazed at my sudden ability to read and especially at the way I sounded out the more difficult words. They wanted to know how I knew so many more words than Gaga had taught me to say. I explained that I always tried to figure out words whenever I saw them, because it was fun.

Mom kept exclaiming over and over again what a "little stinker" I was. She realized I knew a lot more than I let on, because I was always looking and listening and curious about everything. Both she and Gaga acted so pleased with me, saying that it was a wonderful surprise. They also praised Shirley's workmanship on the cardboard reader as well as her obvious teaching ability.

Not long after that surprise, Mom made an appointment at the Alaska Crippled Children's Association (ACCA) to have me tested and to find out what educational opportunities would be available. I got very excited about the prospect of going to a real school. I was fed up with special education "kindergarten" with its games and long hours of therapy. Why had I been stuck in kindergarten so long just because I had trouble walking and talking? What good would walking or talking ever do me if I didn't know how to read or write or spell or do numbers?

I was puzzled by our first visit to the ACCA. Even as an eight-year-old I thought it very strange that the offices of an organization for crippled children would be housed above a store and could be reached only by climbing a narrow, steep, and icy outside stairway and then wrestling open a storm door and a second inner door while trying to stand on a tiny, slippery landing.

Inside we found two large rooms. One for therapy, the other a school classroom. The classroom particularly interested me. I spotted a huge felt calendar with dates that could be taken off and put back on. There were blackboards, tables, desks, and books. I knew this was where I wanted to be—learning in a real first grade instead of being stuck in a never-ending kindergarten.

The tests I took that day were easy and fun. The hardest part was climbing up another flight of narrow stairs to the psychologist's office. Once I got there and was comfortably seated, all I had to do was match some pictures and spot what was missing from other pictures. Nothing to it.

A few days later a tutor began coming to our house every day during school hours. Mrs. Stoner had never taught a child with such profound disability—unable to speak, grip a pencil, or even turn pages by herself. But then I'd never had a teacher who had books and pencils and paper. So we both had a lot to learn. I felt very happy and very grown up because I finally had schoolbooks just like other kids.

Mrs. Stoner was an older woman, very gentle and mild-mannered. She didn't know what to think when she began explaining things that she assumed I didn't know and I would already be two steps ahead of her. Mom had to explain to the bewildered tutor that I'd been playing school with my sisters and had apparently taken my play quite seriously and learned the basics. Mrs. Stoner acted impressed. She said that if I was so motivated to learn, it would make her job easy and enjoyable.

———————————•———————————

Gaga and I left Anchorage and flew back to California for the worst part of that winter, but instead of returning to the beach at Santa Cruz, we went to San Jose, where I could have another tutor for the remainder of the school year. The plan was that when summer came,

Gaga and I would pack up and move to Alaska for good. Gaga would get her dream cabin on her homestead. I would finally live with my own family and go to school at the ACCA.

While I'd always loved living with Gaga, I wanted to be with my family. I wanted to grow up with my sisters. Most of all, I wanted to go to school. I felt that the biggest thing separating me from my sisters and their friends, what made me feel different, wasn't so much the physical effects of my cerebral palsy as the disturbing fact that I didn't go to school like other kids.

Not that there weren't occasions by this point in my life when my appearance and my handicap made me feel self-conscious. I became aware of more and more things other kids could do that I couldn't. I would be invited to a birthday party and suddenly realize the other kids didn't need Gagas to stay with them and help them pin the tail on the donkey.

I began to notice the number of times that people would stare at me, or ask stupid questions without talking directly to me as if I were retarded and couldn't possibly understand. At these times I felt *different* and would cry. But whenever I did, Mom told me the story of *The Ugly Duckling*. No matter how often I heard the story of that awkward little bird who surprised everyone by growing up into a beautiful swan, I always felt a little better each time she told it. It gave me hope that one day I'd discover my own special identity.

I firmly believed that an education was essential for my own transformation from ugly duckling to swan. Going to school seemed my best hope for fitting in. And even if the ACCA was a special school, it was a start. I clung to the dream that someday I would be able to attend the same kind of school as other kids.

At night, in my dreams, I imagined myself playing and chasing my sisters through the woods, dancing with friends, racing a two-wheeler up and down the road. In my dreams I could stand, walk, and even run as fast as Rosemary and Elizabeth. The sensation was so wonderful and free and real that I sometimes felt disappointed to wake up and find myself in the same broken body.

In my dreams I was always normal.

Chapter 5

Breathing Alone

Upon our return to California, Gaga rented a room from an elderly woman about her own age. We shared the bathroom and kitchen with the owner, Mrs. Whaggly. But Gaga and I had a huge front bedroom with plenty of windows and light—a real change from Alaska.

A long stairs led up to the front porch of Mrs. Whaggly's old house. Whenever we wanted to go out, Gaga took my cart down first. Then she returned to the top of the steps to help me down using our "step-wait" method. I took a step while holding on the handrail, and then I waited for Gaga to take a step.

By this age I already had a more efficient, hand-over-hand method of using a handrail while slowly sidestepping up or down stairs, like a clumsy crab. But Gaga thought it was too dangerous for me to negotiate stairs by myself, so we always did it her way.

Gaga never did let me experiment as much as my mother did. Mom tended to let me go. That's how I began to learn that I was not as helpless as Gaga and everyone else thought I was. During our stay in Alaska, when Mom and Gaga were busy, I learned to do a number of new things for myself.

For example, when left to my own devices, I learned to drink from a cup. We had a large wicker clothes hamper near the window in the kitchen. I could manage to climb into the hamper and then stand up with the sides of the hamper around me. On the counter beside the

45

hamper was where Mom always kept a pail of fresh drinking water and a heavy blue rubber cup for dipping the water. I began picking up the cup and pretending to drink from it—just to see if I could. When I got bored with pretending, I wondered if I could really do it—hold the cup with water in it and actually drink it by myself. So I gripped the cup tightly, plunged it into the water, lifted it slowly and shakily to my mouth, and choked down a big gulp of water. I got more on my shirt than I did down my throat. But after that initial success, I refused to let anyone else hold my cup for me.

To keep me from drowning myself, Mom had the good sense to put only an inch of liquid in the cup at a time. She also bought me a "Tommy Tippy" cup like babies use. That worked even better because the tight-fitting lid with a hole in it allowed only a few drops into my mouth at a time. Even then, my way of drinking could be a wet and messy chore. So Gaga insisted that I give up my cup the entire time we lived with Mrs. Whaggly. After all, we were sharing the dinner table with others who Gaga felt had more civilized expectations than we experienced in Alaska.

I was willing to make that small concession in exchange for what I considered a much larger victory. Gaga finally allowed me to figure out how to wash, brush my teeth, and dress myself. I persuaded her to let me try by reminding her that when we went back to Alaska I would be going to school and "school girls" should know how to do those things for themselves.

So Gaga would spread out a rubber sheet in the middle of our bedroom floor. Then she placed a basin of warm water on the sheet, handed me a toothbrush and other necessities, and set out my clothes. She did as I insisted, faithfully observing my "Don't-watch-me rule." Whenever I was teaching myself a new task, I couldn't tolerate being watched, so she'd sit and read the newspaper while I took my "bird bath" and dressed. She never allowed me to take a shower or regular bath for fear I'd slip and fall.

My first attempt at bathing and dressing myself took more than an hour. Dressing, in particular, became a challenging case of trial and error. I finally got my T-shirt over my head and shoved my left arm through the proper sleeve. But oops, my right arm wouldn't cooperate. I couldn't lift it into position to get it through the other sleeve. So I had

to take off the shirt and start over, making sure that I got my right arm in first. That worked.

I soon learned that the only way to get a dress on was to get both arms in the armholes to begin with and then flip the dress over my head. I refined this technique until I could get into almost anything by using my "flip" method. I was pleased with my initial triumph and in the weeks to follow even gained enough coordination to turn down my ruffled anklets by myself.

Try as I might, I couldn't get the hang of buckling my shoes or buttoning my sweaters. I could manage both tasks in my mind, but I just couldn't do it with my hands. Yet the new success I did have in bathing and dressing greatly encouraged me. With that, plus the prospect of school in Alaska next fall, I felt I was well on my way to being an ordinary kid.

——————— • ———————

Gaga found me a tutor by advertising in the San Jose newspaper. Mom had insisted on this and sent extra money to cover the cost. A retired school teacher, Mrs. Osgood brought me new books to read every two weeks and exclaimed that she could never keep up with my reading. But arithmetic was a very different story. When it came to adding or subtracting more than two numbers at a time, I was at a complete loss. Mrs. Osgood patiently went over my math again and again and always praised me extravagantly when I finally got a problem right.

——————— • ———————

Time slipped quickly past. With summer fast approaching, it was nearing time for our big move to Alaska. Occasionally Gaga would tell Mrs. Whaggly about her dreams as we ate dinner. Despite her age, Gaga was still quite a dreamer. Looking at her face you knew she could "see" that homesite in her mind. Her cabin would have space and light. Outside would be a huge vegetable garden with chicken wire to keep out the laying hens. She excitedly told a smiling Mrs. Whaggly that she was finally going to be the adventurer she had always wanted to be. She said she deserved that much after herding kids (her own and her daughter's) for going on sixty years.

One rainy spring Friday Gaga announced, "Today, Posey, we're going to start packing for Alaska. She handed me a box and instructed me to sort out what toys I wanted to take. I'd just begun to sift through my things when she realized we were out of canned milk. Irritated with herself for forgetting it when we were out the day before, she decided to walk to the corner store before it closed for the weekend. She had never left me at home alone before, but said she didn't want to risk my catching cold before we left for Alaska. So she wrapped a scarf around her neck, pulled on her coat, and said, "You stay right here in the room while I'm gone. Don't be scooting around the house and bothering Mrs. Whaggly. I'll be right back." Then she hurried out the door.

As Gaga tried to cross the street in front of the house in the downpour, a car hit her, knocked her down, and sped off without stopping. An ambulance came, but she refused to go to the hospital and insisted that the attendant help her back into the house. She assured him she was going to be fine. She had to be, she said, because there was no one else to look after me. The ambulance attendant finally gave her some crutches and left—reluctantly.

For the next few days, Gaga hobbled around the house on crutches, walking my cart in front of her. She did everything in her usual wrinkle-free, spotless way—refusing all offers of help from Mrs. Whaggly. Mostly Gaga seemed angry at herself for getting hit. She was determined not to let this turn of events change our plans or our departure schedule. Even as she lay in bed resting from her pain, she encouraged me to keep packing.

Since Gaga hadn't called for several days and we hadn't stopped by the local electronics store where he worked, my brother Don popped in one afternoon to check on us. When he learned about the accident, he immediately called a doctor. For the first time in my life I saw my grandmother not in control. I felt terrified as I watched her lying helplessly on that bed, screaming at the doctor not to undress her to examine her. When the doctor ordered her taken to a hospital and Don said that he would take me to my aunt and uncle's house, I started to cry. Gaga roughly told me to stop, that I had to be a "good girl."

But I didn't know how. I was scared.

Mom's brother, Uncle Jim, and his wife, Aunt Mary, reminded me of brand-new furniture still wrapped in plastic. Perhaps because they never had any children of their own, they seemed starched and unused. Uncle Jim could even work in his garden without seeming to get dirty.

Neither Uncle Jim nor Aunt Mary had ever tried to communicate with me. Whenever we visited them, they always talked to me through Gaga. So I felt suddenly very alone and angry to be in their care. I had no one I could talk to, no one who could even understand my questions, my needs, or my fears. Out of fear and frustration I screamed hysterically and out of control. Aunt Mary fed me ice cream to try to calm me. Sometimes it worked. Other times I'd get distracted playing with the tiny new ceramic doll that Gaga had found in an oatmeal box the morning before she went to the hospital.

Mom finally arrived from Alaska, having been delayed several days by bad weather that closed the airport in Anchorage. Also, communications were down to the island where Pappy was working, so she had been unable to reach him for some time to let him know about this emergency trip. As it was, she had to leave my sisters alone in the house and ask the neighbors to check in on them till she or Pappy got back.

The evening after Mom arrived, Gaga died. She went into a coma soon after reaching the hospital and never regained consciousness. The doctors said a blood clot in her injured leg had broken free, traveled to her heart, and eventually killed her.

I refused to cry. I was afraid that if I ever let the tears start, I'd never again be able to stop crying.

Mom and Aunt Mary took turns sitting in the car with me during the funeral, because I didn't want to see Gaga in her casket. Watching her lying helplessly on our bed, screaming at the doctor had been terrible enough. Seeing her cold and still in a casket was more than I thought I could bear. I felt as if I was dangling over the very edge of an emotional precipice. At the slightest crack, a dam would break and I'd be swept over the edge in a flood of endless tears that would surely drown me.

It was strange and sad that only family attended the funeral. None of our friends from Santa Cruz or the new friends we made in San Jose came to the service. But when Mom got into the car to sit with me at the close of the service, she tried to comfort me by saying Gaga was surrounded by flowers—just the way she would have wanted it.

———•———

A couple times over the last year or two of her life, Gaga had talked about dying and tried to ready me for the possibility. But nothing I ever imagined prepared me for this terrible reality.

The sky seemed ablaze behind the dark silhouette of that funeral chapel as afternoon slowly faded into a pale-pink summer twilight. The outer world looked calm and peaceful in contrast to the turmoil raging inside me.

My old world had suddenly crashed to an end. We had always been part of the same sentence. *Gaga and Posey this. Gaga and Posey that.* Never one without the other. There would no longer be a Gaga and Posey anything anymore.

Since the beginning of my memory Gaga had slept with me. She fed me. She bathed me. She took me to the bathroom. For almost ten years we belonged in the same breath. Now Gaga breathed no more.

Now I would have to breathe alone.

Chapter 6

Pappy

The day after the funeral I overheard Aunt Mary asking if Mom had decided what to do with me now that Gaga was gone. "Why don't you put her in an institution?" she wanted to know.

Mom angrily informed Aunt Mary that she would do no such thing. She was taking me home with her to Alaska that very afternoon. Come fall, she'd enroll me in the ACCA school. And the family would survive as we always had—one day at a time.

On the plane flying north that evening, I asked Mom why Aunt Mary always talked *about* me and never *to* me. Mom smiled and shook her head. She didn't know.

"I think there's something wrong with her," I said.

Mom grinned when she finally understood what I was saying. "I suspect you're right, Posey. There probably is something wrong with her." Then Mom and I both laughed.

It felt good to laugh.

When Mom and I walked into our Alaskan home, Rosemary and Elizabeth were in the kitchen quietly painting with watercolors. I knew Mom had called to tell them Gaga had died, but they seemed to be calmly handling this situation like the little adults I perceived them to be.

51

At the ages of eleven and twelve, they both seemed so wise, so adult, and so much more emotionally controlled than I thought I could ever be. I had an irrational volcano rumbling inside me. I never knew when it would erupt in a fiery rage or a flood of tears. So once again I found myself envying my sisters, not for their physical abilities—to sit up straight, clearly articulate more than a handful of phonetic sounds, and eat without drooling a stream of half-chewed food down their chins—but for the ease with which they ruled their emotions.

Elizabeth took my coat and put me at the table on a chair. Though only a year older than I, she was husky enough to lift or toss me wherever she wanted me to go.

The first picture I tried to paint was a torn disaster. Then Rosemary showed me how to make smaller, gentler strokes. Before long I was actually getting most of my paint inside the lines. While we painted, Rosemary and Elizabeth quickly filled Mom in on their adventures during her absence. The weather had turned wickedly cold and froze up the water pipes that Pappy had finally installed. But our next-door neighbor, Lars, thawed the pipes with his blowtorch before any damage was done.

Mom listened quietly to the report as she bustled around the kitchen preparing something for us to eat. There was comfort in the smell of navy beans cooking, in sharing a meal again with my family, and afterward in watching Mom sit down in her favorite chair to read the paper.

———— • ————

At bedtime, Mom set up another army cot for me right between Rosemary's and Elizabeth's. I was determined not to cry, but ever since I'd outgrown my crib, I had slept with Gaga. Going to bed without her reminded me how much it hurt to have her familiar presence so suddenly torn away.

I sobbed half the night, and cried even louder when my sisters told me to shut up. I was furious with myself for crying, but I didn't know how to stop. My lack of control only frightened me more. By the middle of the night, the fire in the wood stove died out and a terrible, lonely cold settled into my bones. I couldn't help comparing my dark new surroundings with the bright, cheery room Gaga and I had shared at Mrs. Whaggly's.

The unfinished bedroom I shared with my sisters was used for storage as well as for sleeping. Wires strung from ceiling rafters held a long pole filled with the entire family's hanging clothes. Boxes and other clothes were stacked in every available space. In one corner stood the room's only source of heat, a small wood stove with tinfoil tacked on the walls around it for fire protection.

Even in daylight that dismal back room had a dreary sense of hopelessness. At night, in the dark, with the clutter piled higher to clear enough floor space for three army cots, the shadows took on ominous, sometimes spine-chilling shapes. The insulation in the walls looked like grotesque goblins with their tummies bulging out from between the open studding. Even when I scrunched my eyes shut in fear, the comforting warm memories of Gaga and California seemed very, very far away.

Just weeks after I arrived, Pappy came home from the bush and declared that he wanted to stay home and find a new job in town. He was tired of life in the bush. He wanted to become a family man again. Maybe he'd even start fixing up the house.

Pappy took a job at Fort Richardson as a civilian mechanic in the army motor pool. But he called himself a "sillyvian" because he worked for the "silly service." Pappy never could seem to leave words alone. He was always twisting them around like a clown twisting balloons.

He maintained an acute love-hate relationship with his job. I think he enjoyed the work itself—he'd always liked working with his hands. But this job gave him a close-up, firsthand look at government waste and inefficiency. He often came home complaining loudly about having the same vehicle in the shop three times in the past week because the officer who drove it took no responsibility for the proper care and use of equipment that the taxpayers sacrificed to provide.

Mom often tried to soothe Pappy as they shared their ritual evening coffee together and discussed everything from his job to the evening news. Pappy never seemed short of definite (and often loud) opinions. He liked reading books about politics and made up his own sayings about world affairs. Mom had to frequently remind him that not everyone he worked with would share his views, so he needed to be careful what he said and try to be tolerant of the people around him. But I don't think Pappy ever heard her.

On the long, light summer evenings, after his coffee and conversation with Mom, Pappy would work on the house or tackle some project out in the garage as he listened to classical music on the radio. Whenever he had the family vehicles in good running order, he made time to dote over his own swamp buggy.

Pappy's contraption was part truck, part dune buggy, with twice the personality of any commercially designed vehicle. The canopied truck bed was mounted on airplane wheels that enabled Pappy's "Tundra Queen" to cover miles of roadless wilderness. Painted blue (though Pappy insisted it was green and would not let us argue the point), the vehicle had a huge winch mounted on the front that allowed Pappy to do everything from winching it up the side of a mountain to dragging a bull moose he'd shot out of a ravine.

I always had trouble bracing myself on something stable so I could hoist my body up into the high cab. Whenever I rode in the buggy with Pappy, I felt as if we were in an airplane taxiing down a runway. It seemed high enough to see for miles. But the most distinctive feature of that buggy was the big old clawfoot bathtub Pappy strapped to the back whenever he went camping or hunting. He insisted on his bath—no matter what. Mom was forever disappointed that his hunting buddies never took a picture of Pappy sitting in his bathtub out in the middle of the Alaskan wilderness.

This was the first time in my life I could remember living in the same house with my father. It wasn't easy for either of us. All those years of one-on-one attention from Gaga had some lasting negative effects. I was used to living in a world centered around me and having all my needs quickly met. When something didn't go my way, I usually reacted by crying or by screaming and pitching a fit.

Pappy, too, was used to having things *his* way as man of the house. When they weren't, he got irritable. It took more control than I had some days not to burst into tears when he spoke roughly to me. And the smallest things seemed to bug him. Like when he thought I took too long in the bathroom. Or when I got the wheel of my chair stuck in the floor where a board had rotted out in the threshold between the kitchen and the hallway at the very time Pappy needed to get to the bathroom. Then our tempers would ignite.

Pappy never had any patience for my emotional outbursts. My crying got on his nerves. He only made things worse because an angry look from him was all it took to set me crying for hours. Then he'd get mad at me for crying, and I'd be angry at him for upsetting me, and angry with myself for getting so upset and for making him angry.

It took some time for the two of us to get along. We had never before learned how to love or live with each other. Both of us had to work at it. And I remember thinking, *If only I were normal, Pappy would love me more.*

⸻

I think a major breakthrough in Pappy's attitude toward me took place as he watched me garden. I'd pestered Mom for a patch of my own until she finally assigned me a bare spot along the back fence by Britchy's grave. She marked off the borders of my area with 2 x 4s and told me to break up all the dirt in my little square of ground. I was in dirt heaven whenever I could be outside digging, planting, or pulling up weeds.

My garden kept me busy for many hours every week all summer long. The only mistake Mom made was in assigning me a spot so near the back fence where our childless neighbors, Lars and Jean, would lift me over the fence to show me their carefully manicured backyard paradise—a true gardener's showplace. They gave me tiny vegetable plants early in the season, and they all grew into giants by fall.

Pappy thought my garden was great. He marveled over the size of my plants, teasing me and saying that he thought I must have dirt in my veins. He made me proud. It was one of the highlights of our some-times difficult relationship.

Perhaps one of the barriers between us was that no matter how hard he tried, Pappy never developed the knack of understanding my speech. What little bit he did understand encouraged him to mimic me. He soon got so good at it that he could often fool Mom and get me in trouble for talking out of bounds.

Because I was never easy for anyone to understand, Mom had a rule. When I had something to say to her, I was supposed to come where she was, get her attention and then start saying what I wanted to say. Face-to-face communication was always a little clearer, so it was a reasonable rule. Mom would get irritated with me when I forgot.

One day Mom stormed into the back room to find out why I'd been yelling for her. I was about to accuse her of hearing things when we both heard what sounded like my voice coming from another room: "Mom, where are my yippers? My feet are cold!"

Mom rushed down the hall to investigate. A few moments later I heard Pappy's laughter. He had mastered the high pitch of my voice, my *Y*'s for *J*'s and even my *S*'s just the way I said them. He even had my mannerisms down, tilting his head to the right like I did and prancing sideways like me when I tried to walk without thinking carefully about what I was doing.

Mom failed to see any humor in Pappy's antics. She scolded me for encouraging him when I began to give him a few pointers. But the two of us enjoyed teasing Mom and even threatened to arouse her wrath with the suggestion that we might consider entertaining company with our joint act.

Mom didn't think our performance would be suitable for "polite" company. I laughed and told her our company was hardly ever "polite" and most of them wouldn't enjoy anything fun anyway.

Mom told me that wasn't a very respectful thing to say about our adult friends. But Pappy was still grinning as he hurried out the door.

On those few warm summer days when the thermometer threatened to hit 70°, Pappy loaded all us girls and any of our friends who wanted to go, into the back of his pickup and headed to the lake for an afternoon of swimming or boating. I loved those outings, but Mom disliked the water and always stayed on dry land so she could count heads.

During these recreational outings I began to get used to being with Pappy, and he with me. I began to understand why learning to live with each other was so hard. All my life Gaga and Mom had taken care of me and made the decisions regarding my care. While he trusted them to know what was best, he had also allowed them to shut him out of the first ten years of my life.

I was his daughter. He was my father. But we never really knew each other. So it took time to discover that we did indeed love each other—even if that love had been buried under awkward and unusual circumstances.

Chapter 7

Trapped

The towering birch tree shading our kitchen window turned golden. The morning air had a crispness to it. Our five assorted dogs and fifteen cats added new layers of hair. Cocoa, Elizabeth's horse, began growing his scruffy winter coat. Labor Day arrived, and the next day school started.

Rosemary and Elizabeth got themselves dressed, finished their breakfast, and headed out the door. Then they climbed the back fence, cut through the neighbor's yard to the next street, and headed for school a few blocks away.

I remained in my chair at the kitchen table as Mom carefully braided my hair and then tied the braids with scotch-plaid ribbons. This was to be my first day of "real school." I was so excited I could hardly sit still. I'd imagined this day ever since I started daydreaming.

I wasn't the least bit interested in breakfast. When Mom finally tired of trying to hit a moving target with spoonfuls of oatmeal, she gave up on feeding me and began a verbal checklist. "Schoolbag. Hankie. Sweater. Last check for potty. Clean face. Clean hands." Then she walked me out the door to the pickup.

The schoolroom looked just as I remembered it from when Gaga, Mom, and I had visited the ACCA almost a year before. How recent that visit seemed, and yet how much had happened. A lifetime had passed.

Mom left after escorting me over to a chair at a table where other students were sitting. Miss Paul, strikingly beautiful with her hearty Russian features and rosy complexion, introduced me to the class.

———————◆———————

Our very first assignment was to fill in the big felt calendar with the days of the month that had passed so far. Then Miss Paul handed out stenciled drawings of a calendar with a picture to color at the top. Every day we would practice writing a new number.

Most of the other kids could use pencils. I had great difficulty gripping mine, steadying my hand, holding the paper down, and then writing small enough to get my numbers in the space provided. To make matters worse, I invariably wrote my numbers backward.

Miss Paul must have been a genius to decipher my writing well enough to catch all my backward numbers, though she sometimes had to double-check with me before grading my work. I never understood why I had such trouble reversing numbers; letters never gave me any trouble. But I remained optimistic because I was so excited and proud of myself to finally be in a real school.

In an attempt to help me write more legibly, Miss Paul attached a small lead weight around my wrist to keep my hand from jerking away whenever I tried to make the small, precisely controlled writing movements. She also fattened up my pencil with clay to help me grasp it better. Even then, my handwriting was readable only in the morning. By afternoon my written work looked as if ants had been square dancing in ink across my paper.

Though I struggled with any task demanding coordination, the actual learning was the easiest part of school. It would be a long time before I could write numbers and letters small enough for my workbooks and worksheets. But when it came to reading, I had no trouble because it required no dexterity—except to turn the pages—which often proved tedious and frustrating.

My biggest frustration with reading resulted from being such a fast learner. I expected to move to a higher reading level and progressively advanced material every few weeks as had happened when I had tutors. But this was the real world in the early years of special education for children with disabilities. Money for resources and adequate textbooks did not exist. I had to review my reading texts again and again.

———————•———————

Much to my dismay, I still had to make time in my school day for speech and physical therapy. I thought therapy should be secondary; academics interested me so much more. I had been frustrated with "kindergarten" in California, where the emphasis was on physical therapy and no one wanted to teach me to read or write. And all the grown-ups in my life had placed such an emphasis on learning to walk and talk, they seemed to see walking and talking as ends in themselves.

Not until I started school at ACCA did I find the incentive I needed to strive for success with speech and physical therapy. I finally realized that if I was ever to fulfill my dream of going to a regular school with able-bodied kids, I'd have to learn to get around and communicate much better. Now I saw how therapy fit into my own goals. My attitude improved immediately, and I began making more progress.

Speech therapy made the most sense to me. I very much wanted to talk like everyone else because I had so much I wanted to say. The first order of business in speech was to learn to drink from a straw. Not just another dumb exercise—my therapist explained that the ability to suck is basic to forming the lips to make certain sounds.

Pappy helped me by carving a special mouthpiece out of a spool and gluing it to a plastic straw. I was better able to hold the larger wooden mouthpiece between my lips than the skinny little straw. Once I mastered using a straw, I used it more than my tippy cup. I had better control of swallowing what I sucked through a straw than with the dribbles of water from a cup.

I had the same problems I'd always had with speech therapy. The straight drilling of words and sounds bored me. And since I was fast becoming a human thesaurus, I had little patience whenever my therapist wanted me to try the same difficult word over and over again. *Why struggle with an awkward word when I knew a dozen ways to express the same idea?*

Like all the speech therapists I ever had, this one insisted that I learn to say all sounds as clearly as possible. Even if I never got the hang of the "Sammy Snake" sound or a number of others. I must have heard that therapist tell me a million times, "Slow down. Think about each sound before you say it." But in at least one way I was just like most eleven-year-old kids in the world; I hated to slow down for anything. Especially when I was talking.

———————•———————

At the ACCA school, for the first time in my life, I had a consistent, prolonged program of physical therapy. Every time I got into physical therapy in California, I moved, or something else interrupted or ended the program. So my steady progress surprised me.

Within a few months I could walk some distance with the help of sawhorse crutches. Pappy made the crutches out of scraps of pipe that he painted fire-engine red. My crutches were the talk of the school. Their eight sturdy legs gave me a sense of security.

The physical therapists told my parents that the sawhorses were just "the first step toward independent walking." With the progress they saw, they felt certain I'd be walking on my own within a couple of years.

Step two was having a doctor prescribe a custom-designed steel-and-leather brace with a special body harness around my chest to correct my rag-doll posture. Those braces were a pain—in more ways than one. If I had had three hours to put them on every morning, I might have managed all the straps and laces myself, but Mom or my sisters had to help me into the complicated and uncomfortable contraption.

Just keeping up with the maintenance and making routine adjustments on the braces was expensive and frustrating. The therapists finally removed the chest adaptation because it restricted my breathing. The next time we saw the doctor, he infuriated Mom by accusing her of taking it off because she didn't want to bother with it.

It seemed that no one could ever anticipate my teeter-totter physical condition. On one visit I'd be able to sit one way so the doctor would order costly adjustments to my braces. On the next appointment my body would be shifted another direction and my braces would need very different adjustments. Some weeks it seemed Mom and I spent as many hours in the brace repair shop as I did in school.

In a matter of time I progressed to the point of walking with Canadian crutches—the kind that fit snugly around the forearm. But they made me feel like a string doll, trying to balance precariously on rubber-tipped matchsticks. Every time I was startled, my arms jerked and my crutches went sliding. The only place I ever felt secure using them was in our back room at home, where the tile was so chipped and cracked it provided a great non-skid surface.

Though I never liked the new crutches, I used them because they were a sign of progress. The sooner I mastered them, the sooner I'd be able to walk by myself. Besides, I felt "cool" to be using the same crutches that most of my classmates had.

I pushed myself too fast. Once I started using the Canadian crutches, I abandoned the trusty sawhorse crutches that gave me enough balance and security to practice walking. As it happened, I never did gain any confidence using those Canadian crutches. This insecurity eventually discouraged me about the idea of walking.

I always felt far more disabled walking unsteadily on crutches than I did scooting on my bottom or rolling in the used wheelchair I got with the money my big sister Maxine had sent me from Chicago. Crutches may have enabled me to walk, but walking with crutches seemed too restrictive—too limiting.

For example, I could walk to the sink using my crutches, but I couldn't pick anything up to bring back to the table. In my wheelchair I could spin to the counter, get what I wanted, put it in my lap, and roll back where I wanted to be. None of the grown-ups in my life understood my feelings or saw the logic in my preference for the wheelchair. It seemed terribly important to them that I walk.

Most mornings Shirley or Elizabeth helped dress and strap me into my imprisoning braces. Shirley was particularly patient—even laying my braces and clothes on the furnace for a few minutes to get them warm. Oh, that felt good! I sensed that Shirley liked helping me, so I usually graciously accepted her help and cooperated as best I could.

But there were times when I was upset—especially if Pappy had accused me of being lazy and not wanting to walk. Then I'd squirm and even try to kick whoever tried to lash up my brace. Afterward I'd feel guilty and get angry with myself for not being a better kid. If I could just try harder and be better, maybe Pappy and Mom wouldn't quarrel so much about my physical therapy.

Why were Pappy, Mom, my teachers, and my therapists so concerned about my lack of progress walking? Why weren't they as concerned that after two years of academic work I was stuck using the same introductory reader? Why couldn't they understand what was most important?

Whenever I became really upset, it was Shirley who had the gift of calmness. Without knowing what my basic problem was, she usually managed to settle me down by getting me to think or talk about other things. Soon I'd be laughing and feeling good again. Shirley seemed to understand my frustrations. She and Mom often talked about me and my problems at night after I went to bed.

My dear sister Elizabeth was a lot less merciful than Shirley. Whenever we got into a scrap, she always got in the last word. If I gave her a hard time getting dressed, she would stick my braces out the back door to get them good-and-cold before strapping them on me. And if I ratted on her to Mom, she'd leave them out twice as long the next time.

You didn't want to mess with Elizabeth.

We never had an occupational therapy department at the ACCA, so what I learned in this area I got by asking my physical therapists for help, or learning on my own by trial and error.

We tried a variety of spoons in hopes that I'd be able to feed myself. But we never seemed to get the right one. One spoon turned out to be just the opposite of what I needed. Someone brought in a swiveling survival spoon designed for those with limited movement. My trouble was too much movement. Each time I tried to take a bite, the spoon would turn and dump it. So I dumped the spoon.

Mom eventually built up the handle on a tablespoon so I could grip it. Then I ate out of a large soup bowl set on a wet washcloth to keep it from slipping off the table as I tried to scoop out the food.

The first time I managed to feed myself, my family celebrated. Mom made me an aluminum foil medal to honor the achievement. She also salvaged the swivel spoon, claiming it was perfect to stir her coffee.

While the ACCA didn't have occupational therapy, we did have Mrs. Mac, who introduced the innovative idea of music therapy. She was a sweet older woman, well-schooled in dance and drama. While I enjoyed my regular classwork, I absolutely loved going to music therapy, where I learned to play in the rhythm band. Speech therapy and physical therapy gave me one-on-one attention; but in music therapy I could be part of a group.

Mrs. Mac could have charmed a Siberian wind to smile and dance for joy. Pappy and Mom agreed she was gifted, because she could get any of the ACCA students to do whatever she asked. She took each of our physical problems and designed special dances around them. Patsy was stiff-legged, so Mrs. Mac put her in clogs and gave her milking pails! Her dance offset her stiffness and made it look like a natural part of the dance. She even coaxed Johnny, shy as he was, to dance a Dutch dance with Patsy at the recital we put on for our parents.

I was given a pair of finger cymbals so I could practice moving my fingers separately. Mrs. Mac never concerned herself with my walking. Instead, she designed activities to force me to use my arms, hands, and fingers. Perhaps that's one reason I loved her so. She, too, believed that it was more important for me to learn to use my hands and my head than it was to walk. She taught me the hand motions for "Lovely Hula Hands" so I could be a Hula girl in our dance recital.

My fingers refused to cooperate at first, but the music eventually wove its spell. The more I listened to the rhythm, the more relaxed I felt. All the work with those finger cymbals loosened up my fingers for other tasks. For the first time in my life I was able to pick up small objects with the thumb and index finger of my left hand.

The dance recital itself was the highlight of the school year. Mom and Shirley helped Mrs. Mac by rummaging through the local Salvation Army thrift store to find the makings of our costumes. I wore a tutu for my grass skirt and a paper flower lei. Freddy and Johnny played the drums and wore drummer uniforms. Everyone had a part. Johnny's mother was amazed. She told Mom that she'd have called anyone a liar if they had told her that Johnny would actually perform for an audience and pose for a newspaper photograph.

Some days it seemed what little I gained got lost in having to deal with adverse Alaskan circumstances. Once winter set in, my transportation to school was a challenge. In moderate winter weather Mom could clear the ice off the front steps so she could tote me under one arm and hold on to a ski rope with her other hand as she carefully trudged to the bottom of our treacherously steep driveway. Most of the winter it was impossible to drive up near the house. Some days Mom got so frustrated with conditions that she sent me to school in a taxi, but whenever winter weather turned especially wicked, she just kept me home.

Having survived winter, we faced the new and different challenge of spring thaw. Beneath the magnificently beautiful deep blue arctic skies and the blossoming trees with their sweet promise of summer, the entire state of Alaska seemed to turn into a sea of oozing, slippery mud. All winter, Mom carried me in constant fear of my falling on the ice. All spring, she worried about falling and splashing mud all over both of us. I was never sure-footed enough to walk outside on my own, and both ice and mud greatly limited my mobility.

Many were the days that my frustration with Alaskan conditions reduced me to screaming fits of anger and despair.

———————•———————

Something had to give. Although my school and therapy were the best I'd ever known, I felt hopelessly stuck on a treadmill. I knew that I could never achieve my dreams if I continued my pattern of explosive emotional behavior. I couldn't make the progress I wanted to make when it took so much physical and emotional energy to cope with our living conditions in Alaska. Even the education I was getting didn't seem to be enough to overcome the limiting circumstances of my life.

The ACCA was only a Band-Aid. And I needed a bandage. Not just for my body but also for my emotions and my dreams. I was a very tiny eleven-year-old girl. Profoundly handicapped, nearly helpless, and undoubtedly very naive. But I knew, if not in words, what I felt.

I felt trapped.

Chapter 8

Elsie Shows the Way

One spring day Mom showed my a book she happened to find in the parents' section of the ACCA's meager, underfunded library. Somehow, my little school had acquired an old out-of-date yearbook from a place called the Crippled Children's School, a Lutheran school in far-off Jamestown, North Dakota.

Pictures in the book showed many disabled children and young people in school settings and playing together outdoors. They looked happy and active doing things I only dreamed about. I was especially intrigued by pictures of students working and studying together in their classrooms. The ACCA school was so small that we almost never had group learning activities because everyone was at a different level. One student would try to learn her alphabet while the person next to her worked on sixth-grade geography.

"Oh, I wish I could go to a school like that," I told Mom. I thought the place depicted in those yearbook photos looked wonderful compared to anything I'd ever experienced. So did Mom. As she drove me to the ACCA the next day Mom asked, "Would you really want to go to that school in North Dakota?"

"YES!"

Mom promised to find out what more she could about the school. She also cautioned me. "That's a very big decision, Posey. It would be best for you to think about it for a while. North Dakota is a long ways away."

Mom talked to several ACCA staff members, who thought it might be a good possibility. My classroom teacher, Miss Paul, heartily endorsed the idea. She frequently told Mom that I needed more than the ACCA could provide—and that I needed it soon.

My mother warned me that I would get homesick if I went but that I would eventually get through it. And she seemed convinced I'd feel less stifled and be happier with the education I could get at the Crippled Children's School. Mom also assured me that she and Pappy wouldn't force me to go. It would be my decision entirely.

And a heavy decision it was for an eleven-year-old girl. All those years I'd lived with my grandmother. As much as I loved her, I dreamed of living with my family like a normal kid. Alaska, for all its drawbacks, had allowed me that. *How could I think about leaving my family when I'd hardly become a part of it again? Why did I always have to be separated from my family just to get what other people take for granted? It's not fair!* But then my life had never seemed fair.

I sensed that I was at a crucial crossroads in my life. I knew if I didn't take this risk I'd be trapped forever. And I would live the rest of my life wondering *What if . . .*

When I told Mom my decision, she immediately wrote to inquire about enrolling me for the '58–'59 school year. Now this was getting serious.

At various times in my life, big plans had been made in my behalf only to be changed by unexpected events, but it looked like this big plan was really going to happen. It was hard enough to be brave and determined when we were talking wishes and dreams. It was far more unsettling to hold the actual acceptance letter in my hands. I had to keep telling Mom, "I want to go!" Though my emotions were saying just the opposite.

This wasn't an easy time for Mom, either. But at least some of her motivation came from an unspoken, perhaps even subconscious sense of providence. Before the unexplained appearance of that yearbook in the parents' section of the ACCA library, Mom had often complained about the selection and usefulness of the books. She even vowed to help organize and add to that library if she ever had the time and money to do so. In part because she actually found that yearbook in what she considered a most unlikely place, I think she believed that it was simply meant to be.

My own doubts and dread intensified as Mom began a list of things that needed to get done before my departure. Mom was a list person. At the very top of her list was "Find a traveling companion for Carolyn." I certainly couldn't go by myself. It was going to be expensive flying to North Dakota. And if she could afford the airfare, Mom didn't think she could afford the time away from the new day-care business that she and Shirley had started.

The plan was to find someone already heading for the northern plains and pay them to deliver me to my destination in Jamestown, North Dakota. But before Mom got around to placing a classified ad in the Anchorage paper, something else remarkable happened.

One exquisite late-spring morning, Mom opened up the doors and windows to air out the house as she and Shirley sat with me around the kitchen table. With only two toddlers to look after that day, they talked about letting me watch the kids while they tried to get a lot of spring housecleaning finished before Pappy got home.

But the warm weather beckoned, and Mom gave in to temptation. She and Shirley packed up the car and the kids and headed to the ACCA's annual picnic that we hadn't planned to attend. It was scheduled to be held at Hidden Lake, only a short drive from our house.

We found the other ACCA families with no trouble. Then we spread out our blankets in a spot away from the water so that the babies wouldn't be too near the lake. We were soaking in the noonday sun when a woman we'd never seen before walked over to us and asked, "May I share your picnic table? The others all seem to be full." We made room for this pleasant middle-aged stranger. Something about her intrigued me even before she introduced herself.

She told us her name was Miss Benson, "But I prefer to be called Elsie." She said she was visiting her sister in Anchorage for the summer and had read about this ACCA school picnic in the newspaper. Since she had been dorm mother at a school for handicapped children in North Dakota, she decided to come to the picnic and see what it was like.

Mom, Shirley, and I all stared at Elsie as if she were a ghost. Shirley finally recovered enough to ask: "Th—This school. . . It couldn't be in Jamestown . . . could it?"

I got so excited I nearly fell off the bench.

Elsie got this puzzled look on her face. "Yes, but how . . ."

Mom found her voice and quickly explained that I'd been accepted and would be going to Jamestown in the fall. Elsie shook her head in amazement and smiled a knowing smile as we launched a barrage of questions.

Was the school as good as it claimed? Would they teach me things I wanted and needed to know—like typing and how to button my clothes—as well as academic subjects? Could I be in Girl Scouts like the group I'd seen in the yearbook? Would I sleep in a dorm? How many students would there be my own age? What about meals? How did students get around campus?

Elsie laughed and patiently, cheerfully answered all our queries. At last Mom asked the final, $64,000 question: Was Elsie going back to Jamestown at the end of the summer? And if she was, would she be willing to take me back with her?

Elsie said she planned to begin a nurses' training program in Minneapolis in the fall so she could become a medical missionary to the Navajo Indians.

My heart sank.

"But," Elsie said, "I'll have a little time before my school starts. I'll be glad to take Carolyn to Jamestown. It will be a great excuse to visit with my friends."

When we said good-bye to Elsie, I think we all left the picnic with a sense of amazement, wondering, *What in the world is going to happen next?*

During the remainder of that summer I spent a great deal of time with Elsie. She came by our house a lot of afternoons to talk or to do things with me. Before we left for North Dakota together, she wanted me to learn to trust her.

I did. She seemed a naturally kind and caring person who obviously loved kids. The better I got to know her, the better I began to feel about my decision. She offered my first solid glimpse into my uncertain future. In Elsie I had something more than a yearbook full of pictures.

Elsie so impressed Pappy on her visits in our home that he told Mom, "If she's what Christianity is all about, then I might be interested." I think he sensed and appreciated her honesty and candor.

She told my parents she considered the Jamestown school to be excellent. She had seen severely disabled children achieve amazing progress, both physically and academically. She also told us the school was no miracle factory. The people working there only did what they could. She said the student's desire was always a big factor in determining how much he or she accomplished.

That made sense to my parents. And it gave hope to me. I knew I had the desire.

There was so much to do to get ready. One late-summer day Mom took me shopping for some last-minute items I needed for school. We were looking at hair ribbons when a woman walked up, looked down at me in my wheelchair, and said to Mom, "My sister had a little girl like that. But she was lucky. She died."

I looked at Mom and rolled my eyes. Mom hurriedly turned and wheeled me away from that woman and out of the store before we both burst out laughing. We didn't want to be rude, no matter how insensitive that woman had been.

I had encountered people like her before. She and my aunt would have made a good pair. Mom shook her head and said what she told me many times, "Some people are like that, Posey. You can't let them bother you."

"I know," I responded. "I'll never let an ignoramus like that get me down. Not when I'm ready to leave home and go to a real school for the first time in my life."

Despite my excitement about school and my trust for Elsie, I cried the morning we were to leave. Elsie calmly escorted me onto the plane.

She was gentle but firm, saying she knew it would not be easy, but that I would be okay because I was a strong girl and would do great things with my life.

By the time we were airborne I had stopped crying. But I dared not look out the window for fear I'd see our house and begin bawling all over again.

Soon after she settled into her seat, Elsie slipped a small black Bible out of her purse. As she opened it, she explained that she hadn't had time for her devotions that morning. So she read me a story about Jesus and asked if I'd like him to bless me, too. She said she knew that Jesus wanted to bless me and my experience at my new school because he loved me very much.

I knew about the Bible, of course, but having devotions was a new experience. As Elsie read to me that morning and talked about Jesus loving me and wanting to bless me, I remember thinking: *Doesn't Jesus know that I'm really a bad girl who cries more than I laugh? Wasn't God angry with me for causing Mom and Pappy to argue so much about me? How could he love me? If I weren't disabled, I could be good. Then Mom and Pappy would love each other.* But I didn't see how God could love anyone who was such a mess as I was.

But I didn't say any of that out loud.

———————— • ————————

After landing in Minneapolis, we spent the night in Elsie's dorm room. The next morning she read her Bible and prayed for me again. She told me she believed that God had sent her to our picnic table that day at Hidden Lake so that the two of us could make this important trip together.

The more I thought about it, the more I thought she was probably right. How else could you explain a teacher from the Midwest on summer vacation in Alaska, reading about the ACCA picnic in the morning paper, showing up uninvited at the same picnic we'd decided to attend at the last minute, asking us if she could share our table, and then beginning the conversation by saying she had worked in the very school I would attend that fall thousands of miles away?

We flew from Minneapolis to Jamestown in a small plane later that day. A van met us and took us out to the school.

A huge white mansion surrounded by tall, shady trees and fabulous gardens dominated the campus. The James River, running cool and clear, horse-shoed around the grounds, its banks lined with weeping willows. The scene brought back memories of some old pictures Gaga used to show me of the Old South.

When we drove up to the school, arriving families were already unloading students and their belongings. Everyone seemed to know Elsie. They hugged her and asking about her pig-tailed charge. She introduced me all around. This was like nothing I'd ever seen before. So many people hugging and kissing and acting happy to see each other. I didn't know what to think.

When it was time to go into the school, Elsie took my wheelchair from the driver and began rolling me up the walk. She told me, "I want the honor of walking you through the doors of this school for the first time. I believe that God has something great planned for your life. I want to remember ushering you into the beginning of God's gifts for you."

Elsie made me feel good. While I had no idea how prophetic those words would be, I, too, felt the significance of that day. I had no realistic idea of what lay ahead. But I had hope. That hope told me, *This is a new beginning*.

Chapter 9

Life-Changing Discoveries

Elsie took me right to the junior girls' dorm—a long, open room containing eight beds with identical green-and-white bedspreads and matching window curtains. I was struck by the clean, welcome feeling of the room. All that natural light and fresh air seemed almost too marvelous to believe.

A friendly, older woman bustled into the room to greet us. She told me, "All the girls call me Grandma Gunse." She pointed out the unassigned beds and said that when I picked the one I wanted, she'd show me which clothes locker went with it. I chose a bed in the corner and then demonstrated to Grandma Gunse that I could transfer myself from my chair. As she and Elsie watched, I bounced on my new bed and laughed.

Before Elsie could get my suitcase open and help unpack my things, I told her I had to go potty. I was surprised and delighted to find railings on the walls by the toilet. *What a great idea!* I just had to try this by myself. Elsie held my chair, and for the first time in my life I used the bathroom by myself. When I finished, I laughed with pure joy. Elsie laughed and explained to Grandma Gunse that my home in Alaska was anything but accessible and that I was eager to learn even the smallest feats of independence.

Back in the dorm room as Elsie helped unpack, other girls began filtering in. They all seemed to know "Miss Benson," and Elsie made

73

me feel comfortable by making introductions. Jane, the girl assigned to the bed next to mine, was small with long hair like mine. Katie, a redhead. Sandy, a solidly built girl with Scandinavian features. Jackie, who despite a crooked smile, usually had a pained expression on her face. Susan, with dark hair and glasses, who was proud of her family background and made sure we all knew it. And Doreen, a Canadian student, who had fallen in love with God despite her parents' request that she not be taken to church.

When supper time arrived, Elsie and I accompanied my new friends to the dining hall. About eighty residential students were enrolled for the fall term. I'd never seen so many different kinds of wheelchairs, walkers, and stretchers. Happy noise and laughter filled the air. All of us needing bibs had them tied around our necks with a friendly hug or a kindly pat on the head. This was certainly the huggiest place I'd ever been.

Older students were assigned one area, while we little ones moved into a room with smaller tables. Once we were directed to our places, a woman came around with adhesive tape, writing our names, and sticking them on the table where we sat.

After our meal, Elsie gave me a full tour of the school. Many of the teachers were in their rooms, preparing for the beginning of classes the next morning. We stopped in the third-and-fourth-grade classroom, where Elsie introduced me to Miss Austin, who greeted me, checked her class list to confirm that I was to be in her room, and told me we would start promptly at 8:30 the next morning.

She politely ignored my sudden involuntary squeals of excitement and began talking to Elsie about nurses' training, leaving me free to regain my composure and look quietly around the room. This well-supplied classroom looked just like the pictures in the yearbook—traditional school desks for those who could use them and special tables for those using wheelchairs—typewriters, a towering supply cabinet, and shelf after shelf of books. Here was a place I knew I could learn.

The sky had begun to lose the brightness of day by 7:30 P.M., the appointed time for junior girls to be in their rooms. Elsie took me back to the dorm. Since she was returning to Minneapolis right away, we said our good-byes. I maintained my bravest front until she walked out of my dorm room and it hit me that she was my final link with home and family. From now on, no one in Jamestown, North Dakota, would have any idea about what the ACCA school was like. No one would know what my family, my home, or my life had been like. No one would know me.

I suddenly felt very alone.

But I wasn't alone. No sooner had I begun to cry than Grandma Gunse swept into the room and wanted to know which pajamas I wanted to wear on my very first night. Then she helped me get my tattered doll "Honey" into her PJs, too. As she tucked me into bed, I looked up into her warm, wrinkled, beautiful face and sobbed my heart out.

I wasn't alone in that either. Soon every girl in our room was weeping. And that set off the eight kindergartners in the next room. But Grandma Gunse and her helpers were compassionate. They never scolded us for crying.

The next morning I met another dorm mother, Sarah, who patiently braided my hair and saw to it my hands and face were clean after breakfast. Once she and her staff were satisfied as to our appearance, they escorted each of us to our assigned classes. Sandy, Susan, Jackie, and I went to Miss Austin's third-and-fourth-grade classroom. The rest of our dorm mates were escorted into the fifth-and-sixth-grade room next door.

Miss Austin made sure that we all knew the other kids in the room. There were two day students and four boys in addition to my dorm mates and me. Then she began class for the day by reading from the Bible and praying.

When the first textbooks and assignments had been handed out, Miss Austin concentrated on me. Within a few days she determined that I was not prepared to do third-grade work and gave me a battery of standard achievement tests. I tested out at the high first-grade level for math and low second-grade level in reading and spelling.

Because of my age, I was allowed to stay in the third-and-fourth-grade room with my friends, even though it meant extra time and work for my teacher. However, Miss Austin left all my third-grade books in my desk. So in my spare time I hunted for words I knew in them and tried to piece together enough from my history and geography books to take part in classroom discussions.

Miss Austin quickly concluded my unpredictable writing ability was a major hindrance to my education. As always, my penmanship seemed better in the morning than the afternoon, but it was barely legible at best. She determined that the first order of business during my occupational therapy time was learning to type. Mom had long talked about getting me a typewriter. Now the time had finally come.

That first day in occupational therapy I was afraid to use the typewriter. *What if my jerky hand movements somehow broke the machine?* But the therapist convinced me the typewriter could withstand my pecking and pounding. He showed me how the machine had a special plate over the keys to prevent me from hitting more than one at a time.

In a matter of days I had memorized the keyboard and received my very own typewriter. It was a sturdy, coal-black model, an iron writing machine that looked very durable. Within weeks I lost all fear of accidentally damaging it and pounded out all my lessons on that wonderful machine.

Typing dealt a fatal blow to any hope for improving my handwriting! It also inspired me to learn as nothing else had ever done. I felt like a magician every time I looked at my typewritten work. Those were my words spelled out legibly on paper! I had finally found a way for everyone to understand me.

———————— • ————————

I quickly mastered straight typing and was managing to type the correct answer in the right blank while doing assignments for spelling and history. But I had real trouble doing math on my typewriter. Some of my classmates who had to use typewriters were pros at neatly lining up numbers in straight columns. My efforts at math usually turned into such a jumbled mess it would perplex Miss Austin.

I seemed to have no common sense at all when it came to numbers. What little progress I made was painfully slow. Miss Austin even tried to teach me to use an abacus, but I suspected she was about to give up hope that I'd ever learn basic arithmetic.

I cried a lot over my continuing frustration and failures in math. *How could I make good progress in things like typing and reading and struggle so with anything having to do with numbers?* I felt stupid. I decided that any girl my age who couldn't do any more math than I could must be a dumb ox.

I couldn't yet see that my decision to leave my family and come alone to this school in North Dakota was an act of courage and wisdom far beyond my years. I didn't understand that my desperate desire to learn and grow was a very hopeful sign. I didn't know that if I had talked to any of the teachers or the staff they might have helped me. I never talked about my emotions to anyone. I came from a family that never talked about feelings. So I didn't tell anyone how angry I was at myself. But I often sat by the river and cried.

———— • ————

One day in October it dawned on me that my crying and my continuing bouts of homesickness were getting me nowhere. In that moment, I decided to stop. My abrupt about-face must have bewildered Grandma Gunse. One minute I was crying and demanding to know if I would be sent home if I refused to eat. She didn't know but said she'd go ask the nurse. By the time the two of them returned, I was playing happily with my dorm mates.

I can't explain it. Something just clicked, and I made up my mind that since Elsie (and I think even Mom) believed that God meant for me to come to this school, then I did, too. And if I was meant to be here, then I needed to begin learning all I could.

———— • ————

My occupational therapist told me that once I learned to type, she would let me decide what to tackle next. I told her that I wanted to be able to feed myself all the time without ending a meal looking like Emily Post's worst nightmare.

To achieve this goal, I had to overcome a basic and troublesome law of physics. Most people don't think about this, but food is subject to gravity, which was why I had so much trouble getting a spoon in my mouth with the food still on it.

The therapist's first step was to string my left hand to a weight-and-pulley contraption that would allow me to make a steadier, more controlled movement of my hand and arm. Then I clutched a thick-handled spoon with its bowl bent at a sharp angle toward my mouth. With the weight as a counterforce keeping my arm from flying out of control, I practiced the motions of moving a spoon from a plate to my mouth—over and over and over again. Eventually, when I had the muscle pattern down, I abandoned the weight and pulley altogether. All I needed was my trusty spoon, a weighted bowl that I wouldn't knock off the table, and an absorbent bib (nobody's perfect).

The next feat I accomplished in occupational therapy took only a matter of minutes. My unexpectedly sudden success thrilled me. Then it made me angry. All my life I had struggled with buttons when trying to dress myself. No matter how long and hard I tried, I always had to give up and let someone help. Buttons were impossible.

The therapist handed me a button hook and showed me how it worked. Within seconds I could button and unbutton almost anything. *Why hadn't anyone ever shown me a button hook before?* When I thought of all the hours, all the frustration, all the tears I'd shed over buttons, I got very angry.

This made me wonder how many other simple tools there might be that could simplify my life and provide more independence. *Why waste time learning to do something the way other people do it if there's a simpler way? I'll just have to try and find them for myself.*

I saw positive results in physical therapy as well. My new therapists quickly decided that my complete body brace was all wrong for me. They took it off and ordered simpler braces that supported only my ankles. Then they made me walk a lot more to build up strength until I could actually take a few steps by myself. I had more confidence and stability without my awkward old braces.

———————— • ————————

These life-changing discoveries were reason enough to feel very positive about my new school. I had made the right decision to come here. Then I had a small, seemingly incidental experience that profoundly changed my life. It would take me years to see the lasting significance of the incident, but even at the time I realized that I had reached a crucial milestone.

It happened one day after school. On my way outdoors to play with friends, I saw Dr. Anne Carlsen, the administrator and director of the Crippled Children's School, climbing the long flight of stairs up to her apartment.

Dr. Carlsen was a quadruple amputee. She was born with two stubs for arms (with no hands) and one very short stubby leg. Her other leg was twisted beyond use and eventually amputated to accommodate artificial legs and feet. Despite her physical limitations, Dr. Anne graduated from college by the age of twenty, became a teacher at the Crippled Children's Home, and earned a Ph.D.

I stood watching her laboriously climb those stairs. I realized that she had battled her way through life just as nobly as she ascended those risers. With the stumps of her arms she carefully positioned her crutches on a step and then bade her alien legs to do the walking. Slowly, slowly, she climbed higher and higher—one short step at a time.

She must have known I was watching, because when Dr. Anne Carlsen reached the very top, she turned around and smiled down at me. Without speaking a word she said to me, *You can make it too. It will never be easy. But you can do it.*

In that moment, something opened up my heart and my soul and filled me with the freeing hope and determination that one day I, too, could be a great woman like Dr. Anne Carlsen.

I will never forget that experience. It was burned into my soul's memory forever. I, too, would make it to the top.

Chapter 10

A New Spirit at Work

I determined to put the new spirit that seized me into practice. The very next day I began taking schoolbooks to my dorm room so I could do extra studying at night. Miss Austin noticed the change in my attitude and asked, "What's gotten into you, Carolyn?"

I didn't know how to explain it in words. I didn't fully understand it in my own mind. I just knew that I was different. I soon began writing my own letters home. Up to now I had dictated my correspondence to Miss Austin because I knew how to spell so few words, but with my newfound determination I wanted to become more independent. Whenever I learned a new word, I could hardly wait to go to my typewriter and use it in a letter or assignment.

My two best subjects were English and spelling, because they involved reading. I particularly enjoyed filling in blanks with the correct words in my speller. And I loved "Complete the story" assignments in my English workbook. Soon bored with merely completing stories, I wanted to compose my own. I wrote about my sisters, Rosemary and Elizabeth, and some of the escapades that earned them well-deserved spankings. Then I wrote about my cat, Muffin.

Each term, Miss Austin sent progress reports to parents and included samples of the child's schoolwork. When Mom saw how well I was doing that first year, she started sending me large-print children's books as a reward. The more I read, the more I wanted to write.

My new eagerness to strive toward higher goals spilled over into physical therapy. Though I remained less than keen about my Canadian crutches, I determined to master them. One day I wanted to walk up stairs like Dr. Carlsen.

———— • ————

Although schoolwork and therapy took most of our time and energy, we always had fun things to do after school. Plenty of grown-ups volunteered to do them with us. I loved the green uniform I was given when I joined the school's Girl Scout troop. I earned a merit badge by putting on the play *Cinderella* in which we all read our parts, but I was far more interested in taking nature walks and learning to identify the various trees and plant life around the school grounds.

The school staff and a small army of volunteers saw that our playtimes were constructive. On Saturday afternoons, if nothing else was happening, we played in the school's large stainless-steel whirlpool tank, went for walks into town, or drove out to see the "world's largest" concrete buffalo that served as the community's "tourist attraction." Once a year, the third and fourth graders went on an all-day picnic out to Miss Austin's family's farm.

Whenever we left the school, I always wondered how far we'd have to drive to see mountains. After growing up in California and Alaska, it seemed strange not to feel cradled between mountain ranges.

At times we junior girls made our own entertainment. Even when we started out playing "church," we often ended up in raucous hair-pulling contests that brought down the gentle wrath of Grandma Gunse. Our loving dorm mother heard it all—tattling, arguing, fighting. And whenever she had enough to try her patience, she sat us all on our beds to be silent and think about our sins.

It must have worked. For every night, once we were bathed and in bed, she always said we looked like a roomful of pajamaed angels.

———— • ————

The school in Jamestown provided my first real exposure to church. I once went to a church with Gaga when some of her friends invited us, but Gaga was unimpressed because the service seemed so plain. "They don't even have flowers on the altar," she groused. She walked out of that church in a huff, taking me with her. We never went back.

Church hadn't exactly been a priority for Mom or Pappy either. But they were impressed by Elsie's quiet and gentle faith. She never tried to preach at them; her belief just shone through her loving manner. Since Elsie was Lutheran, my parents indicated on my enrollment forms that I had their permission to attend a local Lutheran church.

An elderly couple drove out to pick me up for church each Sunday. While I never experienced a true sense of belonging in that congregation, I was struck by a sense of holiness and mystery that provided the first sparks of interest in knowing something more about God. The words of the liturgy intrigued me and spoke to my heart.

> *The Lord be with you.*
> *And also with you.*
> *We lift our hearts to the Lord. . . . We lift them to the Lord our God. Let us*
>   *give him thanks and praise. . . .*

The new and unfamiliar ritual raised questions I never felt free to ask. *Why was God "in his holy temple"? Wasn't he supposed to be with us everywhere? Why were we all sinners? And could God really love us all anyway? Why did Jesus have to die on the cross? And why were children not as important as grown-ups?* I asked myself this last question because children were never allowed anywhere near the Communion table. *If Jesus really said, "Let the little children come unto me" and the bread and the wine were his body and his blood, why couldn't we go up there?*

I was also intrigued with the minister's black robe and the white material over it. I wondered if it was the same material Gaga used to make curtains.

Before church each Sunday, the children met in our school classrooms for Sunday school. I felt a little more comfortable asking questions of the nurse who taught third-and-fourth-grade Sunday school than I did in town, sitting in the sanctuary with all those sober grown-ups. The grown-ups at school never acted as stiff and stern as the ones at church. I greatly enjoyed our chapel programs during the week—especially the songs and Bible stories.

Some of the older students at the school seemed to have a spiritual maturity beyond their years. Harriet was one such teenager. I never knew her background, but I merely had to look at her to see that her love for God was very real. Her motto in that year's yearbook was simply, *Living for Christ.* She didn't have to say any more. If only I could have been a good girl like her.

What impressed me even more was the obvious spiritual faith and commitment of the teachers. They were so different from any adults I had ever known. When they had misunderstandings or disagreements, they resolved their problems without getting angry or calling each other spiteful names. When they made a mistake, even with a student, they apologized and didn't try to cover it up or pretend that nothing had happened.

So it was that my experience at the Crippled Children's School was raising my sights, my standards, and my expectations of others as well as of myself.

By the end of my first year I advanced two whole grades and was doing the same-level work as my classmates. I returned home for the summer, able to feed myself and go to the bathroom alone. When Mom instinctively tried to help me, I told her to "Go away. Let me do it."

That fall, Mom took me to Jamestown herself. She wanted to see the school that had done so much for me. And that second year I made even more progress—impressing my teachers as well as my parents.

But after two years of paying for school and my expensive transportation to and from Alaska twice a year, Mom and Pappy concluded that I had learned enough. Now I could be placed in a new public school special-education program in Alaska. In light of my rapid progress in Jamestown, my teachers approved the decision. Everyone, including me, had high hopes for my continued success. And I could live at home and be part of my family again.

What I was to find was a deadly trap, baited with false hopes and unfulfilled promises, but in the years I was to be caught in that trap, the one thing that constantly sustained me was the memory of that day I saw Dr. Carlsen climb those steps. She, and the Crippled Children's School, which eventually changed its name to the Anne Carlsen school, provided me with a dream to pursue and a standard to live up to that I would refuse to abandon.

Chapter 11

The Dropout

In contrast to the warm sense of belonging I felt at school in North Dakota, I felt very out of place at my new school in Alaska. Some of my special-education classmates with behavioral and emotional disorders were so intrigued by my wheelchair they couldn't take their eyes off me. To keep their attention, our teacher, Miss Trent, had to position a portable screen around my desk. While I understood the problem and agreed to her solution, it made me feel all the more isolated.

I hated that screen. Since it was also used as a means of detention or punishment, I worried about what others would think whenever they walked by the open door of our room and saw that it was always around my desk. Anytime Miss Trent forgot to pull it closed, I made no effort to remind her, and in time the others paid less and less attention to me.

But I still felt conspicuous as a fourteen-year-old doing only fifth-grade work. To make matters worse, I owned no typewriter and had to resort again to my troublesome handwriting. I told Miss Trent that the only way I could make any meaningful progress was to have a typewriter with a key guard like the one I had used the past two years. Miss Trent seemed to empathize with my frequent, tearful frustrations. She promised me that when I got a typewriter, she would work my fingers to the bone and we'd make up for lost time. In the meantime, she offered to write my answers for me in the small spaces provided in the workbooks.

But of course Miss Trent had a limited amount of time. She had thirteen other students, ranging in age from nine to seventeen. Four of us were in the higher elementary grades, but since the other three were able-bodied and had only been assigned to special ed to deal with behavioral and emotional problems, they made great improvement and transferred out by the end of the year—which didn't seem fair. I had done the same work, but I didn't get out.

I wanted to complain to someone, but I didn't know where to go. When I talked to Mom about my frustration, I always cried and that only upset her, so I quit talking and suffered the injustice in angry silence.

I had other complaints as well. While most of my classmates were well-behaved, capable of independent study, one boy demanded constant supervision. Paul seemed to live on a diet of jumping beans. Good thing I didn't need the detention screen anymore, because Miss Trent put it around Paul's desk almost every day. Still he couldn't keep to himself. He talked and yelled constantly. If he wasn't wandering around bothering others, he was standing on his desk and pretending to be an airplane.

His frequent and loud outbursts played havoc with my startle reflex, making me jump and mess up whatever I was working on. He was a constant disruption in class and a real embarrassment to us all. His reputation rubbed off on all of us in special education. We were different enough anyway; he created one more barrier between us and the "normal" kids.

———— • ————

Living at home, I had no organized after-school activities. No Girl Scouts. No field trips. No pajama parties. I really missed the social aspect of school. Miss Trent tried to help by introducing me one day to three girls my own age in another special ed classroom next door—a friendly girl named Corrine and her two friends, Carla and Cindy. Polio left Corrine with a limp so severe that she would fall on her face several times a day. In short order we discovered she had more stability when she walked pushing my wheelchair. So I accepted her assistance knowing that I was also helping her. I even allowed her to do those tedious little tasks that required dexterity—like quickly buttoning my jacket before leaving school in the afternoon.

I liked and admired Corrine right from the start. She was my age, but she seemed so much more grown up. She controlled her emotions and never got upset like I did. And she seemed so much better able to accept herself and her limitations. Before long we formed a great friendship, even spending time together on weekends. Her friends Carla and Cindy never did accept me, keeping their distance whenever I was around. But Corrine stuck by me like a real friend. We spent so much time together that people nicknamed us "The Bobbsey Twins."

After I met Corrine, I didn't feel quite as isolated. At least I had a friend. But I was discouraged with school. How was I ever going to realize my dream of becoming a writer one day? Without a typewriter I couldn't even keep up my fifth-grade studies.

I kept bugging Mom to get me a typewriter, but something always came up, or she didn't have the money. I began to think it would take another miracle as big as the one that brought Elsie Benson into my life that day of the ACCA picnic if I was to ever again have a typewriter. Mom meant well, but turning even her best intentions into reality was a long shot. Anything beyond the demands of our regular routine seemed next to impossible.

Then one morning early in my first winter back in Alaska, Mom pushed me into my classroom. There on my desk sat a typewriter—a standard electric model, complete with a heavy plastic finger guard. It had a "Yukon Office Supply" tag on it, but no other papers to explain its appearance.

Mom had a thousand questions for Miss Trent, who shrugged them off and advised us that the less said about it, the better. I told Mom that I didn't care where it came from. Then I spun my wheelchair around in a joyful circle, ecstatic to think that someone had cared enough to donate a typewriter for me to use. And I wondered, "Who in the world would do this? And why?"

To me it *was* a miracle. Stuck without seeing any way out, I suddenly felt as if I'd been given a key that would unlock my whole future.

That old typewriter often broke down, but Mom took the responsibility of having it repaired. She said it was the least she could do since some generous person had gone to such effort and expense to get it for me. I think she was also beginning to realize just how crucial it was if I had any hope of progressing in school. I was now able to be just as independent in my written assignments as I had been in North Dakota. I had regained an inch of freedom.

True to her word, Miss Trent loaded me down with English and writing assignments. But I loved it. I had many ideas waiting to be born on paper. And the words that came out of my typewriter were not slow or twisted.

Despite my accelerated progress, there remained a limited number of hours in the day. Sometimes I think Miss Trent was as frustrated as I. Over the three years I spent in her classroom, I began to understand that we were both entangled in a system that had promised far too much and provided far too little.

Mom assured me when I came back from North Dakota that the public-school program would keep me on track to get through high school and go straight to college. It didn't take me long to figure out that this just wasn't true. The special-education program satisfied itself with the goal of graduating its students with skills needed for only the most basic service jobs—dishwashers, janitors, maybe waitresses.

I presented a serious problem for the system. First, because I actually wanted to graduate from high school and go on to college. Second, because they weren't equipped to deal with anyone physically unable to perform the manual labor they were training students to do.

My goals were never their goals. A system unequipped to work for me actually worked against me. By the time I started junior high it seemed the public-school system was content to accept the extra federal funding they got for me because of Pappy's civil-service job. There was no real effort to meet my needs or help me toward my own goals. My conflict over my seventh-grade schedule provided a good example of the system's inadequacies.

My classes for seventh grade taught such basic survival lessons as reading road signs and janitorial skills. I sarcastically informed my counselor that I had been reading road signs for years and didn't need to waste my time on such nonsense. As for janitorial skills, they might be of some value if I planned to become a maid. But I had my heart set on being a writer. If they couldn't offer me some academic courses, I didn't see any point in continuing school.

The counselor reminded me that it was the law that I go to school, but if I insisted on academic classes, the only one available that fit my schedule was a science lab. So I signed up. It turned out to be totally impractical because it required many hands-on experiments and few reading or writing assignments. I couldn't ever get the slides inserted properly under the microscope. I couldn't handle specimens without crushing and destroying them. The teacher never made the time or had the patience to give me alternative assignments that covered the same material.

I became even more discouraged to find that my junior-high classroom was a zoo and the teacher was content to be a zookeeper. Three huge boys made big balls of clay and actually threw them at each other across the room while the teacher ignored them and continued his lecture. How could I learn anything in that kind of chaos? How could anyone?

———————————•———————————

Things didn't seem any better at home with my family. Living conditions in our house were bad enough before. Now, after experiencing a very different standard at boarding school, I found life in the Martin house nearly unbearable.

At school I was used to the luxury of having clean clothes to wear each day. At home I pleaded in vain for Mom to wash up my underwear often enough so I'd have clean panties every morning. We didn't have a washer or dryer, so Mom took everything to a laundromat, a major chore she hated so much that she only managed it about once a month.

Many times, instead of doing laundry, Mom simply made another trip to the Salvation Army surplus store to buy me something clean to wear.

I realized that there was no chance our dank, dark, ramshackle, and makeshift old house could ever compare with the standard of cleanliness I experienced in the bright, fresh, and airy dormitory back in Jamestown. Evidently my mother had given up hope. When it came to housekeeping, it seemed that she didn't even try.

Dirt and clutter piled up everywhere. Stacks of old clothes and junk reached the ceiling in the back room where I slept. Countless pets wandered in and out of the house at will. Some of the cats routinely used the floor of my closet for a litter box. Since the closet had no light, I could never see their messes until I slipped on them. That invariably made me so furious I screamed at Mom, who might or might not get around to cleaning up after her animals.

There were other frustrations. The independence I gained at Dr. Carlsen's school opened many wonderful doors—doors that now slammed shut. I begged Pappy to put rails in the bathroom so I could help myself, but he never had the time. I told him that if he put a handrail on the front steps I'd be able to get myself in and out of the house. He never did that, either.

He didn't argue with me as much as he used to about my need to learn to walk. Only once in a while did he swear and call me "Lazy!" He seemed burned-out with me. But then I felt pretty burned-out myself.

In North Dakota I'd never felt disabled. I walked in therapy and to class each morning. Everything seemed in balance. Even my dreams fit with everyday realities. While I started out behind my classmates, once my attitude changed I made encouraging progress. I felt like a loser when I started so slowly, but people like Miss Austin and Dr. Carlsen changed all that by giving me what I truly believed were realistic hopes and dreams.

Now my two years in far-off North Dakota seemed like a cruel joke. I felt terribly disabled and ugly. I got so angry over the littlest things—like spilling milk, knocking the rickety leg out from under the bathroom sink with my wheelchair, or making an absolute mess when I ate—that I'd kick and scream and pitch crying fits lasting for hours.

When I finally wore myself out, I'd be angry about getting angry and feel even more alone and trapped.

———— • ————

About this time, a school psychologist reviewed my records and asked Mom to bring me in for an interview. His conclusion was that we (and the school system) had been doing everything wrong. He said he wasn't at all sure it was worth the money to try to educate me.

At first I was angry. *Who gave him the right to make that decision about me? What did he base his conclusion on anyway? He doesn't know me.*

But *I* knew me. I also knew that his criticism of the school system was valid. Everything they did was a costly experiment at my expense. Junior high school was a farce. How could high school be any better? As for college, I could just forget that. I grew so discouraged that I began taking medication for depression. Every day I slept away as much time as I could.

———— • ————

Pappy had a saying for whenever he got frustrated: "I have reached dead center." Whenever I heard that phrase, I pictured in my mind a car stranded on a mound. It couldn't move forward or backward because none of the wheels touched the ground. There was no traction because it was stuck "dead center."

I was fourteen years old when I came home from North Dakota, ready to pursue my dreams. But after three years of public-school special education, I was going nowhere. Given my disability, my lack of educational options, and my family situation, I didn't see how I ever could. I had reached dead center.

———— • ————

March 27, 1964. Good Friday.

I hadn't felt well that morning. Mom kept me home in bed most of the day. I was watching some puppet show on television while Mom and Pappy sat talking at the kitchen table. Mom got up to go outside when I called her in to adjust the TV picture. Just as she bent down in front of the set, the earth began to shake. Before we had time to think *EARTHQUAKE!* it stopped. For a moment. Pappy headed outside to see what he could see. Frightened, I tried to get out of my push chair as I called, "Mom."

Suddenly there was a terrible cracking sound. The whole world began to heave up and down. With one arm around a room divider and the other around me, Mom held me tightly as I screamed. It's a terrifying sensation to feel your home moving underneath and around you. I heard window glass breaking all through the house. Mom whispered in my ear, "Don't be scared, Posey. It'll be over in a minute." Still the earth rolled on and on.

Finally it stopped. We had survived the great Alaskan earthquake. Much of the city of Anchorage was devastated. Entire downtown streets collapsed. Buildings crumbled.

In the weeks that followed, our family and everyone else in that part of the state tried to cope with the aftermath of a terrible natural disaster. I was delighted to find that my schooling was no longer a priority. Mom was too exhausted from coping with the details of life in a disaster area to bother taking me each morning. We never really made a decision, I just quit school after the earthquake because I never got around to going back.

While my family and our house survived the earthquake with surprisingly little damage, my own life was a shambles. My dreams were shattered. And I had not yet even begun to face the emotional destruction caused by an ongoing personal trauma no one else ever suspected.

Chapter 12

Deep Furrow of Pain

During the years I went to special ed in Anchorage, I also attended church with my girlfriend, Claudia. She invited me first to join the youth group and promised there would be many fun activities. I became a regular passenger in the church van that came by the house to pick me up. My rickety wheelchair wasn't a problem. The minister eased Mom's fears by assuring her he would take responsibility for my chair and me.

Even as I grew discouraged with the school's question as to whether I was worth educating, I found a true sense of self-worth and acceptance at church. No matter what the youth group did, I was allowed to participate. We had pajama parties and picnics. We attended youth rallies together, put on plays, and sang. Oh, how I loved to sing!

But the main focus of the young people's group was to study the Word of God. I really enjoyed competing with the other kids in Bible quiz games. When we chose sides for Bible Bowl competition, I was often picked first because I studied and knew the answers. Anytime I had difficulty pronouncing a biblical name, the minister's wife would give me three choices and I would pick the correct one.

The love and acceptance of my peers in that youth group played an important positive role in my life. However, I had some initial reservations about the church itself. Something about it didn't feel right. At first I thought my uneasiness might be due to the building itself.

Located in an old storefront, the makeshift sanctuary symbolized for me the "rural-haphazard" conditions basic to Alaskan lifestyle. So much man-made ugliness in a land so rich in awesome beauty.

In winter, covered with snow, the building actually looked like an idyllic Christmas card. But spring thaw revealed the truth. The shabby building needed much paint and repair. Inside, the church always struck me as gloomy and depressing. Bags of insulation spewed their brown fillings out from between the wall studding. A large old heating stove coughed and rattled in one dark corner. Though I always sat near it, I never felt quite warm enough—coughing and rattling nearly as much as the stove.

Water stains made haunting designs on the ceiling, giving this place of worship a most hopeless decor. Flimsy, mismatched folding chairs sat in vacant, uneven rows—evidence of someone's unrealistic expectations.

In spite of the shabby building, I was even more troubled by what I didn't see. No paraments. No candles. None of the ecclesiastical trappings I became familiar with in that little church in Jamestown. Nor did the pastor here make the sign of the cross as he offered forgiveness to the congregation.

All the minister did was pray, sing, and then preach—very loudly. After the sermon, he invited us to come to the "altar" (nothing more than a bare rail in front of the pulpit), to accept Jesus as Savior.

This was definitely not a Lutheran service. I assumed that was the basis of my uneasiness. Part of me longed for the familiar sense of holiness and mystery I felt worshiping God back in North Dakota. But I told myself that part of my life was gone now. I would stay in this church because my new friends made me feel loved and accepted.

Yet that sense of uneasiness never completely disappeared. In my quiet moments just before I went to sleep at night, I had the recurring feeling that *This is not what God has planned. There's something more and greater stored away for me—something gentle and deep and wonderful.*

I angrily dismissed such thoughts by reminding myself that I always had had noble dreams and believed for too long that I would actually fulfill them. I dreamed of attaining an education and becoming a writer. I dreamed of freedom and breaking the bonds that limited me and defined my life. Perhaps most foolishly, I dreamed that one day I would gain control over my emotions and grow up to be a kind and gentle woman.

A lot of good my big dreams did! They seemed to hurt more than they helped because I felt more trapped than ever. Each shattered dream became another blow, pounding my trap deeper and deeper into hard, unyielding ground.

These deepest, secret feelings surfaced only in the dark and silence of the night. I dared not share them with anyone. Not even God. Because what I was being taught about him convinced me that God would be angry at me if I ever expressed such anger and doubt.

———— • ————

The fundamentalist theology I caught from my new church said that once a person was "born again" all the concerns of our earthly life should be unimportant. We should be forever happy with our lot in this life, setting aside all our practical, everyday concerns for that all-important mission of saving souls. To please God, you had to be a "soul winner for Christ."

This was a confusing burden to me. I already felt unaccepted by others who couldn't understand me or my speech. Preaching at people wouldn't make me any more acceptable. And the fact that I didn't want to be a "soul winner" made me feel that I wasn't the kind of person God would find acceptable.

But I went along, playing the part of a devout teenager who was, in the terminology of my church, "on fire for the Lord." Pretending to be one thing on the outside just to cover up what was happening inside did earn praise from my church friends. It also further weakened my self-image. My hypocrisy underscored those feelings that I was a bad girl with less and less hope of ever changing into the mature person I desperately wanted to be.

———— • ————

I was able to coax Mom to come to church with me a few times. She didn't mind helping with various service projects. She even talked Pappy into fixing the church van. But I knew she was never comfortable in those services, so after a while I quit twisting her arm to come. She seemed to hear her own spiritual drummer during silent midnight walks in the garden with her pride of stray house cats tagging along behind her.

I did get one of our neighbors, a woman known for her heavy drinking, to begin attending church. The minister's wife expressed amazement when the lady accepted my invitation; she'd been trying to get my neighbor to come for months.

I felt proud and encouraged when the minister and his wife praised my efforts. They convinced me I was indeed "chosen" by God to be disabled in order to bring souls into the kingdom of God. Whenever they told me it was "God's will" that I was disabled, I believed them because they seemed to know so much about God and the Bible. I valued their acceptance and never risked confessing to them my feelings of anger or doubt.

It disappointed me to learn there was no special rite of confirmation for the youth. The people in this congregation believed that once a person was "born again" he or she could be baptized and join the church. That was all there was to it.

When I decided to take those steps, Mom drew the line. She wanted me to postpone that decision until I could separate my faith from my need for acceptance and from my growing friendship with the minister and his wife. I thought Mom was being terribly unfair, but she held her ground, saying that when I earned a high school diploma I could make my own decision about joining any church I wanted.

Eventually I became so comfortable in my tiny new church that I even felt free to share with the minister's wife my dreams of writing. She affirmed those goals but told me that it would take a lot of work and would probably require going somewhere else to get the necessary education that I needed and deserved. But, like Mom, she expressed great faith that once I got on the right course, I'd quickly make up for the awkward waiting time I seemed to be stuck in.

It was her encouragement, as much as my family's, that kept me plodding along in special education those three long years. The minister and his wife always made time for me. So I loved and trusted them.

———————————•———————————

During the winter it was always dark when the minister drove the van full of kids home from youth activities or church. Often he made it a point to drop me off last, since I enjoyed the laughter and company of my peers so much. Yet the minister never tried to communicate directly with me. He always relied on others to tell him what I was saying.

After he had been driving me home for some months, he started to rest his hand on my knee as I sat in the seat beside him. I thought nothing of this gesture because he was my "Pastor" and also my friend, regularly in and out of our home, visiting with my parents and working with Pappy on cars. And I was always a "hands-on" person anyway—someone was always moving and positioning me, even shoving my knees to adjust my sitting posture.

Then came the evening when he took an extra long way home, down a dark and overgrown road, far from any streetlights. When he stopped the car, he found another place for his hand. And in that moment I became aware of my sexuality.

I had access to as much information as any teenage girl at that time, but no one had told me the emotions that come with being touched in an intimate way can be so overpowering and confusing.

I began to cry, in part because what he was doing hurt me physically, but also because I felt as if he had pierced the very core of who I was, and the resulting wound had become instantly infected with shame.

He waited until I stopped crying. Then he pulled off my jacket and loosened my clothes so he could get to me more easily. I screamed at him because I felt so powerless, and I screamed in self-fury because of the strange new emotions overpowering me. I kept screaming until he finally stopped, and then I cried because I felt so dirty.

He told me that the pain would go away soon. He said I would feel good when he did it again. He also told me I was a good girl and a good friend for helping him by letting him do this, because his wife couldn't have sex with him at the time. He said it was okay because God wanted him to do this to me. This was going to happen eventually anyway, and it was better that he teach me these things as a minister because if I felt any guilt, he would be able to pray for my forgiveness. He said it was better that he introduce me to sex than have someone who didn't care about me really hurt me or cause me to become pregnant.

He told me that no one else ever needed to know. If his wife ever found out, she would be angry with both of us. Mom and my family wouldn't understand either. Then he threatened me, saying if I ever thought of telling, he would pull all my pubic hair out. He grabbed it and pulled just to show me. I understood.

I think I always knew it was wrong. But I didn't tell anyone what had happened that night. Or the next time he drove me home. Or the next.

As time went on, I hated myself for enjoying his touch. I hated myself even more for being so weak, for touching him and letting him touch me, and for having such a desperate need for love and acceptance that I let him use me like that. I didn't understand all the feelings I had, but I blamed myself for having them.

No matter how many times he told me I was a good girl for "helping" him, I knew I wasn't. I had felt like a bad girl all my life. Any doubts I might have had about that were certainly gone now.

I tried to bury this horrible new sense of brokenness deep in the most private, hidden corner of my soul. I was convinced that no one could ever again love me if they found out what I had done. But I remembered. And in the darkness of my nights, I now had this added reason to detest myself.

Chapter 13

Spring Thaw

I sank deeper than ever into my recurring pattern of depression. I cried for no reason—at least no reason my family could understand. I slept as often and as long as I could. Sleep offered the simplest escape.

When awake, I had to live with two devastating disappointments. First was my disillusionment with school. Whether I failed at school, or school failed with me, the discouraging results were the same. The one thing I'd always seen as the key to my escape, the best hope for a meaningful life, had become part of my trap.

My second great disappointment was with myself. What had become of my dreams? Why wasn't I making something of my life? Where was the hope that someday things would be different? When would I be different? Stronger. More stable emotionally. Smarter. More mature. A great woman like Dr. Carlsen.

All such dreams were shattered one by one during those dark encounters in a church van on deserted back roads. I was now beyond hope. I was a disgrace for causing a minister to sin. Even after the man and his family moved back to the Lower Forty-eight and I knew that I would never have to see him again, there was no denying the horror of the memories or the terrible truth: I was an evil person.

I had no one to talk to about my feelings. Had there been someone, I still couldn't have done it. I didn't know how to talk about my emotions. But I felt them. They were always there. Every day. And especially every night. They gnawed at the corners of my soul. Their constant heaviness dragged me deeper and deeper into my personal black hole of despair.

———————•———————

From time to time I was able to pull out of my depression. Sometimes when I did, I dreamed fantastic daydreams and then devoted all my energies to bringing them to reality. For example, since I was the last kid at home and had the large back room to myself after my sisters moved out, I had a great plan. I talked Mom into painting the room a bright sunshine yellow to capture and reflect what little light filtered in the one tiny, single-pane window. After Mom painted the walls, we went shopping and found yellow candlesticks, plus matching doilies and curtains. Finished, I thought the room looked beautiful.

Along one wall sat a huge bookshelf. I continued to read a great deal. On another side of the room was a table that had weathered out in our yard for months before I got someone to bring it in. After hours and hours of tedious scrubbing, it made a serviceable desk and a good place to work at the typewriter I had talked my teacher into letting me keep before I quit school.

My bedroom became my refuge. In this place I could some days still try to recapture my old dream of becoming a writer.

———————•———————

I suppose Mom did what she did with my room in an attempt to try to encourage me. She didn't know what else to try. I think Pappy was at a complete loss to know how to react to my depression. The frequent sound of typing coming from my room may have been the sole reassuring sign they had that I was still alive.

The only one who expressed any objection to my typing was Sam, our huge white cat. He hated the typewriter. Whenever I turned it on, he would attack it, then walk on the keyboard, and finally lie down across the machine and purr. Maybe he was just jealous.

Every time I swatted him off, he'd run to mew at Mom until she laughingly scolded me. "Posey! Are you abusing poor Sam again?" Then Sam, feeling vindicated, came back into my room swooshing his tail at me. Mom also fed him to appease his hurt feelings, so Sam became an enormously fat and spoiled feline.

Despite Sam's interference, I spent a lot of time at my typewriter. Mostly I pounded out religious tracts in the hard-edged style of my rigidly fundamentalist church. "God is good. Men are all worthless sinners. When we become Christians we die to self and commit our lives to conquering the world for Christ. Nothing else matters."

I think the belief that "self" didn't matter appealed to me. It gave me license to punish myself for my own sin. I could be especially hard on sinners, because I was one. I'd don my religious armor and my smiling Christian mask for my friends at church, but my harsh attitude of self-condemnation colored much of what I wrote about the cut-and-dried gospel I believed in.

My fundamentalist faith became as much a hiding place as my room. I couldn't bear the thought of giving either of them up. Simplistic answers and familiar walls shielded me from the hard, difficult truth of the real world.

I was getting comfortable being trapped.

———————•———————

My sister Elizabeth had a falling-out with Mom when she ran away from home and got married. She made it a point to stop by the house when she knew that Mom was out. That way, the two of us could talk. We often discussed my future. I knew she was right when she bluntly told me I couldn't go on living like I was. I couldn't stay in my room every day reading and writing. Without more schooling I couldn't expect to get any farther than my own front door.

We agreed on the problem. We just couldn't see any reasonable solution. The local educational system hadn't done the job. Elizabeth checked into the possibility of some kind of financial assistance from the state, but there was always too much red tape. Anytime we thought we were onto something, someone or something would yank the rug out from under us, and I'd wind up even more depressed.

What I needed was a miracle. But I didn't bother asking God for one. I knew I didn't deserve it.

A miracle arrived anyway in the form of my oldest sister, Maxine, who flew in from Chicago for what she planned to be a long weekend visit. I hadn't seen her for years, but she was still as tall and as pretty as I remembered.

When she walked into the bedroom to give me a hug and tell me what a pretty girl I was with my long braided hair, I felt as if I were meeting a pen pal for the first time. We'd written to each other regularly ever since I learned to type. Within hours of our reunion we were talking like we'd been doing it all our lives. She understood a surprising percentage of what I said. When she couldn't understand, I spelled the word. When I didn't know how to spell what I wanted to say, she simply played twenty questions until she understood. And she always laughed good-naturedly whenever she tried to guess what I was saying and missed the mark entirely.

Maxine arrived on a Saturday morning just as Mom, Pappy, and I were preparing to head out of town to our homestead for the weekend. We had an old trailer and a lean-to Pappy had built on the property, and we spent part of every week living there in order to satisfy the government's residency requirements. But my sister wasn't sure she liked the idea of traipsing off into the wilderness only hours after arriving in Alaska from "civilized" Chicago.

Pappy assured her that it was safe. He said that Shirley lived alone with her two children on their homestead all week while her husband stayed in town and worked. Our homestead was primitive but livable. Even so, as Pappy packed the car, Maxine found his rifle and suggested we take it along. He talked her out of it, explaining that any big game stayed deep in the woods and wouldn't come out in the clearing around the trailer.

I did warn Maxine that if she thought she heard anything, whether it was a mouse or a bear, she should always check to see where Pappy was. He had an uncanny ability to imitate animal noises and liked to wait until someone was seated helplessly in the outhouse to put on his best performances. Maxine thanked me for the warning, while Pappy just grinned.

I, too, assured her that only small animals ventured near the trailer. "And Pappy's already made friends with them." His favorite was Willie, a weasel who would even ride with him on the tractor.

What we didn't tell Maxine, because we didn't know it, was that Willie had apparently chewed a small hole in the trailer floor during our absence. And that night, after we all went to sleep, Willie weaseled his way into the trailer and jumped onto Mom and Pappy's bed.

Mom was never in a good mood when half asleep, so she wasn't too happy to be awakened by Pappy's whispered plea: "Help me, Ma! There's a weasel on my chest. I think it's Willie!"

Mom's sleepy response was, "Are you sure? Well, I guess you'd know. It takes an old weasel to know an old weasel!" So she climbed out of bed, turned on the lights, took a broom after the weasel and shooed him (Willie, not Pappy) out the door. Then she nailed up the hole and went back to bed.

I thought the whole thing was hilarious. Maxine wasn't at all amused.

———————•———————

Despite such a rude introduction to Alaskan life on her very first night, Maxine decided to extend her stay. In Chicago she was a model and worked in restaurants. Now she realized that she was tired of that routine and wanted to do something more productive. So once she decided to stay in Anchorage, she wasted no time enrolling in a local community college and looking for a job. Despite a hectic schedule of school, work, and involvement with a local theater company, Maxine made time to help take care of me.

Whether it was giving me a bubble bath or taking me on outings to the library or to the theater, she did whatever she could think of to get me out of my frequent black holes. Pappy often praised her, saying that I seemed so much happier since she came home. And I know that Mom was glad to have someone to ease her load and get me motivated again.

One thing Maxine seemed determined to change was my hair. Long and heavy, it took two days to dry whenever it was washed. It looked beautiful when Mom braided it in a wreath around my head, but it didn't stay that way long without a lot of attention.

A shorter hairstyle would be simpler. But some of the women at church called my hair my "crown of glory." So many people commented on it that it was as if my hair was the only good thing about me. It seemed to mercifully hide the grotesque person I believed I was. Perhaps no one would like me if I cut my hair.

I told myself that such fears were irrational. But I still agonized over the decision to let Maxine cut it. Twice I gave her the okay and then backed out at the last minute. When I finally surrendered to her scissors, the rest of the family cheered my courage.

Two hours later I had shoulder-length hair with a soft perm. Maxine sagged into the nearest chair, exhausted. Cutting and perming a moving target was hard work. But I was more than satisfied with the results. I hugged Maxine and proceeded to thumb my nose at anyone who mourned the loss of my trademark braids.

That haircut marked the beginning of a new determination to break free from my trap and pursue my old goals. I would have to face the stormy bouts of depression that threatened to enslave me. And I still feared them. But what I feared even more was being isolated forever in my room, at home, in Anchorage, Alaska, drifting slowly but surely farther and farther away from any promise or hope that a meaningful, productive life might have to offer me.

───── • ─────

Maxine took a job with a new local agency that worked with disabled children—thoroughly testing the kids and then placing them in educational programs or homes that would most benefit them. She soon accumulated new and interesting information regarding financial support, medical care, education, housing, and employment opportunities for physically or mentally disadvantaged young adults. When Maxine told me about a newly established state office of vocational rehabilitation, I asked her to call and see what they could offer me. After submitting a big packet of paperwork, Maxine and I got an appointment.

The counselor reviewed my case history and admitted that he didn't think there was anywhere in Alaska that could adequately meet my needs. He suggested that we look into the United Cerebral Palsy (UCP) Center and the Sea Ridge Nursing Home down in Seattle, Washington. He told us that no one from the state rehabilitation offices had actually been to either place, but the UCP chapter in Seattle was widely respected and thought to have the best resources on the West Coast. And since there was no adequate program available in the state, Alaska's Department of Vocational Rehabilitation would pay for my housing and education in Seattle.

Indeed, the UCP Center facility seemed to offer everything I wanted—an educational program, physical therapy, a vocational training workshop, and even social activities. Those who were able could finish high school and receive an official diploma. The counselor had little information on the nursing home, but his information indicated that several of the UCP's young adults lived there.

I had mixed reactions to this Seattle idea. It offered new hope that there might be a way out of my limiting circumstances. Maybe my dreams weren't dead. Seattle wasn't Alaska, and that was another plus.

But I had seen dreams dashed too many times before to let my hopes soar unchecked. *What if it didn't work out? What if this was just another special program that failed to deliver what it promised?* There were so many unknowns. And it would mean another painful separation from my family. I'd be far from home and alone again.

While I wrestled with this decision, the rehabilitation counselor found a tutor who could work with me every afternoon at the ACCA to help get my academic skills up to the level of a high-school freshman. In the mornings I had speech and physical therapy and then worked on my homework there in a classroom.

Though I was now the oldest student at the ACCA and back in the same setting of almost ten years before, I told myself that it was only temporary. And I enjoyed being in the classroom because the younger children seemed to like me. One little boy told his foster mother that he wanted to be just like me when he grew up. Anytime he couldn't sit next to me, he would pout.

Nearly a year passed before I reached the point of having to make my final decision. In the meantime, the Seattle UCP sent sheet after sheet of application and entrance forms—most of them containing very personal questions about my character and my background. Their seemingly high standards greatly encouraged me. I had visions of something similar in quality and tone to the Crippled Children's School in North Dakota. And since the Sea Ridge Nursing Home never sent any additional forms of its own, we all just assumed it was on the same par as the UCP.

———————•———

The actual decision wasn't easy. But despite my doubts and fears, I overruled my emotions and decided to pursue the only reasonable course. I had to go to Seattle. It was time—after a long decade of disappointment and pain—to leave my family and a home where my dreams had melted away even faster than ice during an Alaskan spring thaw.

Chapter 14

Welcome to Sea Ridge

I flew down to Seattle with Barbara, a friend of Maxine's, who volunteered to get me settled into the nursing home and take me to the United Cerebral Palsy Center. We arrived on a bright spring morning, which I took as an encouraging omen. The Alaska Office of Vocational Rehabilitation had a representative at the airport to meet us. Bruce was a recent college graduate who told me that since I was his first "able-minded disabled" client, he could foresee making some mistakes.

Bruce loaded us into his car for a whirlwind tour of the center. There was no tour guide. So we nosed around the center on our own. We found classrooms, therapy rooms, an arts-and-crafts center, even a machine shop.

The most activity seemed to be taking place in a basement workshop of the main building. Never in one place had I seen so many people with varying degrees of serious disabilities. What struck me most was the range of their ages.

For the first time in my life I confronted the reality of middle-aged, disabled adults. It shocked and frightened me. For years I had told myself that I would get better once I got the help I needed. Now, in the very place where I would pursue those dreams, I found people who had stopped dreaming. These people had lived a lifetime and not gotten better. I couldn't help thinking, *Am I going to be like that one day?* But then I answered myself with a determined, *No! I'll never be like them. I'm going to get better.*

Up a two-flight ramp from the workshop was the center's dental office. I had needed dental work for a long time and took aspirin regularly to dull the pain. The involuntary and uncontrollable movements characteristic of my type of cerebral palsy make dental care an impossible task. But here, the dental nurse explained, they were equipped with anesthesia to put patients to sleep while working on their teeth. I told her that sounded wonderful to me. It seemed that my teeth had hurt me forever. She nodded and smiled, saying that many people with CP had similar trouble. And since this was the first such dental clinic on the West Coast, their office kept busy.

By this time it was late afternoon. We needed to head back across town to find the nursing home. We dropped Barbara off at a downtown hotel on the way. She promised to catch a cab to the home in the morning and help get me unpacked and settled in. I thought Bruce and I could handle the initial check-in, since Sea Ridge was expecting me. Anyway, I was exhausted by the trip and the day's excitement. All I wanted was to eat and go right to bed.

Bruce and I made the slow trip back to the home in rush-hour traffic. While I enjoyed seeing so much of my new city on this very first day, I began to wonder about the daily routine of coming and going from Sea Ridge to the center. How would I cope with such a long drive?

Once we arrived at Sea Ridge Nursing Home, I started across the parking lot with my walker, but I was so tired that the distance seemed impossible. Bruce went inside and returned moments later with a wheelchair and pushed me the rest of the way.

Sea Ridge looked much like a well-kept motel with a neat and clean sidewalk, a carefully trimmed garden, and a large porch where a number of residents sat enjoying the early evening air. Several young people, some in wheelchairs, seemed to be talking and enjoying each other's company. I imagined myself among them in a few weeks, and it made me feel good. I was eager to make friends and begin my new life here.

Around the corner from the well-lighted entry hall we found the nurses' station. A woman in a crisp, starched uniform greeted us with a clipboard of forms to be filled out. I asked the nurse if I could get my own wheelchair, which I'd shipped the day before in a large crate with my other belongings. She eyed me coldly and said sternly, "According to your medical records we received from UCP, you aren't supposed to have a wheelchair here. It's not part of your therapy program."

"What?" I was becoming upset. "That's not right!"

Seeing my mounting distress, Bruce took up for me. He informed the nurse that he was the social worker assigned to my case and he knew of no medical evaluation. He expected some tests to be conducted within the next month. As he talked, I grew more and more alarmed to think that someone had written medical recommendations for me after scanning a few records and without ever seeing or hearing from me. Fortunately Bruce's insistence that he was in charge of my case carried some weight with the nurse. She let him check on my things and bring my wheelchair.

That battle won, I proceeded to tell the nurse that I was hungry. She said that the staff had already served supper and then ungraciously agreed to send something down to my room. She seemed put out with me for disturbing her routine and acted impatient to get back to whatever she'd been doing. Then she made me feel even more unwelcome by saying, "I don't know why you brought so many things when you're only going to be staying with us for a month."

Bruce spoke up in surprise when he heard that. "There must be some mistake. Carolyn plans to live here while she goes to the UCP Center and begins high school." We assumed this had all been arranged, since I'd received letters of acceptance from both the Center and Sea Ridge. When the nurse heard all this, she rather huffily replied, "Well I wish someone had told me all that in the first place!"

Since the home had full occupancy on the "South Wing" where the other disabled young people lived, I was temporarily placed on another hall. I would share a room with a pleasant elderly woman recovering from a broken hip who would go home shortly. I smiled and greeted my roommate, but she didn't understand anything I said after "Hello."

The room looked a little too much like a hospital for my tastes. But it was well-lighted. And right across the hall was a door out to a wheelchair-accessible patio.

Bruce left after an aide arrived with my supper of runny, lukewarm, creamed tuna and a glass of milk. A few minutes later a silver-haired nurse named Fern came into the room to check on me. She smiled warmly when she asked if I'd gotten enough to eat. When I said I had, she got me a washcloth and handed it to me with the good-natured observation: "You certainly look like you enjoyed it."

As she helped clean up my mess, she said there was a church service starting in just a few minutes. "It would be a good place for you to meet people if you'd like to go." I told her I'd enjoy that, so she pushed my chair down to an arts-and-crafts room where volunteers from a local congregation conducted a regular service and Bible study. Everyone seemed interested in the fact that I'd just arrived from Alaska. Most of the residents seemed friendly and did their best to make me feel welcome.

———————————◆———————————

The next morning I awakened feeling like a lonely alien in a strange new world. By 7:00 A.M., the daily routine was in full swing and I was just another new patient.

When an aide served me a bowl of sloppy, thin oatmeal while I was sitting up in bed—the worst possible place for me to eat—I began to cry. I felt isolated. Never before had I been left alone with strangers who treated me as if I were totally helpless.

After breakfast, another aide came in to give me a bed bath. She didn't even try to stop and understand me when I protested that I'd rather bathe myself. I hated to be touched intimately, and that part of my bath was done without dignity. She didn't even use much soap.

I fought and screamed in frustration. All I wanted was to bathe myself in privacy, and I couldn't get the aide to listen.

I wanted to wear comfortable, casual clothes, but by the time the aide finished my bath she was so impatient with me that she grabbed the nearest garments, dressing me in my best suit. It was more than an hour before I finally quit sobbing. In the meantime I decided that I hated this place and that when Barbara came back I would leave with her and return to Alaska.

However, my second morning was better. An older aide named Anne brought my breakfast. She introduced herself and talked to me as she raised the head of my bed and placed the tray in front of me. I took the risk of asking her to lower the bed rail so that I could get out in my chair and feed myself. She not only understood me, she did what I asked. So I then asked if she would please break up my toast and put it in my cereal bowl so the dry toast would soak up the sloppy oatmeal and make it easier to stick to my spoon. She cheerfully did that, too. I felt we'd made remarkable progress in one day.

When Anne returned after breakfast, I asked for a towel and wash-cloth. I took a change of casual clothes into the bathroom and indulged myself with a sponge bath, using lots of soap. Then I dressed myself. I felt wonderful and had begun making my own bed when I overheard Anne out in the hall telling the aide who hadn't taken the time to listen that I was able to dress and take care of myself.

Later that morning I asked for the belongings I'd sent to the home so I could get my typewriter. The head nurse argued that it would be too much trouble since I was only staying for evaluations. I asked why everyone seemed to have the impression that I was only staying a month. I thought I was there to go to the UCP Center and to start high school. That's what I wanted.

The nurse apologized for the misunderstanding. But she added, "I wish the UCP would have told us that in the first place. As soon as we can get a free aide, we'll get you settled."

One evening just a few days later I was sitting on my bed, reading, when two aides walked in and announced they had to move me. My roommate was going home, and two more elderly patients were moving in. They needed my space within the hour. So Fern and one of the aides hurriedly loaded my bed with my belongings and suggested I stay in it as they pushed my bed and my typewriter table down the hall to the south wing. We all laughed at the reactions of the other residents as I rolled through the hall with the greatest of ease.

When we got to my new room, no one was there. Fern laughed and said, "I'll bet Ila Mae will be surprised to find a new roommate when she returns."

I felt like I was invading someone else's home. Why hadn't anyone told her I would be moving in? I wasn't even sure I wanted to live with Ila Mae. I'd just met her briefly on my first day and she didn't seem to fit into the group. When I expressed my uncertainty, Fern assured me Ila Mae was a nice person who also liked to write. "I'm sure you'll like her when you get to know her," she said.

So I got off my bed and started to unpack. I wasn't sure how all my stuff would fit in my new place. I felt squeezed into a room already filled with someone else's things. I got especially concerned when one of the aides wheeled my typewriter into the hall. I had visions of one of the older disoriented patients pulling it off onto the floor. But the aide covered it with a sheet and reassured me with the promise that Anne would help me get everything squared away in the morning.

I was still putting my clothes away when Ila Mae was wheeled into the room. She looked surprised and then bewildered. She was clearly upset that no one had told her what was happening. But she sighed as she told me, "That's the way they do things around here."

I felt relieved that she wasn't upset with me. I think we both felt the same frustration, realizing that someone else could decide that since we both had cerebral palsy, we would automatically get along and share our lives together. But we knew nothing about each other. All we shared was our disability and the belief that this was a very strange way to begin a friendship.

Chapter 15

No Escape from Myself

Sea Ridge certainly wasn't the Anne Carlsen School.

A week after my arrival, I was to begin going every day to the United Cerebral Palsy Center. The plan was for me to get involved in the activities at the center, become acclimated to my new routine for several weeks, and then commence my high school study when a new school year started in the fall. I probably did need time to adjust to new people, surroundings, and routines. I even began to look forward to the prospect of working in the center's workshop on what would be my first real job.

I decided to take my walker for my first day at the UCP. After the confusion over my records when I arrived at the nursing home, I didn't want to get in trouble for showing up in my "unapproved" wheelchair.

I waited on the front porch of the nursing home with several of my new friends for the UCP bus to arrive. It looked like a huge yellow box with a door on the side that lifted up and back. Two male aides jumped out and positioned a ramp as the driver came over to push wheelchairs toward the bus. "Hi, I'm Carol," she greeted me. "You must be Carolyn."

I smiled and said hello as I watched one of the aides begin pushing wheelchairs up the ramp while the other man worked inside the bus, lashing the chairs to the floor with cargo clamps like they use in airplanes.

112

Carol had an extra wheelchair that she rolled toward me as she suggested, "Why don't you get in and let me take your walker? Then you won't have to climb the steps."

Inside the bus I transferred to a regular seat, and Carol buckled me in. She warned me to watch my feet because the aides "are going to park a wheelchair right in front of you, and they aren't always very careful."

Upon arrival at the center after a long drive, Carol helped me out of the bus and walked with me all the way down to the basement workshop, a long, dingy, narrow room where thirty people were already working. Once everyone from our nursing-home group had settled in, a supervisor named Mrs. Kippin brought me an old wooden wheelchair with casters. "This isn't the safest place for people who are unsteady on their feet," she told me. It was beginning to look like I would get no hassle about bringing my wheelchair from then on.

Mrs. Kippin situated me alone at a small table and then brought over a stack of stiff plastic envelopes. She instructed me to tear all the tape and stickers off the envelopes, remove any staples, and then stick my hand inside to check for holes. If I found any hole that I could stick three fingers through, I was to discard the envelope. "Any questions?" Before I could react she said, "Good" and walked away.

That's it? I looked around that crowded basement workshop in disbelief. Everyone seemed tediously engrossed in the same chore the supervisor had just explained to me—awkwardly tearing off tape, extracting staples, and checking the plastic envelopes for holes.

This is a job? No, this is a big mistake! I came all the way to Seattle for this? To pull sticky tape from dirty, wet envelopes that smelled like infected eardrums? Whatever possessed me to leave Alaska?

My discouragement quickly turned to feelings of anger and betrayal. I called the supervisor over and told her there had been a mistake and I wanted to talk to the center's social worker. But he refused to see me and said he wouldn't give me an appointment until a month had passed. All I could do was sit in that workshop and struggle with a dead-end job. There was no one to complain to. No one to explain anything.

At break time, Ila Mae noticed my distress and tried to explain what the workshop job was all about. The envelopes arrived in huge bins from Seattle's various Boeing Corporation plants. They were used in every department at Boeing factories to affix instructions and small parts to projects. When the outside of the envelopes accumulated too much tape and stickers, they were sent to us for cleaning and then recycled back to Boeing.

Ila Mae acknowledged that it was dirty, boring, unpleasant work, but the envelopes provided the biggest single work project handled by the center. This ongoing job kept the workshop open and running every day. She encouraged me to calm down and give the center a chance. Ila Mae warned that if I ran home to Alaska now, it would be even harder to start a new life of my own in the future when my parents died.

I think I realized that she was right, but I still skipped going to the center the second day. My first day's experience had just been too horrible. I told myself that I wasn't so disabled that I had to resort to such unpleasant, menial labor. I learned that there were a few other jobs at the center, but those of us from the nursing home were at the mercy of Carol's erratic bus schedule and got assigned to the envelope job because it could be done whenever we arrived.

———————◆———————

I sat alone in my room at the nursing home that second day, trying to decide what to do. There was nothing for me back in Alaska. But maybe Seattle would be no better. I was feeling terribly depressed when a short, round, smiling man peeked around the door of my room. His grin was contagious, his eyes danced with joy.

"My name's Mr. Goleeke," he told me, "but everyone calls me Mr. G." He was the director of the UCP Center and came to visit because he heard I had a rough start the day before. I had to laugh as he readily acknowledged it was a pretty strange place for a young person to be. He seemed to understand what I was feeling—that looking at the other people at the center I realized what it might mean to be disabled all my life, and that I would grow old.

He told me he didn't have all the answers to my questions or the antidote to all my disturbing feelings, but he urged me to come back and try again. He didn't promise that I would like it, but the respect he showed and the encouragement he gave made me feel better. His spirit of hope seemed infectious. The next morning I went back.

Back in the basement workshop, I decided to check for tears in the envelopes before peeling off all the tape and stickers. That way I could avoid doing tedious work only to find the envelopes useless anyway. I showed my time-saving idea to the workers nearby, but they just scowled and went on with their routine. It made me realize why some workers did the same job for umpteen years.

During our fifteen-minute break I snooped around and found the center's marvelous arts-and-crafts room. The two women in charge wanted to know if I'd like to start a craft project. My first project was yarn embroidery on burlap. I drew a flower design and then took heavy yarn to sew the outline. When I finished, the women helped me pin in a lining and use a sewing machine. Within a few weeks I had my own designer bag to hang on my wheelchair. Then I started on my second project—a mosaic butterfly.

I soon developed a special relationship with the arts-and-crafts teachers. They constantly teased me about how I did things my own way instead of taking a conventional approach. And they encouraged my creativity. But they had two strictly enforced rules: Don't come running to us when you have a problem in the workshop, and no crying in the craft room—it's supposed to be a fun place. When I abided by those rules, I found understanding and comfort from these two new friends.

———— • ————

Break times provided the ideal opportunity for exploring the UCP. I realized that no one ever volunteered information, so I took the responsibility to see that I got what I needed from the UCP program. If no one was going to show me the ins and outs of the center, I'd find out for myself. That's how I discovered the physical therapy room and let the therapist know that I wanted to be part of his program.

The out-of-date PT equipment at the center lent a friendly old charm to the therapy room. The therapist allowed us all to work at our own pace and concentrate on whatever interested us. I began experimenting with crutches again. For two years I was to work with crutches, although I always felt more confident with a walker. The big problem was my relentless startle reflex triggered by loud or unexpected noise. So the therapist and I eventually agreed to give up once and for all on the crutches. We concluded that for me, a wheelchair was the most reasonable and efficient mode of locomotion both at the center and around the nursing home.

A couple of weeks after I discovered physical therapy, I added speech therapy to my list of regular activities. The speech therapist himself had cerebral palsy, but he could walk and had little problem using one of his hands. Jim was young, handsome, and acted as if he thought he was God's gift to women.

Fortunately, he was married. I regularly told him he was full of beans, but he made speech therapy fun. I talked him out of doing traditional drills with me, because my speech is so erratic I found repetitious drills frustrating and ineffective. I can say a word perfectly one minute and the next minute the same word may be unintelligible.

So we spent most of our therapy sessions just talking. Jim seemed interested in everything. He asked me to teach him something from the Bible, so I started going through the gospel of John in the King James Version.

Before I knew it, I'd completed my first month at the center. It was time for my initial appointment with the staff social worker. I had never met the man, but he began by gruffly telling me, "I've seen your kind before and you can't fool me!" According to him, I thought the world revolved around me. I was spoiled and doing a slothful job of working at the center and doing little to adjust to life at the nursing home. He told me that if I didn't get my act together, and soon, he'd see to it that I wouldn't get to start school in the fall.

His swift and harsh criticism stung deeply. I did not like this man at all. He acted as if he held the keys to heaven and hell in his own hands. Back at the nursing home I reported to Ila Mae about the appointment. I cried as I told how he threatened not to let me go to school. I told her I definitely wanted to return to Alaska if I couldn't go to school.

Ila Mae didn't much like the way the social worker had talked to me. She acknowledged that I wasn't exactly a model of maturity, crying whenever I got upset and threatening to go home whenever anything discouraged me. "But you've been here less than two months. What does he expect?"

Ila Mae got so irritated she went all the way to Mr. G. to complain. Mr. G. soon came by my worktable to say that I could certainly go to school in the fall. He promised to see to it. Then he winked at Ila Mae and told her that "the kid," as he called me, would undoubtedly grow up to be a fine woman. Then he told my roommate, "I'm giving you the task of seeing to it." Ila Mae rolled her eyes and shook her head. I had to grin at the two of them.

In the years to come, Mr. G. often made me feel good about myself. During much of that time all the UCP clients would have monthly parties in a nearby fieldhouse. Whenever he went, Mr. G. made a point of getting me out of my wheelchair and dancing with me across the gym. He always conveyed the feeling that he believed in me. The fact that he was the director of the UCP Center often seemed so frustrating, but it helped me realize not everything was totally good or totally bad.

That fall, I did start school. And I was pleased to find that the UCP had the same high standard of education as the Anne Carlsen school. I was assigned to help Ila Mae with the center's monthly newspaper. It was called *The Spastic Scholastic*. When I half-jokingly suggested we rename it *The UCP Scandal Sheet*, it was agreed. We had reporters from all over UCP, and our regular news ranged from reports on monthly parties to the goings-on at our nursing home.

The creative-writing teacher assigned me to write my autobiography. I began in September and didn't finish until December. In it I had nothing but positive things to say about my family and my background. I even praised the Alaskan minister and his wife for their kind and generous treatment of me.

My biggest problem at school was learning to deal with the teacher's constructive criticism of my writing. Up until then, my mom had been my only critic. She often sent me back to my typewriter with the first draft of some writing all marked up, good-naturedly admonishing me, "Posey, if you're going to be a writer, you better be a good one!"

Somehow my teacher's criticisms and corrections seemed harsher. I often left class in tears.

I couldn't seem to deal with the pressures of school on top of the work at the center and the constant daily chaos of life at the nursing home. I was always upset. One day the teacher firmly suggested that I drop out of school, "Until you get your life together!" She said that once I did, she would gladly accept me back into the program. She felt that I wasn't emotionally ready for the demands of high school.

I came back to the nursing home that afternoon, kicked the door of my room open, threw my stuffed animals off my bed, and cried for three solid hours. I wasn't angry with the teacher. As usual, I was angry with myself. Once again I was failing to rise above my emotions.

I came all the way to Seattle to escape the limitations in Alaska. Now I was caught again in the same maddening trap. I couldn't escape myself.

Chapter 16

In the Zoo

One harsh reality I faced was the realization that the institutional system in which I lived gave me little control over my own life. Understanding this hard truth was one thing; learning to accept it would take much longer.

In the late sixties and early seventies, federal and state governments in their bureaucratic wisdom began providing special funding for nursing homes that took in mentally retarded residents. Such facilities were reclassified as Institutions for the Mentally Retarded (IMR homes). The objective was to relieve overcrowding in government institutions, reduce government costs, and bolster the private nursing-home industry. Nursing homes like Sea Ridge would enjoy an immediate injection of government funds that could provide added staff and additional staff training. But the new IMR status meant that elderly patients would no longer be admitted. Sea Ridge quickly became a very different kind of place to live.

Our new residents arrived two or three a week—delivered in state cars and accompanied by state workers. I was shocked. Many of these people, all former residents of state mental institutions, were uncivilized and wild. Some would urinate or defecate on the floor even as they were dragged into the nursing home scratching, kicking, and biting their attendants.

It took an act of courage for my friends and me just to get to the front door of the nursing home. Some of our new residents crawled on the floor, blocking the halls, grabbing at walkers, and even sticking their hands through the spokes of our wheelchairs. Adult-sized babies with the mentality of one- or two-year-olds had to be watched and rescued continuously. A few seemed good-natured and playful, but I quickly learned to play with them carefully. They were strong and could easily get too rough and actually pull me out of my wheelchair.

One new resident, Frank, seemed both functional and civilized. Older than most former state patients, he was a devoted Catholic who attended an in-house Mass held every Friday. Very soon after his arrival we learned he was also an accomplished "jewel" thief. He wouldn't take just any necklaces, bracelets, or pins. He stole only those with crosses or other religious symbols. Whenever anyone in the nursing home reported such jewelry missing, the aides would check Frank's room and always find the evidence.

While Frank's burglary jobs were a disruption to our lives, he was never destructive—which was more than I can say about some of our other new neighbors. Johnny was one of those adults with a baby mentality. One afternoon when he was left unattended and got into my room, he climbed up on my bookcase to reach a pair of ceramic elephants I was painting as a craft project. Johnny broke one of my elephants, scattered my books and papers around the room, tore the covers and sheets off my bed, toppled a pile of my clean laundry onto the floor, and ate a whole bowl of fresh fruit I kept on my bedside table.

I got angry when I came home to find my room destroyed. A cleaning lady had started to clean it up, but after she finished and left, I sat and cried. I felt violated. I felt trapped again. I didn't understand this new system and had little control. I smashed the second elephant on the floor and began wadding up the stack of wrinkled pages of my writings. What was the use of thinking about going back to school if I was doomed to spend the rest of my life in a place like this?

Even then, in the midst of my discouragement and pain, someone was there for me. Anne, the craftswoman, came into my room with a broom and a dustpan. As she swept up the broken shards of my ceramic elephant, she tried to encourage me. "You are our writer, Carolyn. If you give up now, no one will ever know what it's like to live here. I firmly believe that one day you will tell the world about this place."

Then, being the plain-spoken, earthy woman she is, Anne grinned and said, "Just think about the mess Johnny's poor aide will have when all that fruit goes through him tonight. I bet she'll keep a closer eye on him after this."

That made me laugh. Then Anne and I talked about all the changes going on at Sea Ridge. She agreed that whenever major changes take place in an institution, no one seems to know what's happening until after the fact. So at Sea Ridge, bits and pieces of rumors and information floated through the home like cottonseeds on the wind, spreading unrest and uncertainty that might have been avoided had someone explained what was going on.

Anne wasn't sure what to think about the changes herself. She didn't want to give up her crafts room, but she was excited about her new role as "activities director" and looked forward to learning new things as she worked with our new residents. She told me, "I'll be switched if I understand what the Lord is doing here. I don't know if I even like it. But we can see things only from our little point of view. God can see the total picture."

I clung to that bit of wisdom because the nursing home was all I had. I went back to Anchorage every summer to visit my family, and those short visits were enough to remind me of why I'd left. No matter how bad things deteriorated at Sea Ridge, I knew I didn't have the luxury of picking up and moving out.

And things did deteriorate. Some of the new residents had to be tied to the railings in the halls to prevent accidents. There were streakers who ripped off their clothes and ran naked down the halls. Sometimes they got out the front doors, and police brought them back hours later after finding them walking around the neighborhood *au naturel* or digging around in garbage cans, looking for food.

The two Annes, the activity director and the aide who became one of the "housemothers," designed and made special "union suits" with zippers up the back to thwart the strippers in our midst. These two patient women also kept us longtime residents supplied with secondhand clothes, because clothes that weren't devoured by the home's industrial-sized washers eventually stank so badly with the overpowering scent of the nursing home that we couldn't stand to wear them.

Both Annes worked hard to provide for our continued well-being, doing everything from training new aides to diapering the most troublesome residents. They even began doing our hair as the changing atmosphere rapidly depleted the ranks of regular volunteers who used to come in every week to handle such routine but time-consuming jobs.

Staff turnover became a serious problem. New aides arrived, burned out, and left almost before we could learn their names. But the two Annes stuck with us. Sometimes it seemed that the whole place depended on them.

Finally the home's assistant administrator instituted a change that had a positive impact on all of our lives. The most disruptive and unmanageable residents were all moved to one wing that could be locked off from the rest of the home. This was a major improvement, but the rest of the home continued to take in more and more new residents as old ones moved away.

As a result of the major room reassignment, I was put in a room overlooking a small garden. On wet winter mornings fog would slumber there, giving it a haunted, lonely, and enchanted feel. On those mornings I would sit and stare out my window, letting my imagination wander out into the fog and shut the door of reality behind me. In this private refuge I encountered a recurring image of myself running across a huge field of wildflowers. In this dream I always wore a long, white dress made with elegant lace and pink ribbon for a belt. I was free from the nursing home, free from the secret agony of my abuse, free, independent, and dignified—with my dream of a formal education completed.

Those early morning meditations became a kind of prayer for me. In some wonderful way I don't claim to understand and can't adequately explain, God made no distinction between my daydreaming and my prayer. He heard the longings of my heart and answered my soul with a peaceful, reassuring image that was both comfort and hope. An idyllic daydream became a promise, the beginning of a miracle, but that miracle began in a strange and frightening way.

One day I went to get some towels at the far end of the nursing home. Rolling back to my room I saw Barry, a former patient from the state mental hospital. He had gotten loose from the railing and dumped his breakfast tray on the floor. He had somehow managed to strip himself naked and was down on all fours, eating off the floor. As I watched, he began picking up dirt swept into a nearby pile and ate that, too.

A full-grown man. Naked. Eating dirt off the floor. It was something out of a horror movie. But it was part of my everyday world. It was happening in my home. In the days that followed I couldn't turn that image off in my mind. It burned into my deepest memory. It burned into who I was and who I am.

I asked myself, *Is this what God wants for my life? What about school? What about that educated, free, and dignified person in my dreams?* Those were just daydreams, but Barry and the nursing home were all too real. I concluded that I would drown in that sad cesspool of humanity if I stayed much longer at Sea Ridge.

Still I saw no way out. And the more I thought about it, the more I felt like a demolition ball smashing again and again into in an unmovable stone wall. I was as bound to the nursing home as were those pathetic human beings tied to the railings in our halls.

Chapter 17

"No! Don't Tell Me . . ."

Physically, my roommate Ila Mae was much more limited by her cerebral palsy than I was. Since she was a full-care patient she had no choice but to relinquish total control of her appearance and hygiene to the sometimes uncaring and usually harried nursing home aides. She fought a daily battle of wills with the staff just to keep from smelling like an institution and to keep her soft, honey-colored curls from becoming a snarled and tangled mess.

When I arrived at the nursing home, Ila Mae used a small, outdated wheelchair. The only way she could move herself at all was by pushing herself backwards with her feet—the same way I travel. But where I could move at a pretty good clip, Ila Mae could creep along only inches at a time. Her lack of mobility proved to be her biggest frustration. When she finally bought herself an electric wheelchair she gained more independence than she'd ever thought possible. I called her new wheelchair her "freedom wagon." And that it was.

Despite our differences in background, outlook, and personality, Ila Mae and I managed to not only get along, we became close. But what a strange combination we were—Sea Ridge's version of the Odd Couple. She was orderly and neat; I was plagued by untidyness. She was thirty-three; I was only seventeen. I called her the "The Old Lady"; she called me "The Brat."

124

I'd come up with some crazy ideas and Ila Mae would pretend to be shocked by my antics. But I often noticed a twinkle in her eye when I teased her.

One of my favorite tricks involved what I called the "zoo tours"—groups of outsiders who periodically came through the nursing home acting as if they were observing caged animals. I liked to eavesdrop on these groups, who often assumed from my physical appearance that my brain worked no better than my hands and feet. They'd make insensitive comments about how sad we all were and how grateful they were to be "normal." That was my cue to roll my eyes in disgust, to let them know I'd understood every word they'd said and make them feel like jackasses. Some people were embarrassed and would apologize. But others just walked away in a huff—as if they alone had a right to intelligence.

I felt particularly irritated one day when I saw two women look into our room and one said to her companion, "Oh, look. There are typewriters and books in this room." She seemed as surprised as if she'd found such furnishings in a monkey cage. "It must be a staff lounge."

After the tourists left, I talked Ila Mae into letting me make a sign for our door that read, "Beware. These creatures are human!" That melted the plastic coating off the tourists in the next zoo tour.

After four years as roommates, Ila Mae went to Missouri to live with her sister. I enjoyed living by myself for a while, but as the home grew more crowded I soon had to have a roommate again. I asked if I could room with one of the calmer, more contented retarded residents. Some of our new residents, once they were dressed and fed, seemed happy to go about their daily routine and expect little else. If I could live with someone like that, I thought I might have more emotional energy to deal with the center and even begin to think about school again.

Within a few months, Arlene came to Sea Ridge. She was a middle-aged woman who had lived with her parents until their sudden death in a car accident. Arlene was a solidly built model who used the rock-and-roll method of locomotion. When she rocked, her wheelchair rolled. Acne covered her face and often broke open and bled. She always seemed grateful when the nurses put medication on it. Her face was also disfigured by a severe misalignment of her teeth and jaws. Despite her appearance, Arlene was in her own way a real sweetheart.

She expected little from me. If I'd only get her favorite book for her when she wanted it and let her "talk" to me a while every morning, she was happy.

I tried to teach her to use the call light to get the aide when she needed to go to the bathroom, but Arlene never understood the connection between the little switch and the aide's walking into the room. Her loud, middle-of-the-night calling "I gotta go potty, Mama!" seemed more direct and usually brought the desired response.

Arlene was a fascinating person, and I had many unanswered questions about her. She had a very strict, self-imposed routine that enslaved her. There was a set time every day for everything, including eating and drinking. She never snacked or drank between meals. Anything that disrupted her routine sparked a tantrum.

I discovered this quite by accident one day soon after she moved into my room. Feeling miserable with the heat that summer afternoon, I got myself a glass of water and made the mistake of offering one to Arlene. She knocked the glass out of my hand and went into a tantrum lasting eight hours. For two or three days afterward, she would scream angrily whenever she saw me. Finally she began to sob and wanted a hug, which I gladly gave.

After that first incident I watched more closely and noticed that she seemed annoyed whenever her schedule was threatened, or her routine changed or delayed the slightest bit. Maybe her routine was so important because it was the only thing she could control, the only thing she understood in her private domain of confusion and pain.

I understood the frustration that comes from the inability to control one's own life. So I could live with Arlene.

———————•———————

One fall morning, I told Arlene, "I think I'm going to see about getting back into high school." Almost four years had passed since the teacher at the center told me I wasn't ready for her program. Now I wanted to try again.

Arlene seemed to approve of my plans. But then her voice always rose with joy when she received any kind of attention. The more I talked, the louder and faster she babbled until she got so happy she cried her fake tears.

"Arlene, you phoney!" I teased as I stood up and hugged her. I couldn't help wondering which one of us fate had cheated the worst. Was it Arlene—who was so helpless but so loving, innocent, and accepting of her circumstances? Or had fate played a more horrible trick on me by putting a perfectly good mind that could understand and dream in a dysfunctional body that prevented me from attaining those dreams?

After hugging Arlene, I went to the center for the day. When I talked to the teacher, I was pleasantly surprised by her reaction. Mrs. Richards said she had been expecting me back for some time. While she still had some concerns about my emotional maturity, she was now confident that I could succeed in her classroom.

Mrs. Richards was an unusual person. Raised by Catholic nuns, she now professed to be an ardent atheist. She was easily offended by my faith and told me so whenever the subject came up. She tried to run her classroom as if it were a model of the outside world. She told her students that they wouldn't always live in the shelter of the center, so she expected us to be men and women. While I often had a strained relationship with her, she was indeed an excellent teacher, sometimes rigid and demanding, but with her own distinct brand of stern compassion.

She feuded constantly with the center's administration. She thought we should be paid for the time we spent in school. After all, we got paid for our time in the workshop. Arguing that education should be the center's top priority, she thought that paying us for going to school would be an incentive that would benefit everyone at the center. She was not to win that fight.

Another fight she determined to win was teaching me math. She told me she dearly wanted to disprove the widely held belief that people with cerebral palsy have severe problems in mastering mathematics. I told her that I didn't think she'd ever disprove that theory by me.

As usual, I did well in subjects requiring reading and writing, and I continued to struggle with math. But when I made an A on the final test in a required business course, Mrs. Richards was perplexed. How could I do so well in a business course that included math and have such a hard time in my regular math course?

I told her that my brother Bob owned his own construction company and my sister Elizabeth kept his books and often discussed his ventures with me. So I was familiar with business subjects. From that Mrs. Richards discerned my usual pattern of learning. I got interested and could understand concrete mathematical concepts when I saw how they applied to my life. From then on she made up problems for me using math that I might actually use in daily living. She'd have me figure the width of a piece of burlap I could use in a craft project, or ask how many plastic envelopes I could clean up in a certain amount of time in the workshop if I did three every five minutes.

With Mrs. Richards' patient help I soon could handle fifth-grade fractions. But she remained concerned because I needed more math credits to graduate, and our continued efforts in math seemed to be a losing battle.

Unlike my earlier struggles with math, this time I didn't get down on myself. I was able to maintain enough perspective to pull back and realize that I was doing well in all my other areas of study. I was even learning the value of having a demanding judge like Mrs. Richards critique my writing. I learned to divorce myself from my own words, to pretend that I was a reader who knew nothing about the author, and to judge my own writing. Did it have depth? Did it make sense? Would the first paragraph make me want to read the rest?

Soon Mrs. Richards was praising me for my objectivity. She said that it showed her how much I was growing. One afternoon she pointed out an awkward sentence in an essay and asked me to revise it. Two hours later she walked from her desk to where I was still working. Seeing that I'd rewritten the sentence nineteen different ways and still wasn't satisfied, she laughed and exclaimed, "If you aren't the writer!"

Her words made me feel eight feet tall.

———————————————

Now that I was back in school, I felt more at peace with my circumstances at the nursing home. I had purpose and direction again. I was moving toward a goal.

My sister Elizabeth was right. She warned me I could give up and get sucked down into the system that surrounded me, or I could pursue the freedom trail of education. She could be very blunt: "Since you can never sling hash for a living, I suggest you buckle down and get yourself a good education. I don't care how you get it or even if you ever go on to college, but set your sights beyond the nursing home and the center. If you don't, I'm telling you, you'll be sorry."

Two more years marched into eternity. One early spring day I asked Mrs. Richards if we could map out a revised set of goals for me. I wanted to look over my school records to see where I needed to go. Since I had finished my assignments for the day and Mrs. Richards said it would take her a while to pull my records together, I went on to work and said I'd check with her the next day.

Later that same afternoon Mrs. Richards called me back to the classroom. She said that she didn't want to wait to give me the good news. "You only have two more courses to take in order to graduate," she told me. "And as far as I'm concerned, you can read the textbooks and take the finals."

I couldn't believe it! How had I managed to complete so many requirements without realizing how close I was to finishing? Mrs. Richards laughed and reminded me that I'd been steadily plugging away for a long time. And the best news was that the state board had just lowered the general math requirement. I already had enough math to earn my diploma.

So it was true. All I had to do was read two texts and pass the exams. "You better get started right away," Mrs. Richards said as she handed me the books. "I'm tired of looking at your funny face."

Soon after my arrival at Sea Ridge I'd begun attending a nearby church that had been recommended by friends in Alaska. My Sunday excursions to worship there offered my only regular escape from the narrow confines of my everyday world. The young pastor and his wife, Lloyd and Betty, had become encouraging and supportive friends.

So, the first thing I wanted to do when Mrs. Richards gave me the good news was to call Lloyd and Betty to tell them they were about to have a high-school graduate on their hands. Mrs. Richards let me use the phone in her office.

I could almost hear Betty's smile over the phone. "Well, I declare," she exclaimed in her Southern accent, "I always knew you would do it." She told me she wanted to hear all the details and would come by the nursing home later to help pull me back down to earth.

When I got back to Sea Ridge that afternoon, I gave Arlene a big hug of gratitude for wanting only to be loved and asking so little of me. She had even slept through all the late-night pecking on my typewriter. Having her as my roommate really had made a tremendous difference.

When Betty arrived, I had her call Mom and Pappy. Mom gave me her typical smart-aleck response. "No! Don't tell me," she said. "You can't be graduating from high school. You're supposed to be an imbecile. But I guess I shouldn't be surprised. You never did do what you were supposed to do."

Mom was more than proud. She promised that she and Pappy would be down for the graduation ceremonies.

———— • ————

Since I was the only graduate at the center that spring, we had the ceremony the way I wanted it. At my request, the center invited Lloyd to speak. One of the songs I selected was the classic hymn "A Mighty Fortress" because it reminded me of the Anne Carlsen School and the Lutheran teachings that I still remembered in my heart.

I graduated on a gorgeous June afternoon in Seattle. I had never felt more alive. Pastor Lloyd spoke about my hope in Christ and how it was the undergirding of my desire to accomplish the most with my life. I hoped Mrs. Richards was listening.

When Lloyd finished, Mom and Pappy wheeled me to the front of the room to receive my diploma. I was so excited that Mom had to pry my hand open and put the diploma in it. All my friends laughed with understanding.

Chapter 18

Trying My Wings

The year was 1972. I had graduated from high school at the age of twenty-seven after living in my Seattle nursing home for eight years.

My brother Ken was unable to come to Seattle to see me receive my diploma, so for a graduation present he sent me a round-trip airline ticket to San Jose, California, and invited me to stay with his family for a month. He said he didn't want his four children growing up without knowing one of their aunts.

Ken's wife, Carmie, met my plane at the airport. Four pairs of mischievous wide eyes stared curiously as she pushed my wheelchair into the terminal. Within seconds of introductions my nieces and nephews were all arguing over who would carry what for me.

That afternoon I told Carmie I'd help set the supper table. This was going to be my first real meal with Ken, and I wanted it to be special. By the time I learned to feed myself and could eat with the family, Ken had already grown up and moved away from home. I put a tablecloth and flowers on the table, and Carmie got out her best dishes and silverware.

While I worked around the table, the kids drifted in from playing, one by one. Each one looked at me and then walked into the kitchen to ask their mom the same question: "Why is she setting the table with the good stuff?"

After the fourth inquiry Carmie rounded all the children together. "I want you to listen carefully because I only want to say this once," she announced sternly. "If you want to know what your aunt Carolyn is doing, you need to ask her. If you don't understand what she says, she'll be glad to repeat herself until you do. Your aunt is a great woman, and you need to learn to talk with her."

From that time on, that's what those children did. And they stuck with me until they understood every word I said. By the time Ken got home from the fire department that evening, we were all having enormous fun talking and laughing over my verbal hits and misses.

Ken had changed in the years since I last saw him. He was beginning to gray. And he had a flashy handlebar mustache that seemed to scream, "I'm the head honcho around here and nobody better forget it!" A pair of wide rainbow suspenders gave further evidence that he was still a character.

He bombarded me with questions. "What's your next step? College? Tell me about the home. The center? What do you see ahead of you there?"

I answered as honestly as I could. I admitted that the nursing home and the center weren't all I'd hoped, but I felt that they were the best facilities I knew about on the West Coast that could provide me with any hope of achieving a meaningful life. It had been slow going, but now I felt like I was going someplace. Back in Anchorage I'd been tossed back to ground zero by ignorance or circumstances.

Ken laughed. "What's the matter? You don't like ground zero?" When I grinned and shook my head, he said, "I'll tell you, kid, I don't blame you."

We had no sooner sat down at the table to eat when I suddenly heard a loud motorcycle imitation, *Vroom, vrooooom,* followed by the sounds of squealing brakes and another take-off. I glanced at Kenny, Jr., and his brother Danny, thinking they'd cracked under the strain of acting civilized for a full five minutes. But they were staring and grinning at their father who, I then realized, had confiscated my special spoon with its bike-grip handle and was cruising an invisible Harley down an imaginary highway.

Carmie ordered him to give back my spoon, scolding him for teasing me during our first dinner together. Ken stopped and twisted his mustache in thought: "Is this really our first dinner together?" When I said it was, he returned my spoon. But a moment later he snatched it back and put it out of my reach, saying that he wasn't going to give it back because he wanted to see how long it took for me to lose patience with him.

I turned to Carmie and told her I could tell she had a difficult job taking care of five children, one of whom was disguised as an adult. She laughed and told Ken, "Your sister certainly has your number. Smart woman."

Ken scowled and handed me my spoon. I took it and grumbled that my mashed potatoes were getting cold.

That playful dinner episode sent a silent message to Ken's children: It's okay to play pranks on Aunt Carolyn. The very next morning, Danny, a freckle-faced redheaded nine-year-old who looked like a model for one of the cherubs on the ceiling of the Sistine Chapel, appropriated my briefcase, and said "Good-bye, Auntie" as he headed for the front door.

"Where are you going?" I wanted to know.

He replied casually, "Oh, I'm just taking this piece of junk to the garbage."

I told him he better drop it before I got to him or I was going to run him over him with my wheelchair. When he kept going, I charged. He surrendered at the last minute only to have Carmie scold him for teasing me and ask why he was giving me such a hard time. His only defense warmed my heart. "Because I love Aunt Carolyn, and she's fun to tease."

Another afternoon I made the mistake of leaving my wheelchair out in the hall when I went to the bathroom. By the time I came out, my chair had disappeared. Carmie went on a search and discovered the kids had it outside and were charging their friends ten cents a ride.

One day while Ken was at work, Carmie drove me to Santa Cruz to see where Gaga and I had lived. We went on a weekday, so the beach was as abandoned and forlorn as I remembered. But twenty years had passed. Now the waves seemed smaller. And the cottage where we had lived looked old and naked without the patch of flowers under the windows. I fell in love all over again with the peaceful loneliness of the place. I remembered the dark winter days when the rain and the roar of surf combined to give the oceanfront an air of mystery and power. I remembered Gaga.

Even the sad memories felt good.

———— • ————

I went back to Seattle warmed and encouraged by the renewed relationship with Ken and his wonderful family and by my brother's parting words. Ken said I could do anything I wanted to do if people would just give me lots of time and space and stay out of my way. "And if ever you need anything, anything at all," he told me, "just let me know. And I mean that."

He backed up those words a few months later when my old typewriter finally gave up the ghost. Ken sent me a new one.

———— • ————

Those of us who worked at the UCP Center felt it was ours. The center had been started by the parents of some of the employees as a place where their disabled children could work. They needed somewhere to belong and feel productive in a society that wasn't ready to accept the disabled. Many who came to the center believed it could accommodate all their needs for the rest of their lives. It was a safe and familiar place. Perhaps too safe and familiar.

Like the nursing home, the center fell into dire financial straits. As with the nursing home, the state and federal governments stepped in with money to bail it out. But the money had countless strings attached. Change swept the center like a runaway bulldozer. Those of us who labored in the workshop were given productivity evaluations. If we fell below a predetermined standard, our work hours were reduced and we spent the time in a new department called the developmental center, where we worked on social skills and our interaction with others.

The new system also greatly altered my daily private life. Because physical therapy was no longer offered at the center, I had to get PT at the nursing home after we came home in the afternoon. The increased expectations and faster pace so exhausted me that I fell asleep many nights during the evening news and wouldn't awaken again until it was too late to write or do anything else. The new system was demanding more and more of my energy and leaving less for me to pursue my goals.

In quiet moments at the nursing home I tried to talk myself out of becoming bitter and resentful over the changes that altered my familiar identity as a "workshop employee" and forced me into new and different situations. Yet there were things I enjoyed about the increased interpersonal interaction at the center. News magazines were read to us, and we'd have political discussions that stimulated my thinking and convinced me to give the new system a chance. I really wanted to grow. Maybe learning to better accept change was a necessary part of the process.

* * *

Another change of thinking began with an isolated event that took place about this same time. One day an older volunteer at the center invited me to a special program of liturgical dancers who were performing in the developmental center. I'd never heard of dancing in worship, although I did recall the biblical account of King David dancing for joy before the ark of the covenant. However, dancing was frowned upon as sin in the churches I'd attended.

I was curious. So I agreed to curb my reflexive condemnation and perhaps expand my spiritual horizons by going to see this unusual program. Male and female performers were dressed in simple, flowing white robes and danced to the hymn "Jesu, Joy of Man's Desiring." Their movement seemed the height of magnificence and grace. I lost myself in the pure beauty of the moment and knew God could only be pleased with their performance. And I think deep down, that moving experience started me thinking that there must be more to God and relating to him than I so far understood in my narrow, limited exposure. However, I was perhaps too consumed with the physical demands of daily life to devote much thought or energy to spiritual growth.

In pursuit of my ongoing dream to become a writer, I enrolled in English 101 at a local community college. But college was a strange new world. All my previous educational experiences had taken place in special settings where allowances were made for my disability. Not college.

I never realized that colleges had separate buildings spread out over vast acres. I felt frightened, alone, and completely out of place on my first day of class. There was no one there to push me around. No one to double-check and see that I had my assignments printed and placed carefully in my book so I could get them out when I got back home.

The first big assignments for the class were to write fifty lines of free verse and a piece of fiction. Both assignments were to be copied and passed out to everyone in the class so that we could critique each other's work. That seemed well within my capabilities, so I eagerly began to work when I got back to the nursing home that very first afternoon.

It turned out that my English 101 professor made it a creative-writing course, thus I enjoyed all the assignments. I wrote poetry about gardens and about growing as a person. I wrote some fiction about a family living on a homestead—someone tried to swindle them out of their property, but they won a court case to gain the original title to the land. I earned an A for the class, and some of my classmates said they thought I ought to submit my story for publication.

In winter quarter I took another English course—interpretive literature. But I'd never done the kind of writing the professor required, so I struggled in there. My advisor found a student to assist me, but I had to repeat the course a second quarter to get a B.

Throughout that first year in college I had a special work-study grant requiring that I write an article for the campus newspaper about education for the disabled. I also wrote a campus resource pamphlet for disabled students. Also, I cataloged the library's entire collection of college catalogs. I earned enough money to pay for both my courses, but when the year ended, the college couldn't find any more work-study jobs I could do.

Pleased as I was to prove I could manage the academic work in college, the daily logistics nearly overwhelmed me. I had to get to and from campus, then move around campus, and find someone who could take notes for me. Each quarter, the same problems had to be solved all over again. By the end of the year I was so discouraged that I abandoned my dream of a college degree. I'd never be a writer. What I really needed was to find a job.

While I tried to be upbeat about these plans, secretly I was angry and disappointed with God. I prayed that he would take away the bitterness, and I tried to deny it. My inability to shake my anger made me feel even worse about my failure and about myself.

About this time, a new center for the disabled opened in Seattle. When a recruiter visited Sea Ridge, one of the staff suggested that I check it out. I liked what I saw and a few days later began working at the Crestview Development Center.

This center was located in an abandoned school, surrounded with trees and big lawns. In the back was a gravel playground and beyond that a woods. I loved the quiet, lonely feel of the place, but what first impressed me was the fact that the center's bus was always on time. Unlike the UCP Center's haphazard schedule, the emphasis on timeliness at Crestview made me feel important and respected.

The workshop was smaller, thus the staff had time for us each as individuals. Our primary job was washing and bagging headsets to be used by airline passengers. Only a few of the workers at Crestview were physically handicapped. I was the only worker who wasn't mentally challenged as well.

Because fights and arguments broke out regularly among the employees, the atmosphere in the workshop was almost always emotionally charged. Upsetting as the constant conflict was for me, I quickly learned that most of my co-workers desperately longed to be touched and hugged. That I could do, regularly dispensing hugs and affection during our breaks.

The center's staff treated me with respect, and because I was a good listener they even shared their concerns and frustrations about their jobs. I particularly enjoyed going on many field trips from the center. My wheelchair was heavy and created extra bother, but the women on the staff always acted glad to take me along to art shows, lunch, and shopping.

A professional dance teacher taught a class at the center once a week. I watched in amazement as some of the most passive, unresponsive workers at the center came alive with the music. I'll always remember Vernel, a severely retarded man who had the physique of a dancer. He never had a lesson and had been institutionalized since childhood. But he had a gift for dancing. He loved to dance free-style, stepping and moving with startling, perfect grace. It was as if, when he danced, he slipped away into another world, a world where he was whole.

I danced, too. I asked for, and the center installed, a ballet bar that I could hold on to and wiggle with the music. That was all my "dancing" amounted to. But I loved it. And in my wildest imagination I saw myself as an exquisite ballerina.

———————◆———————

Summer faded into fall and Crestview's schoolteacher returned to hold classes for all who wished to continue their struggle to learn. When I told my supervisor that I'd like to do something to develop writing skills, the teacher put me to work preparing lesson plans for her students. We took a graded word list and wrote stories for those at a first-grade (or whatever) reading level who wanted to read something that would not insult their common sense or their dignity.

On a few occasions the teacher trusted me to conduct classes in her absence. Some students wouldn't come because I wasn't the "real" teacher, or because they couldn't easily understand me. But others came, and we managed to have class.

I developed some teaching skills and in the process learned some valuable lessons from my students. Some of the young men keenly wanted to learn to read. When they couldn't, they'd pound on the table or even run out of the room in frustration. I was touched by their tremendous desire to learn. And their determined examples challenged me to begin thinking seriously about going back to college.

At Sea Ridge I faced another problem. Over the years, Arlene's tantrums over disruptions in her schedule grew worse and worse. In her growing depression, Arlene began to want to be near me at odd times of the day. Sometimes she'd merely sit quietly and offer her hand for me to hold. If I gave her my hand, she would take it, put her head down on it, and then break down and sob.

She always made it clear when she wanted me to put my arms around her and love her. She continued to express herself through babblings, but now when she realized I couldn't understand her, she cried real tears. She had fake tears for playing, but these were real, agonizing tears, full of pent-up pain and grief. Sometimes I cried with her because I felt her dejection. It hurt to see her lost and alone in her wordless pit.

Slowly Arlene's pain and depression began to isolate her—even from me. She'd sit for hours in her wheelchair, her head bowed, looking like the last rose of summer. I watched her drowning in her own despair, but I had no life preserver to throw. All I could do was love her and try to show her that she was important to me.

Arlene's family, the staff, and I all agreed it would be better for everyone involved if she were placed on another wing where there could be more structure and a more regular daily routine. By this time her tantrums could last all day long.

I knew this decision was best. I needed a break from the demands that Arlene had begun to place on me, but I still felt as if I was abandoning a helpless friend. I felt ashamed.

I knew that I was going to miss Arlene. What I didn't know was that her leaving would pave the way for one of the most meaningful, most special relationships in my life.

Chapter 19

The Elf and the Fireclock

Donna was Sea Ridge's first "baby." Seven years old, she was the size of an average one-year-old. She needed the care of an infant. Donna ate through a feeding tube inserted in her nose because she never learned to swallow. Her fuzzy tangle of brown hair was as impossible to comb as a Brillo pad. Long thick lashes highlighted her big beautiful brown eyes. But those eyes were vacant, without sparkle or awareness. Even when she offered her plaintive infant's cry, Donna's face seemed a blank slate, revealing no feeling.

Before Donna came to Sea Ridge, her hip had been broken. So the first few days after her arrival she lay in a cart by the nurses' station. The nurses covered her full-length cast with a tea towel because other coverings were too big.

I volunteered to take Donna as my roommate because she pulled at my heartstrings. I'd never seen any living creature who looked so abandoned and helpless. But when the aides moved her into my room, I worried and wanted to ask a thousand questions. "What do I do if she cries? If she throws up, should I come and get someone or should I first try to clear the vomit away from her feeding tube? How will I know if she's cold?"

One of the aides laughed. "You're acting just like a new mother, Carolyn. Don't worry. Donna will be just fine."

140

I wasn't so sure. Donna looked helpless, fragile. I thought she should have been wrapped in cotton.

The room seemed a little cool to me, so I put an old fuzzy lap robe over Donna to make sure she stayed warm. I went back to my reading. A few minutes later I heard Donna begin to laugh and blow spit bubbles. I went over to see what was so funny. Evidently she liked the feel of the fuzzy material.

Donna's laugh amazed the night nurse when she brought in my evening pills. She said that no one had heard anything but crying out of Donna since she arrived here. "We just put her in here tonight and already she's laughing," the nurse marveled. "You're good for her, Carolyn. We should have done this a month ago."

I can't adequately describe in words the feelings I had when Donna broke through with her laughter. From that very beginning my little roommate made me feel needed. I soon learned that when I felt needed I could cope with anything. When I felt needed, life had new meaning and direction.

The first objective was to train Donna to swallow. Aides came at mealtime to try to get her to take strained food. The sensation of food in her mouth evidently frightened Donna. During the first few feedings she screamed and fought with all her tiny might. Even after she began to accept food, her tongue would thrust it back out before she swallowed. Or she would stick her fist in her mouth.

It took more patience and love to feed Donna than some of the aides could manage. These "hirelings" gave up feeding her after a few bites. Other more-committed aides would take her in their arms and patiently coax her to take the food and swallow. I complained to the nurses about those aides who didn't make much effort and commended those who succeeded. That made me unpopular with some of the staff, but I didn't care.

The day came when the feeding tube could be removed. Donna could eat strained food. I had to laugh when she learned to wrinkle her nose over things she didn't like—beets and spinach. But, oh how she loved chocolate pudding!

When Donna's cast finally came off, she could sit up in a wheelchair and wear something other than oversized hospital gowns. Dressed in the used clothing some of the staff brought for her, she suddenly looked more like a real little kid than a tiny, helpless victim.

The next step was to enroll Donna in a special-education program. Given Donna's limitations, "education" really meant "therapy," so her teachers developed an individualized educational program, complete with all the carefully stated goals and steps required by the government for anyone living in state-funded facilities. Goal one was to train Donna to keep from constantly licking her hands and putting her fist in her mouth.

After that they would work on letting her feel different sensations and respond to them. But getting her to react to anything was a task. Each time she did something new, I felt the same kind of pride and joy I had that first night in my room when she surprised us all by laughing at the fuzzy blanket.

Gradually, Donna came alive. She began making what I called "a Donna sound" (a favorite was something that sounded like *suuuuu* whenever she heard me or when other people came into the room to talk to me).

I always talked back to Donna because I wanted her to feel important and loved. Whenever she sounded off, I responded in playful, teasing tone, "Oh, yes? And did I ask for your opinion, Elf?"

As the months rolled by, Donna became louder and louder— almost rude. She seemed to think her voice needed to be heard whenever any conversation was going on.

I amazed myself with the patience I had with her. I never got angry or even irritated. Everyone teased me for being an overly indulgent mom who let her kid get away with anything. I reminded them that Donna was a zombie when she came to live with me and now she was making real progress. Besides, I told them, they shouldn't expect little kids to be angels.

Most of the time Donna remained cooperatively quiet whenever I wrote, read, or worked on some craft. But every so often I stopped to talk and let her know that I was still in the room. That usually satisfied her.

One evening Donna got uncharacteristically crabby. She cried and cried. Nothing suited her. I checked her diaper. It was dry. I rearranged her pillows. Still she remained upset. Finally I went and got an aide who suggested that I try rocking her for a while.

That was just what Donna wanted. She settled right down and began laughing and blowing spit bubbles. I told her she was spoiled, that I had a book I wanted to finish reading, and she had thrown a monkey wrench in my plans by being such an imp. She responded with sweet contented noises that told me she could not have cared less.

Loving and caring for Donna brought happiness and contentment unknown to me since coming here more than a decade before. The responsibility for mothering Donna gave me new determination to make the most of my situation both at the home and at Crestview.

After struggling all my life, I finally felt like a conqueror.

———— • ————

Not even the good things in life can completely shelter us from the bad. Along with joy and discovery there is also sadness and loss.

Alan was a bright and reserved young man who moved into the nursing home after I did. For some reason I never understood but always appreciated, Alan adopted me as his sister. In doing so he helped me build new bonds of friendship at the nursing home.

Alan tried going to the UCP Center but had too much pain to keep up the effort. He had a rare hereditary condition that kept twisting his body tighter and tighter into a circle. The doctors had no way to correct the problem. He eventually had to use an electric wheelchair that reclined, but even then he wasn't able to be out of bed for long periods of time.

When he first came to us, Alan had a small business making and painting wooden duck decoys. They were beautiful and lifelike works of art. His father had made him a small workbench. On his good days, which grew fewer and fewer over the years, Alan worked on his decoys for hours. Some days the reassuring and steady tap, tap, tap of his hammer would be the most encouraging sound I heard.

Another thing that kept Alan busy was his fireclock routine, which he performed at night. Our nursing home had a safety system like none I have ever seen. There was a round steel box in a leather carrying case and a huge key attached to the box. On each wing of the home there was a station where the key had to be inserted so that some kind of reading could be recorded in the box. Alan volunteered for this duty and when winter evenings grew long he came by every hour or so to check the fireclock just outside my room.

To pass the hours of darkness, we often told jokes or exchanged witty dialogue about our circumstances. Once I asked Alan if he ever got tired of taking the fireclock around every night. He shook his head and told me that he enjoyed my company too much. "Sometimes," he said, "you're the only positive person I can find around here."

I had to laugh at that and assured him that I wasn't always in a good mood. In fact, I had a lot of days when I would have gladly walked out and never looked back.

"Good!" Alan replied. "Then I'm not the only one who feels that way about this place."

One night at supper time I told Alan I needed to check on Donna and make sure that we had clean bibs in the room. Alan teasingly said, "If I didn't know better, I'd think Donna was really your daughter, the way you take care of her." I ignored that comment and announced that I'd see him the next day as I headed for my room. But that was the last time I saw Alan. Early the next morning he was rushed to the hospital with an obstructed bowel and soon died.

When I heard the news, I denied my grief all day. But that evening as I read and wrote in my room, I missed the familiar buzzing of his electric wheelchair. There were no more jokes. No friendly conversation. I imagined his voice calling me: "Hey, lady. Are you still in there? You've been quiet for two hours." I cried the rest of the evening.

Every night after that I sadly listened to the footsteps of the head nurse carrying the fireclock. She never had time to stop and talk.

Chapter 20

I Prefer Flowered Kleenex

If my first encounters with Christianity had been in the nursing home, I probably would have had nothing to do with it. As it was, the things I observed being done in the name of Christ made me shudder.

Nursing-home ministries were a dime a dozen. Group after group came and did its thing and went. While some of the Christian groups that passed through Sea Ridge seemed genuinely warm and compassionate, there were others who appeared so rigid and sour that I wondered why they bothered.

The worst were those who couldn't seem to help projecting a definite air of spiritual superiority. I never minded showing them what I thought of their holier-than-God attitudes. Some were brave enough to rattle my cage and tell me all that I needed was faith so God would heal me. When I slammed my door in their faces, they hastily judged me to be a child of the Devil and pretty much left me alone.

It made me furious the way these people treated Arlene when she was my roommate. On warm summer evenings she always liked to sit out in the breeze on our patio and "talk" to me. Neither of us knew what the other one was saying, but we enjoyed ourselves and laughed a lot.

However, on their evenings to hold "church" for the nursing-home residents, these people I called "plastic Christians" would cart Arlene off the patio without stopping to try to figure out if she wanted to go. I thought their actions intolerably rude and thoughtless. I angrily told them so. Not that my protests did any good. They never even tried to understand what I was saying.

Determined to protect Donna from the likes of them, I bared my fangs if any of them dared to come close to her. I instructed Donna to spit up on them if they tried to take her.

It wasn't just patronizing attitudes and spiritual platitudes that bothered me. Their faith appeared to be all talk and no action. I came to that conclusion from observing them during their church services. They sang and preached about God's love and grace, but I never once saw them demonstrate those beliefs by attempting to wipe the snotty noses and drooling chins of their nursing-home congregation.

So I ignored them. And over time, they learned to leave me alone.

One hot summer evening I sat barefoot in an old nightie to keep cool while eating supper on the patio. It was a lazy feeling evening. I was savoring the quiet. Birds scrambled for my dropped crumbs. Suddenly one of those spit-shine Christians walked up and invaded my solitude. He was new and didn't know my reputation. I hoped that if I kept eating and ignored him he'd have enough good sense and manners to get lost.

Not so.

I have to really concentrate to eat. I follow these steps: (1) get my food on my spoon, (2) keep it balanced once it's on there, until I, (3) get as much of it as possible into my mouth. While I ate, this rude young man simply stared like he'd never seen anything like me before. He knew nothing about me. I don't think he even knew my name. But he knew a Scripture verse he evidently thought was the answer to my needs.

Standing there, his perfectly coordinated body towering above my wheelchair, his piety practically oozed out all over me as he further demonstrated his ignorance and insensitivity by quoting: "In everything give thanks for this is the will of God concerning you."

I screamed. I told him to get out of my space and leave me alone. Then I whirled my wheelchair around and would have gladly run over him if he hadn't fled before I had a chance to spit in his face.

Much later, when my rage subsided and I finally calmed down, I decided that the entire incident, the man's ignorance, and even his misapplication of Scripture, was a perfect illustration of another biblical passage: "The dumb ass spoke" (2 Peter 2:16 KJV).

My final battle with the plastic Christians came late one evening. Donna had gone to sleep, and I was typing. It was so hot I was working in a shirt and panties when a man showed up at my door and announced that he was from such-and-such a church. He had been sent to get some of my writings for their church newsletter. I told him that I had no request from anyone about that, but the man ignored my response, came into the room, and began rummaging through a box of papers on my desk.

I yelled at him to get out. When he didn't move, I kicked him in the shins and screamed. One of our volunteers, a sweet older lady we called Gramma E., heard the commotion and came bustling in. She ordered the man out, and he quickly fled when he saw the sheer anger on her face.

When I calmed down enough to talk, I explained to Gramma E. what had happened. I told her that I felt like the man had treated me like some kind of freak and wanted to show off something I'd written as if it were part of the freak show.

Gramma E. stayed with me, comforted me, and even tucked me into bed. Then she gave me a good-night hug and promised to help me store my writings somewhere out of sight so that not just anyone could get to them. The next day she got a restraining order against the man.

It shouldn't be too surprising that I became skeptical of any Christian groups that came to the nursing home. So when, a year or so after those two ugly incidents, a new group came to start a Tuesday afternoon worship and Bible Study, I stayed in my room. I wasn't going to be hurt by any more do-good Christians.

But the wonderful music this group played echoed softly down the hall. Someone knew how to play the piano the way it was supposed to be played. Someone else accompanied the piano on a violin. I had never heard the song, "Morning Has Broken" before, but I fell in love with the gentle, calming melody that day. All the music seemed so full of joy and peace.

The next week I decided to peek in to the service. They were all women—middle-aged. All mothers no doubt. They looked harmless. I think it was partly because I saw no men in this group that I instantly felt safe. I decided to stay for the service and soon learned all these women were part of a fellowship organized to train women to conduct church services in nursing homes.

This group not only told us that we were important to God, they showed us we were important to *them*. They listened to us and loved us one at a time. They even made a point to remember our names and the events that made up our lives.

What's more, they brought their own supply of flowered Kleenex for wiping our noses and chins. For me, their flowered Kleenex spoke more loudly than anything they could say. These women believed in a hands-on gospel. These were Christians I could trust.

I wasn't the only one who responded. This was the only service held at the home that the staff bothered to attend. We met in the day room off the east wing, and the entire hall would be packed with residents and staff who crowded in to listen to the gospel in word and music.

The women who led the service always encouraged us to sing and not worry about how we sounded. They said the Lord loved to hear us praise him with our hearts.

I felt certain that the Lord found special joy in my friend Robert's praise. I know that I did. Robert was a tiny black man with cerebral palsy. He was never able to pronounce any words correctly, but there was no doubt that Robert loved to praise the Lord. Amazingly, when he sang, his words and his voice became perfectly clear. If you only heard him sing in church, you'd never have guessed he had a speech problem. I loved to sit where I could hear him and see the joyous freedom on his face when he sang.

Ross was another resident who responded to this ministry. Before these women began coming on Tuesday afternoon, this frail little man sat in the hall alone all day, every day. He seldom moved. But after he began coming to the services, he seemed to slowly come alive. In the following months he began to smile at people, and I noticed his coming to the craft room instead of sitting in the hall. He still couldn't talk, but he began to make friends. He had caught a small spark of hope from hearing the gospel, and it grew into a small, steady flame within him.

So the impact of this new women's ministry never ended with the conclusion of the service. When I went back to my room afterward, warmed by hugs and feelings, my afternoon work always came alive with creative new ideas.

I grew to dearly love one middle-aged woman in particular. Her role in the group was very clear. Iola was a gifted expert with hugs and Kleenex. She was a no-nonsense mother who accepted no excuses as to why there was any uneaten food on the lunch tray in my room when she came to get me for the service each Tuesday afternoon. I told her that I'd rather be hugged than eat, but she was never satisfied until every bite was gone.

Iola arrived on the scene at a crucial point in my life. I had just learned that my pastor and his wife were leaving Seattle. For years Lloyd and Betty had been the only "outside" friends I could go to and cry out my frustrations with the nursing home and the centers. They listened and loved me patiently through my times of darkest discouragement and despair. They supported me spiritually when I was angry and ready to give up on God. They provided an emotional and sometimes a physical escape from my everyday environment. How would I survive without them? If I couldn't talk to someone about my deepest feelings, I felt I would soon just come apart from deep inside. And I had no one else I could talk to like I talked with Lloyd and Betty.

Until Iola.

I found it easy to talk honestly to Iola. She had no pretense. When she found me discouraged and crying, she was patient and loving. And it always felt so good, so comforting to have her listen as I attempted to verbally sort out the puzzle pieces of my life.

As I shared more and more of my life with Iola, I think she sensed there was something deeper, something I wasn't yet willing to talk about, something she didn't feel qualified to help me deal with. One day when we were talking, Iola told me her Lutheran congregation had just called a new associate minister. She said if I would give my permission, she'd like to tell Pastor Jim about me and see if he would come and meet me. She thought he might be able to help. She wanted me to think about the idea and let her know.

———————•———————

Perhaps it was just knowing that Iola and her friends were Lutherans, but their Tuesday afternoon services triggered some longing in my soul. For the next few months, when I'd lie awake at night unable to sleep, searching the far recesses of my mind for bits and pieces of the old Lutheran liturgy, I would say the Creed and parts of the old Kyrie in my mind. Something in the familiar rhythm of the liturgy often caused me to cry. It was a good cry.

Gradually my recurring daydream began creeping into my midnight recitations of the liturgy. I saw myself again in that beautiful white dress with the pink ribbon, running across that great field of brilliant wildflowers. In the dream I not only had my college degree, I had dignity and self-respect.

I tried to keep that vision alive in my mind by imagining that it was really true. One night I decided that it might someday be possible if I could take just one step at a time toward the goal.

The very next day I wheeled myself into a nursing-home bathroom containing a portable closet with a cross on the door. This was where visiting ministers and priests left robes and stored worship materials. I knew there were some old Lutheran hymnals in the bottom, because I saw them once several years earlier when snooping around. I pulled one of the hymnals out to discover that it was the very same edition we used at the Anne Carlsen School.

It was like finding ice water in the desert.

I began to read the old liturgy. I remembered the mystery of the rhythm. I felt the power of the words:

"In the name of the Father, and the Son and of the Holy Ghost, Amen. . . .

"Beloved in the Lord, Let us draw near with a true heart and confess our sins unto God our Father, beseeching him in the Name of the Lord Jesus Christ to grant us forgiveness. . . .

"... Our help is in the name of the Lord who made Heaven and earth ...

"... Oh, most merciful God who has given thine only begotten Son to die for us, have mercy upon us and for his sake grant us remission of all our sins, and by thy Holy Spirit increase in us true knowledge of Thee. ..." The page was torn there.

The words sounded so ancient and beautiful. The recurring phrase, "Lord have mercy, Christ have mercy" had an especially calming effect on my spirit. Saying them helped me feel that God did indeed understand all my feelings of wretchedness. He knew the pain of those long-buried memories I'd never shared with anyone. I could even believe that God understood that longing I had to wear the white dress of my daydreams.

The Lutheran women who came to the nursing home didn't use the liturgy in their service, but they always reminded us that the Lord forgives our sins no matter what we have done. God loves us with an everlasting love. Each of us is worth the death of Jesus on the cross to keep us in his love.

That message began to settle home in my heart. A few weeks after I found the old hymnal in that closet, I asked Iola to call Pastor Jim.

Chapter 21

Theology of the Inch

When I applied the caring, loving, "mother's gospel" of Iola and her friends to my parched and forlorn spirit, it soaked down deep into my soul. I had heard about God's love, but my experience with these gentle women convinced me it was time to believe it and to test it. The first big test was to go see Pastor Jim.

Iola went with me. Our driver parked right in front of the church office, and the two of them walked me in. Pastor Jim greeted us at the door. Iola asked him to get a chair with arms so I'd feel more secure when I sat down.

Pastor Jim was a tall, thin man in his late twenties who looked like he enjoyed sports and he worked at staying fit. His unassuming, soft-spoken nature gave the impression of a man at ease with himself and with the world. His study was a jungle of big beautiful plants and a collection of projects in process, an unpretentious roomful of warmth and honest friendliness. As I noted an opened bag of potting soil sitting on newspaper in a corner, he explained he'd brought the plants down from Canada with him and was hoping they would survive the move.

With the introductions of plants and people made, Pastor Jim asked me to show him how to use my alphabet board. He said he thought he could understand most of what I said but admitted he was new at this and might need help. Iola told him that she found it helpful to jot the letters down when I resorted to spelling something on my board, so he got a pad and pencil ready.

Iola simply sat back and let the two of us communicate with each other. Sometimes Pastor Jim would get stuck and plead with Iola for translation help. He stumbled through some very strange sentences but stuck with me and seemed to understand pretty well for a first-timer. He did laughingly admit that trying to understand me was a little like playing a game of "Frustration."

Before that appointment, I'd given Iola permission to fill Pastor Jim in on my growing discouragement over conditions at the nursing home and some of my questions about the future. So he told me he wanted us to talk about that. But he didn't have any neatly folded blanket of Bible verses to throw over my depression or my loss of hope. He said he didn't have any easy answers for me or my troubling circumstances.

However, he did empathize with me on a personal level. And after we talked for a while about my feelings of frustration he made this observation: "It seems to me, Carolyn, that you're in a situation that was never intended for you. I doubt any nursing home is ever going to allow you to grow to your full potential. From what you and Iola have told me, you have every right to be unhappy at Sea Ridge."

He encouraged me to start gathering information and exploring alternatives. Pastor Jim clearly believed in the theology of the inch—tackling problems and pursuing dreams one small step at a time. While he admired and affirmed my long-range goal of attending college, he suggested that I decide on one thing that was most upsetting to me right now and develop a plan for dealing with that problem immediately.

One current frustration was getting my supper served and situated so that I could eat it. The nursing home had just hired several new aides who exhibited little common sense and even less commitment to their jobs. Their primary motivation seemed to be to finish their assigned tasks as quickly as possible so they could take a break. They would whiz into my room, perch my supper tray precariously on the top of the typewriter, and make a run for the door. Although I always had my tray table cleared and set for my meal, they never seemed to make the connection that I needed the tray set in front of me so that I could eat. And they were always long gone before I could ask for help with any food that needed cutting up. So I would have to go out in the hall to find another aide to help me. By the time I could actually begin eating, my food would be cold.

Pastor Jim listened patiently to my complaints. Then he gave me the assignment to try to get my supper-serving problem solved before he saw me again the following week. He left the details up to me.

We also talked about some of my spiritual concerns, my sense of loss that Lloyd and Betty had moved, and some of the questions and anger I had directed toward God. Pastor Jim assured me that no matter what doubts I might have, no matter what feelings I had toward God, God understood my pain and my emotions, and he accepted me the way I was, without condemnation, because Christ had died for me.

Pastor Jim talked about Christ's dying on the cross, saying that because of that experience, God could feel and understand our pain. He pointed out that Jesus himself had never prayed, "Father, I am thankful for the cross," but rather had prayed asking God if he couldn't "let this cup pass from me" and avoid such suffering.

At the close of our time together, after we set a time to meet at the nursing home the next week, Pastor Jim prayed with me. He asked God for a show of love and grace that would guide me through my depression and bring me to a place of assurance and rest where I could feel accepted and affirmed by the wounded Christ. Then he offered me the peace of the Lord by making the sign of the cross. I loved this! It was a tangible, physical gesture of God's peace and love for me.

That week I tackled my mealtime problem with what proved to be a very effective strategy. The next time the aide set my supper tray atop my typewriter and turned to hurry out of the room, I knocked the tray off and ground the food into the floor with my feet. Then I called the same aide back to my room to clean up the mess. The next time she put my food on the typewriter, I repeated the process. By the end of the week I had made my point. But I continued to drape a big towel over my typewriter as a reminder that any food left there would go flying. The aides not only carefully placed my supper in front of me on my tray table where I could eat it, they now stayed and cut up my food for me, too.

When Pastor Jim came to visit the following week, he asked how I was coming on the supper problem. So I told him how I solved it. He grinned, and I detected a rascally shine in his eyes as he admitted that my solution wasn't one he would have thought of, "But it obviously worked!"

The next step in our game plan was to work toward a short-term goal in my writing. I hadn't been doing much creative work for a while. Pastor Jim asked if he could read some of my writings to find something I might be able to adapt for his church newsletter. Together we rummaged through my files until we found a short article about a flower blooming in the springtime, titled, "What Is a Miracle?" He asked me to rework that for him. He said he needed it the following week. And since he liked to write, he made some good suggestions on how to improve the piece.

That's how our friendship began. I would talk about my concerns or plans for the future, and Pastor Jim would listen encouragingly and remind me that I needed a step-by-step strategy to bring my dreams to reality. He never did the work for me. He enabled me to make slow, steady progress by encouraging me and believing in my dreams with me.

After more than a dozen years at Sea Ridge, I could hardly imagine living anywhere else. And I didn't think I could ever seriously consider leaving Donna, but at Pastor Jim's gentle urging, I agreed to explore my alternatives. I talked to my supervisor and to the social worker at Crestview about a new United Cerebral Palsy residential center that had recently opened in North Seattle.

I learned that the "Res," as it was commonly called, was another congregate-care facility. It was designed for those with cerebral palsy and therefore offered much more for the disabled than a nursing home ever could. While that sounded encouraging, I resisted the unpleasant thought of change. And I still couldn't leave Donna.

However, I did decide to visit the Res and have lunch there with Ila Mae, my former roommate, who had returned to Seattle and now lived at the new facility. She proudly told me it was the kind of home she, her late parents, and others who helped found UCP had dreamed of having for years.

Lunch was a simple bowl of soup and a sandwich. But I was impressed by the extra crackers made available so that I could crumble them in my soup to make a consistency that would stay on my spoon. It seems like such a small consideration, but at Sea Ridge the soup was like water, and there were never extra crackers. Whenever we had soup, I got very little in me.

After lunch, Ila Mae took me on a tour. The Res was a big rambling building set around two courtyards, with many windows, a lot of natural light, a spacious community dining room, and an impressive therapy area near the center of the facility.

Residents' rooms seemed airy and convenient with built-in closets, vanities, and shelves all designed for easy wheelchair access. What impressed me even more was the fact that even total-care residents were dressed in street clothes and smelled clean—without the familiar nursing-home odor.

The Res had just worked out the details for interested residents to attend nearby Shoreline Community College. The staff provided transportation to and from campus. The year I took college classes, I always had to arrange my own rides. Iola, her friend Ruth, and others from the women's Bible study had driven me and then brought me home when my class was over.

Pastor Jim acted pleased when I reported all I'd learned on my fact-finding visit to the Res. He said it was important to be able to make decisions based on facts. He felt that learning the facts necessary to make an informed decision was certainly preferable to doing nothing in hopes of avoiding the pain of facing a hard choice. Sometimes I wasn't so sure.

But Pastor Jim told me that pain was going to be a part of life, no matter what I did. I couldn't avoid it. No one can. He encouraged me to pursue the higher goals I'd set for myself despite the difficulty.

I knew he thought the Res would be the best choice for me. When I told him there would be at least a year's wait to get into the new facility, he reacted with obvious disappointment. I was relieved by that news. It offered a welcome reprieve from a difficult decision, but when Pastor Jim asked me what I was going to do to cope with my depression in the meantime, I knew that I still didn't have any answers.

I had been taking medication prescribed over the phone by a doctor I felt cared little about my well-being. I received regular Medicare statements indicating that he had seen me when he had only reviewed my charts. On the rare occasions he examined me, he acted as if I were a leper, and deaf and dumb as well. So I had no confidence that the medicines he prescribed were helping at all. If anything, I felt more depressed. A lot of days I slept more than my usual afternoon nap time.

So when Pastor Jim asked how I would cope with my ongoing depression, I couldn't explain my conflicting feelings. I didn't fully understand them myself. For the first time in my life I felt very tired and old. My life was a nightmare, and I couldn't make myself wake up.

One late fall evening as I stood at my window ready to draw the drapes, I saw an ominous bank of dark clouds sailing across the sky toward me. I felt compelled to stand and watch as big drops of rain in a frenzied dance bounced off the young cherry tree next to the patio. I love storms, but something about this one felt angry and unfriendly. A lonely chill went through me as if to say, "A storm is coming. Before it has passed it will rip your heart out."

Those icy raindrops were the forerunners of an unseasonable front. Toward morning Jack Frost did his beautiful but deadly work. When I opened my drapes to let in the early morning light, I saw the coating of ice and knew that the young cherry tree was too young and too weak to survive.

I went to work at Crestview in a quiet and thoughtful mood.

My supervisor told me that she needed me to bag headsets. I needed to hurry because we were behind our quota from the day before. Whenever I did this job, I used a counting tray to help me keep track of what I was doing. The tray sat right in front of my wheelchair and had ten spaces that I filled with one bagged headset at a time. Then no matter how long it took me to get ten headsets into their bags, I wouldn't lose count before I dumped them all into the larger ten-count storage bag. It was mindless work that gave me time to think.

On this particular day I noted a number of tour groups coming through the center. I couldn't help wonder what the people on the other side of the glass were thinking as they watched us. *How do they see me? Do any of them think of me as a woman with hopes and dreams beyond this workshop? Do they assume I'll be happy to work here the rest of my life?*

Cold rain fell throughout the morning. At lunchtime a terrible brawl broke out in the cafeteria. I have no idea what ignited the volatile emotions of my mentally handicapped colleagues, but within seconds a collective ball of rage and frustration swept through the room, smashing bodies to the floor and shattering windows. In panic I wheeled myself to the door and escaped outside into the storm, where I began to cry so hard I feared I'd never be able to stop. This was not what I wanted out of my life.

I could live with the prison of cerebral palsy. But the doors were double-locked by the very idea that I belonged where I was—struggling to work with my hands while my head and heart longed to be put to work. I knew then that more than anything I wanted an education so that I could use the mind and writing ability God gave me before they shriveled and died—like my poor frozen cherry tree.

When I got back to Sea Ridge that afternoon, I reminded myself of what Pastor Jim had said—that God understood and felt my pain. I told myself that God saw what happened at Crestview and knew how utterly alone I felt, how desolate my life seemed. To force myself out of despondency, I made a list of immediate goals, a simple to-do list for my weekend—finish article, read book, clean up room, straighten up Donna's dresser, fold her clothes.

I started in on my list but was too depressed to concentrate. My frustration resurfaced, belittling my feeble and insignificant goals and haunting me with the terrible fear that this was all my life would ever be.

By Sunday afternoon, yet another front blew in. Rain and wind assaulted the garden again. The storm inside me also raged on.

Upon my desk sat a clown-faced mug with a cold, ceramic smile that mocked my pain. I snatched up that mug and smashed it against my desk. When it shattered into pieces, I picked up one of the jagged shards and sawed it across my right wrist. A small ribbon of blood appeared on my arm, but I didn't have the strength or the coordination to cut very deep at all.

What frustration. What bitter irony. *I can't even kill myself.*

But in that moment I realized I didn't want to die. I prayed desperately to God for the will to live and to never again give up. I hurried into the bathroom to clean up my arm. I wrapped the bloody paper towel and the broken pieces of the clown mug in a paper bag, which I buried in the bottom of my wastebasket. Then I donned a long-sleeved shirt, went to bed, and almost immediately fell into an exhausted sleep.

When I awakened the next morning, it was still raining. I made sure that Donna had her rain bonnet on when the aides came to wheel her off to school. Then I dressed myself and went to work. When another tour group came through, I watched the people on the other side of the glass and wondered what they'd think if they could see through the window of my soul.

Chapter 22

No Looking Back

I saw Pastor Jim the following week and told him what had happened. He felt that my suicidal feelings were beyond his ability to deal with, so a few days later I went to see the counselor he recommended.

The man seemed a compassionate listener, but his volunteer office staff proved unbelievably ignorant. Before my appointment I'd written a letter about my recent crises and had a friend drop it off. This way we wouldn't have to spend a long time during my first appointment getting the basic facts communicated. I took it for granted that my letter would be read only by the man to whom I'd addressed it.

At the end of my appointment, the office staff pulled my letter from the file and discussed my plight right in front of me as if I were blind, deaf, and had no feelings. They had obviously never seen anyone as disabled as I was. They didn't know what to make of me and actually wondered out loud whether I could understand what the counselor had said to me. I was humiliated. And angry. And too embarrassed to make a fuss or even let them know just how insensitive and cruel they were.

Afterward I prayed, *Father, forgive those who treat me as if I am a nonperson. Because I am too angry and hurt to forgive them in my own strength.*

The following week, I told Pastor Jim what happened and said, "I'm never going back to that office again." He said he didn't blame me.

The next week when Pastor Jim came to visit he served me Holy Communion. Because I was only a child when I attended that Lutheran church back in North Dakota, this was the first time for me to take the sacrament. The abbreviated ritual seemed a profound and wonderful mystery—to imagine Christ's body and blood as an ordinary piece of bread dipped in wine (this was the easiest way for Pastor Jim to serve me the bread and wine). To think of God's Son, his body broken so that he could take on my brokenness and my pain.

The realization seemed almost too wonderful to believe. But because I did believe it, as I took that piece of bread and that thimbleful of wine, I found a new source of strength to continue on the long, slow journey toward my dreams.

———————— • ————————

Long after the winter of 1978 gave in to spring showers and warm sunshine, the storm in my heart raged on. It blew strongest at night when I couldn't sleep.

I had finally applied to the Res and was on a long waiting list. My head told me this was the right decision, but my emotions wouldn't quit arguing. I wanted to hold and protect Donna forever. I feared for my continued sanity and my life if I stayed, yet I felt cruel and heartless about leaving her.

Donna needed someone to speak for her and to make sure she was dressed warmly enough on cold winter days. She needed someone to coax her to eat when she didn't feel hungry. She deserved someone who cared enough to help her blossom and grow.

I knew that no matter what I did for Donna, her condition would not change. There would be no first words, no small voice demanding, "Leave me alone. I want to do it myself!" There would never be any little nods in answer to questions. Too many times I'd searched for something—anything—in Donna's big brown eyes. But there was nothing. The most she would ever do would be to lie in her bed or sit strapped in her wheelchair. She giggled, blew spit bubbles, shook her head, and flailed her arms. Whatever was locked inside Donna was in there to stay.

How often I wished I could have shared my gifts with her. While I had my share of imperfections, at least I could think, communicate, plan, and pursue dreams. *What was life like for Donna? Had she ever made the rudimentary discovery that she existed?* I didn't know. And I never would.

I asked Pastor Jim all the hard questions posed by my aching heart. I felt so wicked for thinking about abandoning Donna that I often cried when I talked to him about my plans. But he never spared the harsh truth when we talked. He firmly reinforced the facts I already knew. "Ten years from now Donna will still be lying in that same bed and sitting in that same wheelchair," he told me. "But ten years from now you could be graduated from college and writing something that will be making a difference out in the world."

Over and over again he told me he believed that the dreams I had were part of God's will for my life. He told me that doing God's will is seldom easy and sometimes unpleasant. Yet doing the will of God is always good and always right.

So I told God that I was going to trust Pastor Jim to be his spokesperson for me on this issue.

Then one morning as I ate my breakfast, played with Donna, and thought about what tasks I should tackle at work, an idea flashed through my mind: *Why not have Donna baptized?* While I believed Donna was already a part of God's family by virtue of divine grace and her inability to reason for herself, the act of baptism would be an outward, physical sign that I was placing Donna in the loving arms of Jesus forever.

Of course Donna's baptism would never guarantee that she would have a rain bonnet when she needed it, or would always get enough to eat when she was crabby and made feeding difficult for the aides. But it would be a reminder to me that she was committed to God's care, and I needed to trust her to him.

When I suggested my idea to Pastor Jim, he seemed pleased. I was taking another step toward letting go of Donna. He did wonder about permission required for such a baptism, since Donna was a ward of the state. After we cleared that hurdle, he raised another point—the denomination I'd been attending didn't practice infant baptism. I had never given that issue much thought until Donna came into my life. Now I wondered why so many people try to limit God. Surely the big, compassionate Creator was flexible enough to accept and appreciate my intentions on this score.

The day of Donna's baptism dawned warm and beautiful. Her aide dressed Donna in a baby-blue dress that gave her the look of an innocent little angel. We held the baptism in the backyard of the nursing home, with flowers covering an old picnic table that served as the altar. The font was a small plastic bowl full of water.

The unlikely setting was made especially significant by the small group of friends who gathered around and by a very real sense of God's presence. Dodging back and forth among the guests was a small redheaded girl I'd never seen before. I prayed silently for that child, thanking God for her obvious brightness, and asking his blessing and protection for her, that she would never have to spend her life in a nursing home as Donna did.

My prayer and my musing came to a halt when Pastor Jim began the service in the name of the Father, Son, and Holy Ghost. He asked me the same questions he would have asked Donna's parents if she'd had any. He shortened the spoken part of the service and allowed me time to respond. In my promise, I affirmed my faith in Christ and accepted the responsibility for telling Donna that God loved her by showing her that I loved her.

Then Pastor Jim prayed a blessing on Donna's life, that the Lord would keep her and bring her into eternal life. He also asked that when the time came for me to walk out of Donna's life that I'd be able to look back on her baptism and thank the Lord for his promise to love and take care of her.

After the service we all sat in the shade and talked. Pastor Jim told me once again that he believed whatever pain and joy the future would bring for me, it would be even more wonderful than my dreams. God could outdream me. He would give me purpose and work I would certainly be able to do.

Donna decided she'd had enough of being quiet while we talked. She began blowing spit bubbles, kicking, and making Donna noises until all conversation stopped and she was again the center of attention.

Then, when she began to fuss as if she'd had enough of the afternoon, we took her inside, and Pastor Jim laid her gently back in her bed.

———————•———————

My decision was made. I would leave the nursing home. But the Res informed me their waiting list was even longer now than it was when I first checked. I wouldn't be able to move for more than a year. After struggling so long to make my decision, the wait seemed interminable.

But a few months later, when October splashed orange, red, and yellow all over the nursing home's backyard, I realized how quickly the seasons were passing. I decided that while I waited I could begin pursuing another old dream.

I told Pastor Jim that I wanted to be confirmed in the Lutheran Church. He told me that it was never his intention to steal me away from my own denomination. I assured him that it was something I'd wanted to do since I was a student at the Anne Carlsen School. Now as I contemplated leaving the nursing home and moving to the Res, my confirmation would be a wonderful and timely sign of yet another beginning. A fresh start.

What I didn't tell my Lutheran friends, because I still couldn't verbalize the horrible memories and emotions tied to my past sexual abuse, was that I saw my confirmation as the first crucial step in a secret journey away from the ugliness of the past. If I could make a new spiritual connection with the Lutheran Church, then maybe, just maybe, I could begin to break some of the guilt and shame that still bound me.

So to me the idea of confirmation had a double significance. It would unite me with my new friends as it publicly symbolized a new beginning in faith. It would also signify my hope for a very private beginning.

———————•———————

The adult confirmation class was large, and the senior pastor led it. Iola volunteered to sit with me in class as my interpreter. One day during class I felt so weak that I kept sliding out of my chair. When Iola began seriously questioning me after class, I insisted I would be all right, but she said that she could tell by my voice that I was tired and in pain. "I bet you only picked at your breakfast and were awake half the night again. Am I right?" I had to admit that she was.

Iola drove me directly back to the nursing home, put me in bed, and sternly informed the nurse that I was sicker than I let anyone know. While I hadn't felt well for a long time, it always seemed useless to say anything to the nurses. They would just tell my doctor, and he would prescribe something without even trying to listen to me. I figured if I could just keep going until I transferred to the Res, someone there might listen.

When I tried to explain all this to Iola, she got visibly upset and asked why I couldn't get another doctor. The very next morning she and Ruth returned and announced that they were taking me to the hospital for a checkup. But when Iola packed a clean nightie and my robe in my wheelchair bag, I panicked.

Ruth tried to calm me down and get me to listen. "Sweetie," she said, "you haven't been feeling well for a long time. I know you're trying to go on with your life like nothing is wrong, but you're only fooling yourself. There's another doctor who wants to see you. Iola and I will go with you. We'll make sure that he understands you and knows that you understand him. Okay?"

I agreed to go. The doctor made a brief examination and then prescribed complete bed rest and told me he wanted to do a more complete checkup once I had settled down and regained some strength. He then admitted me to the hospital.

I protested and even after I was moved into a room I tried three times to climb out of the bed and leave. Ruth and Iola restrained me. Finally my panic eased, my reason returned, and I apologized for acting so shamefully. After they graciously accepted my apology I said, "Will you ladies please go home and get some lunch. It's almost three o'clock; you must be hungry. I'm going to be fine now."

They laughed and hugged me, saying, "Now you sound more like yourself. Snuggle down and get some rest like the doctor ordered."

The doctor returned to give me a thorough examination the following afternoon. He stayed to talk with me for more than three hours. He had no experience communicating with anyone who had a speech difficulty, but he caught on fast. He was gracious and treated me with respect.

The doctor told me he was going to change my medications. My previous physician had me on heart medicine to treat my complaints about chest pain, but this doctor said he found no indication of heart trouble at all. What he found was a little arthritis and numerous symptoms of stress and exhaustion. He was most concerned about my depression and wanted to talk about what was going on in my life.

I told him about my frustrations with the nursing home and with Crestview. I told him about my difficult decision to move to the Res where I hoped I could get more therapy, better care, and have a chance to attend college. I told him that after I graduated from college, I dreamed of having a home of my own and finding a place for myself in society.

After hearing me out, the doctor said, "Anyone who has as bright and active a mind as you do would naturally experience a lot of stress in your circumstances. But I'm impressed that you're already taking steps to help yourself. I wish more of my patients were as courageous as you and would take that kind of responsibility for their own lives."

Then he asked a very candid question. "Carolyn, how do you cope when people don't take the time to understand you? If I couldn't express myself in a second, I'd go stark crazy. You have so much to offer. If only you had a faster way to get your words out."

We talked for a while longer. When we finished, I thanked this thoughtful man for his patience and his empathy. When he left I slept soundly all afternoon. His compassion had given me a new sense of peace and hope.

The next day the doctor came back to say that he had me on the emergency waiting list at the Res. As soon as a space was available, I would be notified, but for a few more days he wanted me to stay in the hospital and regain my strength. He even gave the nurses orders to feed me because it was so hard for me to feed myself.

After he left, I lay in bed and prayed, telling God how wonderful it would be to get word from the Res before Christmas and be able to begin the new year with a brand new beginning.

One night in December after I was released from the hospital, an old nursing-home volunteer stopped by to see me. Dorothy smuggled in some homemade applesauce, which she fed to me before helping decorate a miniature Christmas tree that we then placed on my bookcase.

I told her how torn I felt about leaving Donna in the same state I'd found her seven years before—as an abandoned child. Dorothy very bluntly told me I had to stop thinking like that. "Donna is a cute little kid," she said, "and precious in the sight of the Lord. But if you stay to take care of her, you'll be cheating yourself. Remember when you told me you thought you would die if you had to stay here much longer? You have to move on. You have to follow your dream to become a writer. Go back to college. Some day your writing will help people like Donna and others who have to live in nursing homes like this.

"It won't be easy, but Carolyn, if you work at it you can make your dreams come true. Donna will always be this helpless even if you devote your entire life to her."

A few days later I got the answer to my prayers. I received a call from the Res saying I could to move in on the second of January 1979. The Lord had given me a new beginning for the new year.

During the short time I had left at Sea Ridge, Iola, Ruth, Dorothy, and I cleaned out my room—fifteen years of accumulated living. I was surprised when Ruth noted that it had been that long. We tossed out loads of junk and packed the rest. When the assistant administrator stopped by and observed that all our preparations reminded her of the time her own kids left home for college, it seemed an apt comparison. For almost half my life, Sea Ridge had been my home. I'd also known joy and accomplishment here as well as pain and frustration. Every room, every hallway, was crowded with memories.

Donna was on Christmas vacation from school and seemed particularly crabby as my friends and I packed away my things. I wondered if she sensed I was leaving. *How could I let her know I still loved her? That I had to leave? That God would take care of her?* I had no idea.

The second day of the new year I awoke very early and prayed that God would send his angels to protect Donna. As usual, I helped the aide dress her for school. It seemed as if time had worked like a weaver's shuttle over the past seven years, weaving my life and Donna's so tightly together that leaving now felt like an irreparable ripping right through my heart.

I tried not to cry as I went out with her to wait for the school bus and say my final good-bye. By the time she came home, I would be gone.

The room looked bare and sad as I folded my blankets and got dressed. I heard Iola and Dorothy coming down the hall. They grinned as they walked into the room. "Good morning, sweety. I guess this is it," Dorothy said as they both gave me big reassuring hugs.

We prayed together that the miracle God had begun in my life would continue in this new chapter. And I prayed, "Thank You, Lord, for the beauty and the tragedy of these years in this nursing home. Please give me a spirit of cooperation for the residents and staff at my new home, the Res."

Then we walked out of Sea Ridge into the teeth of a terrible winter rain and windstorm. I determined not to look back because I didn't want to cry.

Chapter 23

The Res

The wind whipped the rain so hard it felt as if we were driving through a carwash. Radio news reports warned that the Lake Washington Bridge might have to be closed. I hoped that the friends with me would be able to make it home safely. I reached over and took Iola's hand. She smiled and said nothing.

I thought about all the storms that had raged inside me over the years and wondered if they'd ever subside. And as the rain bombarded the hood of the car, I remembered again that stormy day so long ago when I lost Gaga.

One of the nurses met us at the front of the Res, holding the door open wide and saying, "Do come in out of that terrible rainstorm!"

As Iola helped remove my jacket and straighten my clothes, the nurse told me, "I've heard so much about you, Carolyn. I'm sure you're going to be a real asset to the Res." I didn't know how to respond. I wasn't sure I wanted to be an "asset" to anyone else. I'd only come here because I saw no other alternative if I wanted to go to college.

The nurse called the maintenance department for help in bringing in my belongings. A few minutes later I was on my way to the room I would share with Ila Mae. She was working at the UCP workshop and would be home later. But the room already had a familiar feel with her old quilt on her bed, her books and papers on her desk, and her favorite photos and pictures hanging on the wall.

When I had put most of my clothes in my drawers and closet and concluded my official admissions appointment, Iola, Ruth, and Dorothy left for home. No sooner had they gone than I tossed my donkey quilt over my stripped bed and fell sound asleep—totally oblivious to the daytime commotion of the Res. My first few days in any new setting I usually have trouble relaxing enough to sleep, but this was a sleep of release. I had no idea whether I was about to stand or fall, but I had finally taken a giant step forward. It felt very right.

I awakened when I heard the familiar hum of Ila Mae's wheelchair coming down the hall. (Every wheelchair has its own distinctive sound.) I kicked the empty boxes out of her way and welcomed her with a squeal and a hug. She exclaimed, "It feels so natural to see you here. I like it."

I told Ila Mae that I must have dozed off for a few minutes. Just then the evening nurse came in and greeted me, "Well, sleepyhead, you finally woke up. Hi, I'm Margie. I came in three times to check your vital signs, but you were sound asleep. So let me put Ila Mae on the toilet, and I'll check your vitals now. Whenever we get new patients here, we like to make sure they're alive."

I asked if being hungry was a vital sign. If it was, I was very much alive.

Within minutes of the time the nurse finished with me, a parade of old and new friends came by to welcome me. I quickly realized that I was now part of a very diverse community—both in terms of our disabilities and our goals. There were writers and artists and politicians. There were churchgoers and atheists. We had married couples, gays and singles. Some were quiet and reclusive, others clearly were movers and shakers. We had some who constantly fought for increased independence and others still tied to their parents. I met people whom I immediately knew were nonconformists and others who allowed themselves to be carried along by whatever was the current trend.

We were an incredible mosaic of humanity with vast differences. As Ila Mae and I made our way to the dining room, I thought about the common but incorrect assumption that all disabled people want and need the same things.

Caught in a traffic jam on our way to the cafeteria, Ila Mae and I parked our wheelchairs to the side of the hallway to wait out the rush. To pass the time, I stood holding the railing and danced to the beat of the music piped in over the intercom. Ila Mae just rolled her eyes for the umpteenth time in our long relationship.

Someone yelled down the hall, startling me so that I let go and fell down. As I pulled myself back up into my wheelchair, I heard a man's obnoxiously loud voice demanding, "Who is that character dancing? I never saw her before."

Ila Mae laughed, and as he approached, she introduced us: "John, this is Carolyn. I think you two deserve each other because you're both crazy."

John protested that he couldn't be as crazy as I was. "At least I was standing here in a civilized manner," he said. "But you were jumping around like you have a definite problem."

Even if I hadn't seen the mischief in his eyes, I would have guessed he had a jovial nature. He had the look of a man who'd raided more than his share of cookie jars in his sixty or so years of life. White hair fringed out around his ears, but the top of his head was as shiny and smooth as a polished glass ball.

I soon learned that John was a businessman. He and his family were members of the church next door to the Res. He had begun a special ministry for the residents here and was in and out of the facility all the time. He invited me to one of his group's services before he left.

While we were waiting to be served in the dining room, I quizzed Ila Mae about John. *Was he on the up-and-up? What did he want from us? A sense of achievement and a salve for his guilt over being able-bodied?* He may have claimed to be a Christian, but I wasn't about to accept him at face value.

Ila Mae seemed surprised by my cynicism. "You used to trust everyone," she said. "But you act as though John is some sort of criminal."

I told her about the plastic Christians who had come to Sea Ridge, and especially about the man who walked in when I was dressed in my underwear and tried to loot my writing. I told Ila Mae that I felt I had to protect myself until I knew that someone was trustworthy. She smiled in understanding.

Supper was pleasant. The aides even offered seconds on milk. I felt especially good about being able to talk to people without having to guard my food like an animal. At the nursing home I often lost food to some of the retarded patients who snatched anything they could reach. I so enjoyed this leisurely, unpressured meal with friends that I told them if I got used to such civility and decorum, there was no end to what I would be demanding. Everyone laughed. Ila Mae grinned, "You civilized? This I have to see!"

When we finished our dessert, I left the table with my tummy full of food and my heart full of friendship.

After supper I had more unpacking to do. Two aides, a young man and a young woman, appeared at my door. They wanted to know if I needed any more help getting settled. Tom and Mary introduced themselves and explained that they were both students, trying to work their way through the Lutheran Bible Institute with plans of becoming Bible translators. Mary said they'd heard about me through Pastor Jim's father, who was a professor at the institute. They recommended a local congregation for me—Bethel Lutheran of Shoreline—as being very near the Res.

I marveled at the effectiveness of the Lutheran grapevine. Mary chuckled. "See, we keep track of you."

I shook my head and grinned as I complained: "I've just arrived, and I'm already infamous." But I appreciated their interest—especially when Mary and Tom wanted to know what I hoped to accomplish at the Res. They seemed to take it for granted that I had bigger plans for the future.

While I filled Mary in on my goals, Tom dragged in my green desk and set my typewriter on it. That banged-up old desk looked unsightly. When Mary asked me if it was strong enough to be used anymore, I assured her, "That old desk is a lot like me—stronger than it looks and a bit out of place in such a crisp new setting." We all laughed like old friends.

At bedtime Ila Mae and I were finally alone. She again told me, "It's so good to have you here." Then she candidly added, "Grant you, the Res has its problems. It's still an institution. It's not exactly what we envisioned when we began planning it years ago. It's less than we need but far better than what we had."

Before I climbed into bed, I pushed aside the curtains to look out our window. The moon cast its silvery light through scattered clouds drifting silently across the blackened sky. It was going to be a cold, dry night after such a wet and windy day.

I felt as if I'd journeyed a thousand miles since leaving Sea Ridge that morning.

Chapter 24

Danger: Bionic Woman

Almost before I knew it, Confirmation Sunday arrived all sunny and cold. As I dressed for church, I remembered once again my days at the Anne Carlsen School and realized that now, more than twenty years later, I was about to reclaim the spiritual heritage I had known there. After a long and painful detour, I was again moving forward on my spiritual journey, away from the ugliness of the past.

The sun shone down through the skylight high above Bethel Lutheran's sanctuary, beaming over my classmates and me as we stood around the altar—a warm and wonderful symbol of grace. Iola, who'd driven up from South Seattle for the day, stood beside me, allowing me to lean on her for support as Pastor Larson asked those sober questions from the confirmation rites.

"Do you believe in God, the Father, and in Jesus Christ, His Son, and in the Holy Spirit?

"Do you renounce Satan and all his ways?

"Do you support and believe in the work of the church?"

After each question we responded, "I do, with God's help."

Then the pastor prayed as he placed his hands on each bowed head: "Father in Heaven for Jesus' sake, stir up in Carolyn the gift of your Holy Spirit, confirm her faith, guide her life, empower her in her serving, give her patience in suffering, and bring her to everlasting life."

My promises seemed so frail compared to the Lord's promises of unconditional love and forgiveness. I told myself that I did believe those promises. And I was grateful that God knew my desire to please him even when I struggled with my anger and depression.

———— • ————

During the reception following the service, I was greeted with numerous hugs and kisses. Pastor Larson accused me of being the talk of the church. He chuckled as he told Iola, "All I hear about Carolyn is how she has a thousand dreams and is forever working to achieve them. I've been encouraging her to be a pioneer at the Res, but people here seem to be catching her spirit of hope, too."

That made me feel good. I went home that day feeling that my confirmation was worth the long journey. It was a mountaintop I'd finally reached, even if the struggle continued in the valley during the months and years ahead.

———— • ————

I grieved over my separation from Donna. At mealtime I'd think about her—wondering if she had a bib, or if the aides had enough patience to make sure that she got enough food. Vulnerable and unsure of myself after being uprooted from fifteen years at the nursing home, I determined to do something useful with my time until I could enroll at Shoreline Community College.

I talked to the physical therapist about starting all the paperwork required to get the state of Alaska to approve an electric wheelchair for getting around campus. I told her that I expected to use it only at school. I didn't intend to sit in it all day and lose what muscle tone I had.

During my early months at the Res, I took my walker every morning and went to the therapy room for exercise. Then I'd walk back to our room, using my walker and what some of the nurses teasingly called "The Carolyn wobble."

In the following months, as more and more residents acquired electric wheelchairs, I had to change my routine. Many of the residents were safe, sane drivers who realized that their chairs could knock a person flying. But too many drivers had poor coordination and acute startle reflexes—a scary combination in crowded hallways. Others seemed to think that those of us who walked could get bashed and remain saints at the same time. What really infuriated me were the hit-and-run drivers who had the ability to apologize but never bothered.

Don was a sweetheart—a grown man with a little boy's mind. He could sit for hours, content to watch the numbers on the time clock pop up. When he got his electric wheelchair, he never quite mastered the concept of simultaneously driving and watching where he was going. He did always apologize and burst into guilty tears whenever he ran me down. Yet he, and other drivers not as sensitive, were a big reason I eventually confined my walking to the parallel bars in the therapy room.

During my wait for spring quarter to start at college I also volunteered to work again at the UCP Center, this time as a teacher's assistant. One afternoon at the center, I saw that the speech therapist had a new device called a Canon Communicator. The size of a transistor radio, it consisted of a small rectangular keyboard with a thin paper tape, like a ticker tape, coming out one end. Whatever letters or words were typed on the keyboard printed out on the tape. An ungarbled message could come through on what amounted to a miniature typewriter.

Amazing. One of my wildest dreams could come true. With a gizmo like that I wouldn't have to carry around an alphabet board or have someone who knew my speech patterns translate for me.

Communication had never ever been easy for me, not even with people who spent enough time with me to know that my J's, S's, and Z's all sound like Y's—that when I put my hand on my back I mean past tense, and that when I hold up five fingers I mean the word is plural. Tenses and plurals are often impossible for me to say.

I had invented what I call my three-year-old's vocabulary. It saved time and energy but played havoc with my dignity. For example, instead of saying, "I'm going to the dining room, okay?" I would say, "I go dining, okay?" I could get essential messages across, but it sometimes left my listeners wondering if I were missing vital parts, like a brain.

With the Canon Communicator, I'd be able to say anything I wanted without first running the sentence through the "Can I say this" sorter in my mind. Before I can say any word out loud, I have to think through the sounds and how to say them most clearly. I have to check each sentence against my entire speaking vocabulary to make sure I can say the whole thing with its variations of syllables, tenses, and tongue placements. I hate having to avoid using certain words or having to settle for simpler, less precise synonyms because I can't produce certain sounds. The communicator could end some of that frustration.

The therapist told me to take my time trying her communicator to see if it could actually work for me. The keyboard did seem a little small. And the arrangement of letters seemed foreign. But then I was so used to a typewriter keyboard that I had to rethink the alphabet each time I used a dictionary.

In my mind, the pluses far outweighed any minuses. So I typed out a message for the therapist saying: "I am sure I can engineer my way around any problem. We could Velcro it to my lap tray for when I go to school."

So she ordered a communicator for me right away. But like everything else in life, getting it would take a long time.

———————— • ————————

While SSA (Social Security Annuity) paid for my room and board and gave me twenty-five dollars a month spending money to purchase incidentals, I didn't have enough personal resources to go back to college. That's when my sister Shirley stepped in and offered to pay my tuition if I wanted to try school again.

The first few days of classes at Shoreline Community College convinced me that I faced a big challenge. Two men from the Res enrolled when I did, but they kept to themselves. So except for the aide hired to get us to and from campus and to help us with lunch, I found myself all alone each day on a sprawling campus with my battered communication board and my old manual wheelchair.

Our social worker gave me good advice on how to choose classes to fit my limitations. He said to check out class requirements ahead of time. If one was heavy in writing assignments, make sure that the other one required mostly reading. That way I could manage two courses a quarter and perhaps a third, if I could find something like an art class that had no homework.

Unfortunately, there seemed too many things about my schedule that I couldn't control. My entire first year I was sandwiched into the regular workshop bus that dropped us off at the campus on its way to the workshop in the morning and stopped to pick us up again at the very end of the day. Even though I had only two classes, I had to stay on campus all day. While I could read my lessons, I had no way to write homework without my typewriter.

As soon as we got back to the Res each evening, I'd dash to my room and begin my written work, but by that time of day I'd be exhausted and my frustration would explode at the slightest provocation. If Ila Mae came in needing something, I'd get irritated at her for interrupting me. I didn't mean to be a grouch, but I was. I often ended the evening in tears of guilt over my impatience.

Other days my time was eaten away by routine requirements. The therapist would call me out to put hot packs on my arthritic hip. One of the staff would need to talk to me about something. Everything, it seemed, had to be on the Res's schedule. As a result, it would be seven o'clock or later many nights before I could even begin to peck away at my schoolwork.

Many was the time I considered dropping out of college, but my dream kept me going. Two people also kept me going by phone—Iola and my sister Elizabeth. Iola was firm and tactful: "Sweetheart, I know you hurt and you're tired. But remember I've always told you nothing you do will be easy. If you hang in there, you will be a winner in more ways than you'll ever know." More than a few times when I was ready to give up she would say very emphatically, "Carolyn, you are not quitting school. Got it? Or do I have to repeat myself?" I got the message.

Before long, several of my friends from the Res joined me at college. We got to be quite a group descending on the Shoreline campus each day. For many of us it was our first taste of independence. Some people, though, could only audit courses because they didn't have any way to do homework.

Once I finally received my electric orange wheelchair and my Canon Communicator, I experienced freedom I'd never known before. I took my communicator everywhere and found it did indeed open many locked doors. Sometimes I used it just to spell out a particularly troublesome word. Other times I typed out my entire thoughts. I told my friends I might be the only woman they'd ever meet with a rechargeable mouth.

All I had to do was plug in my bionic legs and mouth each night and the next day I could do the impossible—go to the college library and check out my own books, and register for classes (the office staff was always willing to fill out the forms for me once they knew what I wanted). I could even shop.

Once during a group outing to a grocery store, I wanted a jar of jam from the top shelf. I typed out my request and handed it to a fellow shopper. He graciously got it for me. After thanking him, I went on my way feeling positively upbeat and thinking there was nothing I couldn't accomplish. I wondered whether I ought to pinch myself to make sure I wasn't dreaming.

But as I rolled down another aisle with such delightfully smug thoughts dancing through my mind, a wild shriek shattered my mood and triggered my trusty startle reflex. I nearly jumped out of my chair. A woman behind me screamed, "Get away from her! She may be dangerous!" My first instinct was to find a nearby place to hide from whatever dangerous person had started this panic. I halfway expected a SWAT team to come dashing down the aisle. I wanted to get out of the way of the forthcoming drama.

I turned and looked over my shoulder to see a near-hysterical woman dragging her husband back down the aisle away from me. Then I realized that *I* was the "dangerous woman" who had alarmed this poor lady. On the bus back to the Res I told the therapist what happened.

Mary Ann laughed until tears ran down her cheeks. "You? Dangerous? I mean you really look dangerous with your scarecrow body dressed in ratty blue-jeans and a T-shirt. I guess she must have thought your communicator was a bomb!"

A few days later, someone with an equally warped sense of humor tacked a sign on our door, which read, *BEWARE OF THE DANGEROUS WOMAN!*

Even today, I'll meet an old friend who will grin and ask if I'm still a "dangerous woman." I always reply, "Certainly. Only more so."

Chapter 25

Looking for a Listening Ear

For a few years the Res was featured on an annual UCP telethon. Everything was always upbeat. One year I was interviewed for the program by a local television personality. This newswoman sat on the bed in my room, with my desk and typewriter in view, talking with me about my going to college and my dreams of becoming a writer. I typed out my part of the conversation on my communicator.

The cameraman was interested in the key guard on the typewriter because our segment of the telethon featured samples of adaptive equipment to show what donations are used for. Much later it dawned on me that UCP never pays for personal adaptive equipment—the state and Medicare does. As for my key guard, I paid for it myself.

Telethons are staged and can be misleading, yet I admit I enjoyed my brief time in the limelight. I was always a little sad to see the cameras and the added excitement go. Once they left, the Res quickly returned to its noisy, unrestful, and inadequate self. And as time passed, the Res, like my nursing home before it, gave in to the temptation of added government funds by becoming a qualified IMR home and accepting more disruptive mental patients.

Still, the Res was far better than Sea Ridge. I felt very good about my physical therapy. I truly enjoyed the Res recreation program. We took in everything from weekend camping trips to Saturday morning symphony concerts. And I valued the friendships made possible by the emphasis on social life.

Yet, when I prayed, it seemed that God was telling me that he had something better for me. I think I knew that I could never really be at peace until I trusted someone enough to expose my inner scars. But I was afraid. I hid that fear behind the positive, upbeat display of my faith.

Perhaps I didn't always do as good a job of hiding my scars as I wished I could. Or maybe some people are more perceptive than others. One of my best friends and staunchest supporters among the Res staff was Greg, the personnel manager. He was a tease and a friendly pest. One of his favorite tricks was to catch me walking down the hall in my walker and threaten to yank on the big metal loop on the zipper of my jeans. Zippers are very difficult for me without something big and manageable to hold on to. He told me it reminded him of the loop on the string of a "Chatty Cathy" doll, and he wondered what I'd say if he pulled on it.

One day we were talking in his office. He got very serious and said he could see through me and the religious hedge I'd let grow up around me. He told me that if I didn't change my tune and face the truth, I was heading for big trouble. I got angry and stomped out of his office. But he never knew what I was hiding. I couldn't tell him.

I thought maybe I could talk to our social worker, but no—we were on different wavelengths. Every time I had an appointment to discuss anything with him, we were interrupted by the parents of some resident barging in to demand assistance for their adult child. He always apologized for having to dismiss me, but I never could get past the feeling that our needs as residents were less important than the concerns of those people who paid the bills.

If the Res was no place to expose my emotional nakedness, neither was it a safe place to undress and bathe. In addition to the small bathrooms in our rooms, we had four large community bathrooms, each equipped with roll-in showers and a bathtub with handrails.

When I moved into the Res, men and women used separate bathrooms. But gradually things deteriorated. With a lack of adequate staffing, male orderlies started bathing and dressing women residents in the common bathrooms. Some male residents were so lazy and insensitive that they thought nothing of coming into the nearest bathroom to use the toilet while women were bathing. I even saw potential employees being given tours of the bathroom facilities while residents were using them.

For a while I accepted such indignities, but I finally got fed up. The next time a male resident walked in on me in the women's bathroom, I screamed loud enough to scare him and everyone else within earshot. It just wasn't right. We women had a right to privacy.

I began talking to the other women about the problem. A few didn't seem to care. Some evidently liked to be bathed by men because it was the closest thing they had to sexual contact. Some pointed out pros and cons regarding the male orderlies because certain residents were quite heavy and needed to be lifted in and out of the tub. But nearly everyone agreed that we should have more say about who bathed the residents and that the bathroom should not be a thoroughfare.

Our one blind resident especially cheered my attempts to bring reform. She hated being dressed, bathed, and even having her sanitary napkins put on by men. She said they could never figure them out.

So I took the issue to the resident council. From there it went to the chief administrator, who said he had no idea that such a problem existed. He apologized and immediately ordered the maintenance staff to find "Men" and "Women" signs to hang on the bathroom doors. He also let it be known that women had a right to ask for a female aide to help with intimate hygiene care.

We remained so short-staffed that even after that we still often had to settle for whoever was available to help at bath time. But the offending male residents did have to stay out of our bathrooms on threat of being kicked out of the Res. I was never sure how serious that threat was, so we women enforced the new rule ourselves. We were more of a threat.

After winning my campaign for single-sex bathrooms, several staff members and a number of my friends badgered me to run for a seat on the resident council. Mary Ann, our recreational therapist, volunteered to be my campaign manager, making signs and reading my campaign speeches, which were always short and to the point. They had to be because I was trying to concentrate on my schoolwork and hoped that my political life was a short one.

The Res council was the brainchild of our social worker. He wanted it to work for us so we could become self-governing, but we had so many people to deal with that I found the job wearisome.

After I won my election, I did start another successful campaign within the council to get each room its own mailbox for which residents could buy their own padlock and key. It always bothered me that our mail and even our bank statements were simply left on our beds. Any number of people could see our private affairs when we weren't home. Even if some of us had to have help to unlock our mailboxes, they would provide us with more privacy and a bit more control over our own lives.

When the time came to elect delegates to attend the national UCP convention in Kansas City, I was one of two council members elected to go (accompanied by two aides). The local UCP picked up the tab. We had a good time, gathered information, reported our findings to the council, and wrote reports for the *Communicator*, our resident newspaper. Nevertheless, I eventually resigned from my council responsibilities because it took too much time and energy away from school.

I felt guilty about the decision to put my own personal agenda over the group's concerns, but I was determined to put school first. Too, I'd come to the disheartening conclusion that I could never change the Res enough. It would never be the quiet restful place I needed.

———————— • ————————

One morning as I was leaving for school, a new laundrywoman, Jeannie, delivered my clean clothes to my room and began putting them away in my drawers. I asked her to just leave them on my bed because I wanted to put them away myself later. She evidently didn't understand me because when I returned to my room I discovered she'd put all my clothes away.

The next time she came with my laundry, I was prepared. I handed her a note saying I was quite capable of putting my own clothes away. She said "Fine!" but that I didn't need to be a crab about it, and she left the room.

I felt I'd better make up with her. She was a short, stout Norwegian with a look in her eye that said she wasn't about to take anything from anyone. Indeed, over the next few months I learned that her gruff, sometimes-salty manner only partially disguised her softer side.

One day I asked her, "Why, out of 110 residents here at the Res, do you always have to pick on me?"

Jeannie grinned, "You have no idea how much fun it is to tease you. You're so skinny, you look like a cartoon character. And besides, I'm stronger than you, so I know I'll always win."

She smiled so smugly that I decided not to remind her that I'd won the battle over putting my own clothes away. Her feisty attitude sparked my curiosity and made me like her all the more.

Once when I was coming down the hall with my walker, Jeannie walked up behind me and gruffly told me to hurry up and get out of her way. If she'd asked politely, I would have done it. But since she hadn't, I thought I'd teach her a lesson. I slowed down even more and told her that when she decided to use better manners, I'd let her get by.

The next thing I knew, Jeannie picked me up, dumped me unceremoniously into her laundry cart, and pushed me down the hall to my room, mumbling about "Some people's kids!" When she deposited me on my bed, I realized that my wheelchair was in the physical therapy room and my walker had been abandoned in the hall. I pleaded with Jeannie not to leave me stranded. She smiled sweetly and very calmly informed me that if I did not want to get stuck again, I'd better do what I was told. So I surrendered.

On days when depression and frustration got the best of me and I began feeling like a caged animal, I'd often go down to the laundry room to talk with Jeannie or with Jeannie's boss, Betty. Unlike the social worker, Betty was always available to talk. And she made more sense than he did.

One of Betty's prescriptions for my depression was shopping. The first time I told her how discouraged I was, she excused herself, left the room for a few minutes and came back with Jeannie whom she instructed to drive me to a local mall. "Just clock out when you get back," she said to Jeannie.

Did the two of us ever have a good time! We talked about our troubles and shopped. As a single mother with two kids, Jeannie had her own problems and shared some of them with me. That shopping trip was the beginning of a special, lasting friendship.

Before long, when the rec department planned overnight camping outings, it was always a toss-up as to which one of us would be the first to ask the other to go. I loved the outdoors. Jeannie would bring her two children, and they'd help push wheelchairs.

We quickly found that we worked well together. Jeannie treated me a lot like Mom and Elizabeth always did, allowing me to be independent. When she didn't understand something I said, Jeannie would tell me: "Get that mush out of your mouth and talk straight!" And she could mimic my speech as well as Pappy used to do.

I looked forward to my outings away from the Res with Jeannie. One year for my birthday Mom sent me money for a weekend cruise to Victoria on the old *Princess Margarete*. Jeannie and I had a ball sightseeing and getting lost. As always, I felt more alive and less nervous when I could get away from the Res.

And I always had a good feeling before I left for school on cold winter mornings when I'd hear Jeannie yelling down the hall at me: "Zip up that jacket; it's cold outside! And have a nice day!"

Chapter 26

College Graduation

My favorite subject in college was literature, taught by Professor Maxwell, who looked like he had walked right out of a book about medieval knights. A former Jesuit priest, he left the church, married, and then taught literature with a passion. I took his whole series of courses because he convinced me that every writer needs to know and understand everything from ancient Greek mythology to contemporary fiction in order to construct a foundation for credible writing.

Professor Maxwell enjoyed teasing me and seeing me turn crimson in class. Frequently he would greet me in his most flamboyant manner, declaring with phony passion: "Darling, I am madly in love with you. You make my day each time you grace my classroom!" Then he would rush up and hug me.

I told him that I understood why he'd been unable to live a monastic lifestyle: "You're too full of baloney!"

One day in class, the professor assigned us to read and interpret what he said was one of his favorite stories. Titled *The Bondsman*, it was the tale of a man who lived his life bound with rope yet could walk, run, jump, and perform all sorts of feats that should have been impossible. So astounding were his accomplishments that he became the star attraction of a circus.

Though the man always refused any offers to be untied, some people who assumed he was crazy and incapable of deciding his own destiny cut his bonds one night as he slept. When he awakened the next morning, the man found himself completely helpless and could never adapt to being "free."

I was struck by the story and made two observations. I saw freedom as a new disability. And I thought the bondsman was crippled by the loss of his bonds and his lifelong identity that was so intertwined with those bonds. Without bonds he no longer knew who he was. For their unwillingness to appreciate and observe his struggle, I harshly judged the people who freed him. Had they understood that being a struggler was the one thing that gave the bondsman his sense of worth and identity, they might have responded in a more helpful, less self-serving way.

One day at the end of class, Professor Maxwell made a comment that showed both his empathy for me and his very different view of *The Bondsman.* I was collecting my things in order to leave the classroom. He was erasing the blackboard. He turned around and said, "That's a hell of a way to live, Carolyn. I don't know if I'd have the guts to pull it off."

I didn't know what to say, so I merely nodded and left. I was touched as much by this good man's honesty and compassion as I was inspired by his teaching.

Before I knew it, three years had passed. I had earned the ninety-six credit hours required for my Associate of Arts degree in general studies. I felt old, tired, and very proud.

Although the actual graduation ceremony was not until June, I received my diploma through the mail in January. One afternoon I got a call to come to the front desk of the Res. The evening receptionist, Joyce, a grandmotherly sort who took a special interest in those of us who had no family close by, wanted to present me the diploma herself rather than just send it down to my room.

She walked around her desk, handed me the envelope, and after I opened it, gave me a big hug. "You earned this diploma twice over again," she said. "I'm so proud of you."

I laughed and cried at the same time.

Joyce announced the good news over the Res's intercom. I welcomed scores of well-wishers for the rest of that day.

———————— • ————————

Graduation day finally arrived in June. I watched and listened for my brother Ken all morning. Many years earlier, when I'd felt like a piece of driftwood tossed by a stormy sea, I had promised him that if I ever finished college, he could walk me down the aisle to get my diploma. Now he was coming from California to make good on my promise.

Ken arrived mid-morning. Pappy and Mom had reached Seattle earlier and called me soon after Ken arrived to ask if we wanted to join them for the day. Ken told Mom, "By the time Posey has lunch it will be her nap time. I'll just stay here and get everything organized. I don't want to tire her out or let anything else mess up this day. We'll just plan to see you this evening."

When he hung up, I teased him for sounding very much like the fire-department captain he was, carefully planning to avoid any last-minute emergencies. Ken laughed and told me it was my day and that I could do anything I wanted as long as I behaved myself and took an afternoon nap. So I told him that I wanted to just sit on his lap and talk.

I loved to be hugged and held. Sitting on my brother's lap, I was so happy that I literally squeaked with joy. Ken laughed all the harder and noted that while I was now a college graduate, I still had a little girl inside who craved affection. He told me how proud he was of me. He modestly declared how glad he was that Mom had listened to him and allowed me to leave Alaska and come to Seattle. "If I told Mom once, I told her a thousand times, 'Posey has got to make her own mistakes.'"

I wanted to hear more, so he told me that for years whenever I wanted to do something adventurous, something new—like the plan to move from the nursing home to the Res—Mom would unload all her doubts and worries on him. He said that the older Mom got, the more apprehensive she became, and the more she didn't want to, in her words, "rock the boat." After all, the rest of the family outnumbered her eight to one.

"So you decide what you need to do with your life," Ken said. "I'll cover for you with Mom."

I ate my lunch sandwich sitting on Ken's lap. But when I reached for my milk, he suggested I move to my wheelchair to drink it. He didn't trust me with a full glass of milk. When I finished eating, Ken ordered me to bed for a nap. "It's going to be a long evening," he told me. "We can't have you dozing off in the middle of the ceremony."

My brother knew that no mortarboard could possibly stay on my bobbing head—especially if I got excited. So while I was asleep, he ran out to buy some elastic and a needle and thread. I awakened to find him sewing the elastic to my cap and complaining loudly: "See what trouble you are. If you'd only hold your head still, I wouldn't have to go to all this work."

I offered to ask an aide to help him, but Ken didn't want help. He preferred to complain.

After dinner, Mom and Pappy arrived with my oldest brother Don and his wife, Ruth. Ken handed out written directions to the college and asked Ruth to help dress me. But she couldn't understand a word I said, so Ken took over while Ruth watched and laughed at his feigned toughness and his running commentary. He stood me up and removed my dress while saying: "Shut up while I dress you. It is very simple. First, you rip off her arms and smack her with them if she wiggles. You know she's faking CP to cover up the fact that she's really a belly dancer. Here, Ruth, you put this dress on her while I get the gown. She can put her own shoes on; when I do it she always yells at me. She's so picky. She never wants her toes doubled back under her feet."

By this time Ruth and I were laughing so hard tears streamed down our faces. Ruth declared that she would never ever let Ken dress her.

———————— • ————————

From my place among my fellow graduates, I spotted my sisters Elizabeth and Shirley in the crowd. They arrived by train just in time for the ceremony. I remembered how they had been my very first teachers. Once they got me going on the right track, they always said that there would be no stopping me.

The program began, and an hour or so later my name was called. Ken pushed me to the center aisle and locked the brakes on my wheelchair. He waited by my side as I struggled to get my feet under me and stand up, then the two of us together walked down the aisle. I moved slowly in my own unique, Carolyn wobble. By the time we reached the front, everyone in the hall was standing and cheering. Most were crying. I had to fight back my own tears and concentrate on walking.

The president of the college came down the platform steps to meet us. He threw his arms around me and kissed me, saying, "I am so glad you came to school here. We're all very proud of you."

Ken helped me take my diploma, and the cheers continued as we turned and headed slowly back to the chair. I caught a glimpse of Professor Maxwell standing in the aisle, clapping and cheering, and immediately suspected that he'd started the whole thing. I grinned at him knowingly.

Fifteen minutes it took me to walk down the aisle and back to my chair. The entire time, everyone in that auditorium had been clapping and cheering. I felt sorry for the people whose names were called after mine. But I felt very happy for me. After so many years of dreams and struggle, those cheers rang loud and long in my ears. I knew that from then on, whenever I faced a challenge that seemed hopeless, I would always remember exactly what these cheers sounded like.

Chapter 27

Independent Living

During my second year of college, the UCP built a smaller group home just across the creek from the Res. This new facility was to train the more able-bodied members of our community in independent living skills. Excited by the thought that this might be my escape hatch to a new life, I inquired about moving to the new group home. My hopes were dashed when I was told that according to UCP regulations, I didn't qualify.

When I sought an explanation, I learned that the group home accepted no residents who required any personal care. According to my medical charts, I wore a back brace that required help for me to get it on. I angrily informed Don, our social worker, that I no longer wore that brace. It had been stashed in a suitcase in the Res basement for two years. But Don didn't want to fight the decision and suggested that I finish up college before considering any other major changes.

Bus travel was one of UCP's prerequisites for independent living, and Don said he would not even consider letting me apply to move to the group home before I'd managed a trip alone on a bus to Northgate Mall and back.

Even though most of the city buses were equipped with wheelchair lifts by this time, the very prospect of such a trip seemed daunting. Except for school, where people at least knew me, I had never in my life been out in public alone. I wasn't sure I ever wanted to be. What if I needed help and no one could understand me?

Finally I made up my mind. If that's what it took to get out of the Res, I'd do it, but I told Don that I wanted to break this new challenge down into smaller parts. First, I'd go by myself in my wheelchair to the end of the sidewalk. When I felt safe doing that, I'd cross the street. Then I'd wheel myself to the bus stop and back.

I carefully noted the return bus stop to make sure I'd know where to get off. But it had a short, steep incline down to the crosswalk and seemed too scary. I decided I'd get off at the next stop where it was level and wheel the extra distance back to the Res. I studied the landmarks because I had such a problem remembering numbers.

After a month of working up to it, I boarded the bus to Northgate alone. Despite being nervous to the point of tears, I refused to back down. I reached the mall safely, actually did a little shopping, and then headed back for the bus stop to return home.

When I got off the bus and safely back on the sidewalk leading to the Res, my emotions finally let down. Like the last little pig in the nursery rhyme, I cried all the way home. I felt triumphant but exhausted.

Although it was after five o'clock, Don met me at the door of the Res, saying that he couldn't go home until he knew I was back. He smothered me with hugs and kisses, saying, "You are one gutsy woman, Carolyn. What you did speaks volumes about you." His praise made the effort worthwhile.

Back in my room a few minutes later, I discovered that I'd lost my lap robe and my billfold somewhere on my journey. Feeling helpless and hopeless again, I began to cry. But just then Joyce, the receptionist, sent word that she had a call from someone at the mall who'd found my blanket and wallet. One of our volunteers, a friend from church, drove to get them for me. When she returned my lost possessions she commented, "You must really want to get out of here to do what you did."

I hugged her in thanks and told her, "I don't like it here, anymore. I'll do anything to escape." She said nothing, but she held me for a long time.

It was early spring, just weeks before that eventful graduation night, when Don gave me the exciting news that my application to move to the group home had been approved. Though the home was on the same property as the Res, just beyond a small creek and pond, it seemed as though it would take me forever to get there with all the new paperwork that had to be filled out. Though a little anxious about the new routines and a little sad to be leaving Ila Mae again, I knew that the time had come to go.

A huge ageless willow drooped over the front walk and shaded my new home. Inside were five private rooms and three small apartments each shared by two people. The studio apartment I shared with a girl named Diedra had its own wheelchair-height kitchen area as well as a bedroom and study space. The group home's huge main room contained a larger wheelchair-accessible kitchen, a dining area, and a living-room area complete with a fireplace. With only eleven residents, the place felt very homey and quiet—an entirely different world from the Res.

There was such a welcome air of peace and calm that I wished I could live there forever, but I knew I couldn't. The group home was a transitional step, a place where I could learn to take the next step— moving into a place of my own.

I'd known my new roommate, Diedra, for years at the Res. She was disabled in her late teens by some unknown genetic disorder. The two of us were on an almost equal physical footing and became good friends, regularly laughing at each other's uncontrollable startle reflex. We shared one end of the group's dining table with another resident named Stan, who had good use of his hands. Whenever anything would startle Diedra or me, poor Stan would end up wearing our food. But then we had to listen to his corny jokes, so we considered it an even trade.

Diedra and I also laughed a lot over an ongoing contest to see who could sling toothpaste into the most unlikely places. Either we'd get a death grip on the tube and squeeze the guts out of it, or we'd actually get toothpaste on a brush only to have something startle us and have the toothpaste go flying. We had our aide, Jackie, keep a running tally of our scores.

I admired Diedra's courage and her strength of character as she battled her disability. I cried when she moved out to get married. While I was glad to see a friend escape the trap, I knew that I would sorely miss her company.

———————— • ————————

The daily routine in our group home was a big change from the Res. Aides were assigned to teach us everything from cooking to how to balance a checkbook. My first aide, Jackie, soon sensed my eagerness to learn and allowed me the flexibility to adapt routines to fit my own needs. She once observed, "You could be your own occupational therapist." She often let me learn to do things my own way.

Residents of the group home were assigned chores such as setting the table, clearing the table after meals, loading the dishwasher, vacuuming and mopping floors. After-dinner cleanup was assigned to one person each night, and whoever got stuck with it had to work all evening. I made the suggestion in a resident and staff meeting that three people be assigned to do cleanup each night. That worked much better. Everyone cheered the change and wanted to hear any other suggestions I had.

I had a real problem getting dirty dishes from the table to the sink. The other residents solved the problem by stacking their dirty dishes on their laps and rolling themselves to the sink. That didn't work for me. Messes always seemed to leap on me. If anything startled me when I had a lapful of dirty dishes, I had double trouble. There'd be dishes and food all over me and all over the floor. I solved the problem by convincing the staff to buy a plastic dishpan to contain my dishes and into which I could brush my whole dinner mess and carry it safely to the sink.

Not all my little problems were so easily solved. For example, the dumpster. We were supposed to lift the container's lid and toss in a large plastic bag of garbage, but the lid was huge, and so high that I couldn't get enough leverage to budge it. Only the male residents could manage it.

I suggested to Jackie that we get regular garbage cans and let the staff empty the cans into the dumpster before the trash was hauled away. She agreed that would make sense, but she explained that the dumpster routine was part of our required training according to the Individual Program Plan (IPP) guidelines established by the state's Department of Social and Human Services (DSHS).

I asked to see these guidelines. Sure enough, the dumpster business was in there. So were a lot of other things obviously written by some able-bodied person who didn't begin to understand the limitations of my disability.

Another unrealistic requirement said that to qualify for independent living everyone had to "learn" how to screw a mop head onto a mop handle. I thought that was terribly funny. I certainly knew how; it was the actual doing of it that was forever beyond me.

When I pointed that regulation out to Jackie, she just shook her head and agreed that whoever wrote the guidelines was severely challenged in the area of common sense. Over the next months and years, the two of us would find great amusement chuckling over DHSH guidelines that couldn't possibly be adapted to the real world of cerebral palsy. And because the guidelines were always written in such a serious, life-or-death tone, we sometimes read them out loud to each other in the most dramatic voices and then laughed as if it was the funniest comedy routine we'd ever heard.

A few days after I moved into the group home, I ran out of clean clothes. Instead of sending my things to the laundry as I did at the Res, I was expected to wash them myself. Since Jackie was busy on another job at the time, she asked one of the other residents to show me how to use the washer and dryer.

I thought that I followed the instructions carefully. But before I knew it, the washer was belching suds out the top, down the sides, and all over the floor. So I kicked off my slippers, pulled up my jeans, and waded into the mess to shut the monster off. Then I had to throw dirty towels on the floor to soak up the suds.

I never did find out what I did wrong. But once that washer learned I was boss, it never spit suds at me again. It did, however, regularly eat my socks. Maybe it just didn't like me.

As I mastered each new household task, I kept refining my methods. For example, I could seldom manage to get a full scoop of soap from the storage barrel into the washer without spilling it. Then I'd be exhausted by the time I got all the powder cleaned up off the floor. I solved that problem by purchasing liquid soap in squeeze bottles. I'd hold the bottle down in the washer and squirt out what I needed without danger of getting it on anything else. That saved a lot of time, energy, and aggravation. And for the first time in my life I could wash my clothes as I liked, without having them scalded to death in a big institutional laundry.

Cleaning floors was my Mount Everest of housekeeping. The first time I tackled the chore, I worked for three hours before finally crawling over to the rug and falling asleep. Floors take so much energy to clean and so little time to mess up again. But as the weeks rolled by, I learned to sweep and vacuum. I never did master the use of a mop, but I designed my own method of scrubbing hard-surfaced floors. One day when I spilled something on the floor, I tossed a rag down and pushed it around with my foot. By the time I'd cleaned up the spill I was thinking, *Hey! Why not do the whole floor like that.* So that's what I did, scooted around in my wheelchair, shuffling my feet to rub up spots and dirt. I called it the "Rag-Mop Shuffle." If it wasn't exactly what the government guidelines called for, at least it worked.

I think I was proudest of mastering the rather formidable task of making tea. It took me many weeks of experimentation. First, I sat and stared at the teakettle for about three hours, thinking through the process. Just grasping the awkward horizontal handle would take three movements and the coordination of both hands. Then I must somehow fill it and maneuver it onto the stove. I eventually concluded that those movements were hopelessly beyond my ability.

As an alternative, I turned to an old-fashioned coffee percolator, the aluminum kind with a glass knob on the top. If I filled the five-cup percolator to the one-cup level, maybe I could eliminate the danger of spilling scalding water on myself. But how would I get the tea bag into the boiling water without knocking the pot off the stove?

I decided to break the rules of proper tea brewing by adding tea and honey to the water *before* putting the percolator on the stove. A friend removed the glass knob from the percolator lid, so I could stuff the tea bag down that hole. One problem: I kept losing the tea bag when the string fell in the water. I solved that by pinning the tea bag in place with a clothespin until it brewed to my liking.

It took me a long time to figure out how to remove the pot from the stove without burning myself. I had to use long kitchen mitts, attack the pot, and wrestle it to the table. But then how to pour it without drenching the entire table? I worked on that one for weeks and finally yielded to a thin drinking straw stuck in the mouth of the pot.

Triumph! After three months of perfecting the technique, I brewed my first perfect pot of tea and got it to the table without spilling a single drop.

After a few more weeks, bored with my achievement, I decided to hold a tea party. But a proper lady certainly couldn't ask her guests to stick all their straws in one pot. I had to find a way to pour. I got a good idea watching TV one day. Some experimental robots locked their elbow joints into a rigid position to perform certain arm movements. So I set some tall mugs down in my sink, and with my elbow joints held stiff, I learned I could fill them about halfway without sloshing tea over the tops of the mugs. Then I could carry them, one at a time, my elbows still locked, to the table.

Hey! If a heap of tin could learn to pour, I could, too.

———————— • ————————

The summer after graduating from Shoreline Community College, I worked on building up my weight, mastering as many domestic skills as possible, and getting a lot of writing done. Though state regulations called for me to take part in some outside activity for a certain number of hours each day (if I was no longer in school, I needed to be working), the administrator of the group home cut me some slack. She saw that I needed time to adjust to the demands of my new living arrangement.

The next fall, I accepted a teacher's-aide position back at the UCP Center. One morning at UCP I caught a glimpse of a woman being led down the ramp and into the developmental center. The woman had an unusual pair of crutches propped against her body. Something about them seemed vaguely familiar. A couple of minutes passed before it dawned on me. *Could it be?* Dr. Anne Carlsen had used crutches like that.

I hurried down the hall to find out. There she was. Thirty years older but looking much as I remembered her—calm and radiant. A remarkable woman. I felt funny interrupting her tour, but I knew that if I didn't speak to her I'd regret it the rest of my life.

Dr. Anne talked to me for a few minutes, told me how nice it was to see me again, and wished me well in my future endeavors. Then she was escorted off to other parts of the UCP.

All that day I thought about Dr. Anne and her school. Scenes and memories I hadn't recalled for years raced through my mind. And of course, I remembered standing at the bottom of those steep stairs and watching her climb to the top. Now I'd crossed her path again. This encounter also inspired me. It got me thinking about all the dreams I'd ever had. Some had come true. Others hadn't.

Those surprise moments with Dr. Carlsen rekindled my smoldering dreams. I remembered how far I'd come and began to believe again that just maybe, if I kept working, if I dared to step out beyond the known, I might yet break out of the system and find freedom.

Chapter 28

Writers' Workshops

Late one evening I pulled the string to turn off the light over my desk. For a few moments I basked in the darkness and prayed, "Oh Lord, where do I go with my writing from here?"

It seemed as if the answer floated in with the cool summer breeze blowing gently through the open patio doors. *Organize a portfolio. No professional editor will take you seriously if he has to rummage through your tattered box to see your writings. Don't keep using your disability as an excuse for untidiness. It always has been a sorry alibi.*

I hadn't expected such a quick and blunt answer, but I thanked God and told him that as usual, he made good sense. One reason I like talking to God is that I never have to repeat myself. He understands every word I say.

During my free time I began retyping some of my writing to make it look as neat as possible. Then I had Jackie put samples in a notebook. As I worked, I couldn't shake a strong feeling of anticipation. I felt as if I was preparing myself for something exciting. I didn't know what.

A few weeks later, one Sunday at church, I saw a display table marked, "Summer Learning Opportunities" and picked up a few pamphlets to take home. That afternoon, after I fixed myself a snack, I looked through my booty. One leaflet caught my eye—for a writers' conference at the Lutheran Bible Institute (LBI) out in Issaquah, Washington, a forty-five-minute drive from North Seattle.

I told Jackie that I felt that I should go to this conference. She encouraged me to pursue the idea and even suggested that I consider getting some new clothes to wear to the conference. She thought my usual sweats and T-shirts would be too ratty to wear someplace that might be so important to my life. I laughingly told her that I hoped to be judged on my writing, not my wardrobe. But she had a point. According to my checkbook, I had enough money to pay my registration and purchase a new blouse and slacks, so I filled out an application, typed a check, and put them in the mail. Another aide helped me work out the transportation details.

The day of the conference finally arrived. An aide deposited me and my belongings in the vast, airy lobby at LBI and left. I was completely on my own in an able-bodied world.

The woman at the registration desk surprised me by already knowing my name. She told me that if I needed anything at all to let her know. Then she handed me my schedule and sent me to the first general session.

As I cruised down the bright, broad hallway, I was awed by the fresh, clean, open feeling of the school. Huge windows lined the hallways, giving light to the lush green plants that were everywhere. Many large, fine paintings graced the walls. The school had been built for the Sisters of Providence to use as a convent. The restructuring of the Catholic Church after Vatican II constrained the sisters to sell their buildings and the works of art with them.

I was so excited that I felt the urge to spin a few doughnuts down the wide halls in my wheelchair. But I remembered the phone conversation I'd had with Iola just the night before. She lectured me on how important first impressions could be and instructed me to "At least act like an adult!"

The first session set the tone for the conference—small and informal. Each of us participants took turns telling about ourselves. Several people there were published writers. I shared that I had recently graduated from junior college and that this was my first venture like this alone.

The primary instructor for the conference assigned us all to write devotionals based on Romans 5:12–16, a text that talks about human weakness versus divine strength. I wrote about the time I got a string caught in a wheel of my chair and struggled with it for an hour before I admitted to myself I couldn't untangle it. Then I crawled out to the living room of the group home and asked for help. It is the same way in our spiritual lives. *We sometimes have to struggle until we're free to be help-less.* At that point God can work in our lives to turn our own weaknesses into His strength, which is stronger than any human power.

People at the LBI conference were so encouraging that over the next few months I reworked a number of my articles to send to various publishers. None were accepted until Jackie suggested that I send my article about how I taught myself to make tea to *SCOPE* (a Lutheran women's magazine). They not only accepted it, they wanted a picture of me to run with the story. I was very slowly gaining my writing credentials.

My venture to LBI for that writers' conference paid off in other ways. For one thing, I had to admit to myself that there was a very lonely, hungry child deep within me that craved the kind of love and acceptance I experienced at the conference.

———— • ————

One day I heard a radio announcement about a Christian writers' critique group meeting in a nearby church. I had an aide call for more information. The second Saturday of the next month, I attended my first meeting. Since no one in the group could understand my speech, I had to rely on my communicator. I also took along my tea article and another article titled "A Rare Compassion" about my friend Russell, who was deeply grieved when he met someone without arms or legs. Russell himself, who had severe cerebral palsy, had been cheated by life, yet he had compassion for others.

The critique group liked the story when it was read to them. They applauded. The group leader, Mary Hammock, wrote their comments and suggestions for improvements in the margins for me.

Over the next few months I took many of my articles to the monthly meeting of the critique group. Mostly I wrote devotionals based on my experience of living in the group home. I slanted and polished them in such a way that the reader would never know I was disabled. I consciously hid my real self, particularly my physical handicap, behind the veil of my writing. When anyone in my critique group suggested that I write more about myself, I inwardly shuddered. The last thing I wanted to be was a gimp writer.

———————•———————

By this time I was tied into the local writers' grapevine and getting on a number of related mailing lists. When I received a brochure in the mail regarding an upcoming writers' conference at Seattle Pacific University, I quickly signed up.

With the confirmation of my acceptance came word from the conference director herself, Rose Reynoldson, that I was to be assigned a student nurse who would provide me with whatever help I needed. Rose's thoughtfulness and consideration surprised me.

I had barely arrived at the conference and was still looking for the registration table when I heard someone say, "You must be Carolyn Martin. I'm Rose." On first glance she struck me as a softer, gentler version of Margaret Thatcher—sure of herself and flexible enough to be a good leader. Her silver-gray hair and firm manner told me there was something deep and stable about her. I instinctively trusted her.

She must have had a thousand other conference details to worry about, yet she took me aside where we could sit and talk. She asked to see the writing I brought, made a list of editors I should be sure to meet, and made notations on my conference schedule as to what sessions she thought would benefit me the most.

"I want you to be sure to meet Karen Mains," she told me. Karen, a well-known and widely respected Christian author, was the main speaker for the conference. I was impressed and grateful for Rose's consideration and interest in me. In the first few minutes I'd known her, she made both me and my writing seem worthwhile.

Then Rose introduced me to the student nurse who was to be my aide for the conference. After one look at the hillside campus with its steep sidewalks, I was glad to have her help. She got me to my chosen classes and set up the tape recorder I used in lieu of taking notes.

Late that first evening, after my aide left for home, Rose herself walked me to the dorm to make sure my room was in order. Next morning, Rose arrived early to escort me to breakfast. Since I wasn't quite ready, she pitched in to help me as if it was the most natural thing in the world for her to do.

Noticing that I'd just washed my hair, Rose asked how I managed to do it. My funny bone got the best of me and I responded with a straight face, "With shampoo and water of course, how do you do yours?"

She got this surprised, embarrassed look on her face and then a well of laughter bubbled through. When she finally stopped, she said in an apologetic tone, "I certainly deserved that. And I liked the way you gave it to me."

I grinned and she hugged me, saying that she was glad I could accept her naïveté and make a joke of it. We grew the first inch toward friendship that morning.

That evening I went back to my dorm room early to type up my notes so that I could hand them in for credit. But before I started work, I took a bath, tidied up the room, and plugged in my wheelchair and communicator so they'd be charged up in the morning. I'd just gotten a perfect one-finger rhythm going on my typewriter when I heard a knock on the door. It was a woman named Elizabeth wondering if she could listen along with my tape since she'd missed part of the session.

After a few minutes we began to talk. She'd never seen a finger guard on a typewriter and was curious about mine. I explained that I had hit-and-miss coordination and the guard helps me get my finger on the correct key (most of the time). I was ready to drop that subject and learn more about her, but she evidently felt a need to confess: "I guess I've always just taken it for granted that my fingers would stay on the keys. I've never given it much thought."

I told her that I'd always had such zigzag coordination that I just took it for granted that I had to outsmart it by using special tools and carefully planning out how to do anything that required precision movements. I was so used to it by now that I thought I'd probably go crazy without the daily challenges CP gives me.

I said all that to try to put Elizabeth at ease, but she looked around at my recharging wheelchair and communicator and seemed struck by what else she'd always taken for granted. Not wanting her to feel guilty about that, I reassured her that most people take a lot of things for granted. "I take it for granted that I can't fly. So we're even." She laughed and went on to tell me some about herself. Before long, several other women wandered in to join our gabfest, and we had a party. I never did finish those notes.

———————•———————

The next day, Rose made an appointment for me to talk with Karen Mains, who had read the writing samples I'd brought and was eager to talk about them. She told me that she could see an emerging style in my writing and encouraged me to develop it. What she seemed most impressed with were two short stories about Donna and a piece I wrote for our group-home administrator, entitled, "Getting Acquainted with Our Hands." She also said that she liked the article I called, "My Cup of Tea."

Karen had no doubt that I was on my way to becoming a successful writer. (Now that was what I wanted to hear!) What I didn't want to hear was what she said next: "I think you should do more autobiographical writing."

Later Rose told me of the subsequent conversation she had with Karen Mains. Karen seemed genuinely excited about my work, telling Rose, "I can see it in Carolyn's eyes. She has a best-seller in her."

I felt so positive about my interaction with people at the conference and so triumphant with all the encouragement that I overcame my self-doubts and vowed to follow their advice by writing about my life. The trouble was, I'd read so much "upbeat and victorious" religious biography in which Christians always overcame all their anger and pain to walk off in a blaze of faith, that I tried to copy their shallow, propagandistic style. I tried to hide my pain behind the Cross as if I might somehow embarrass God if I wrote about the truth and admitted the anger and disappointment locked within me.

It was as if I had a fragile, alabaster box full of grief, pain, and anger. I kept it carefully and tightly sealed for fear of its deadly contents. I sometimes allowed a few hints of painful truth to seep through in my writing—enough to satisfy myself that I wasn't a two-faced liar. But that was all.

I had to keep that alabaster box closed. So I began the autobiographical writing with the nursing-home years. That way I didn't have to deal with the disappointments I faced in the Alaska school system, my imperfect family circumstances, and that horrible house, or the rape of my body and soul at the hands of a trusted minister.

What a clever woman I was! I could write this new material about my institutional life for the rest of my writing career. This material was accepted and praised by my critique group.

I didn't realize that the Lord was waiting to expose the truth—not to my readers, my critique group, or my friends, but to me.

Chapter 29

LBI

While encouraged that many people thought I had potential as a writer, I couldn't escape my doubts. And even if I could write, how would that help me achieve my other goal—to live on my own, outside a sheltered environment, in the real world?

I decided to explore the possibility of living beyond the familiar confines of my UCP environment. I wrote the Lutheran Bible Institute to ask for a catalog and enrollment information. Pastor Larson was less than optimistic when I told him what I was considering. He knew enough about state regulations and the UCP system to know how difficult this venture might be, but after raising that issue, he chuckled and said, "Such details never stopped you before, did they?" He shook his head, "You're a pioneer, Carolyn. You've broken new trails at the Res and the group home. Maybe it's time for you to go to LBI and teach the folks out there a thing or two."

I told him, "I'd like the dubious distinction of being the first imbecile to attend LBI." He looked puzzled, so I explained the long-standing joke that Mom and I had. All my life, whenever I achieved some new milestone, Mom and I would laughingly recall the assessment the doctor gave at my birth. So I was "the first imbecile to finish high school," the "the first imbecile to graduate from community college," and so on. By the time I finished my explanation, Pastor Larson was laughing so hard that tears ran down his face.

When he regained enough composure to speak, he said, "At least when they ask me for a character reference, I can honestly tell them you're a character." He said I needed to be sure to take my sense of humor with me to LBI to help teach others to see the absurdity of life.

Deciding that I wanted to go to LBI and working out the details were two very different processes. It took a mountain of paperwork and months of arguing my cause to get permission for me, as a group-home resident, to live on campus at LBI for part of every week. But the group-home administrator fought the battle with me, and the DSHS agreed to make an exception in my case as long as I showed continuing progress and fulfilled all my responsibilities in the group-home program.

That hurdle overcome, I still had to be accepted at LBI. On a glorious yellow-and-gold September afternoon I met with the school's Community Life committee for an interview.

No one asked about my previous education or my reasons for wanting to come to LBI. Their questions were more practical in nature: Could I juggle the requirements of the group home and meet the school's academic requirements? What if I got sick—who'd be responsible for my medical care? What about my diet?

I answered every question as honestly as I could. I didn't know how well I could handle the double requirements of the group home and school, but I thought there came a time in everyone's life when he or she had to step out and take a risk. As for getting sick, most people get sick from time to time. When they do, they sometimes need help. And I'd be able to eat anything that could be mashed enough that I could keep it on my spoon.

The committee members laughed and concluded that since I didn't seem worried about my prospects of success, they would accept me in the same spirit that I accepted myself. I could begin at LBI in the winter quarter.

That fall, as I anxiously waited to begin this new adventure, I signed up for a series of adult forum classes held at my church. The classes were to be taught by Professor Josee Jordan, who also happened to be the director of the Christian Education Department at LBI.

Wearing a black suit, her black hair salted with gray, Professor Jordan struck me as a calm, very professional person. As she spoke, I could feel her interest and personal investment in what she taught.

We got acquainted after the first class. She showed a real fascination for my communicator. And when I told her that I planned to come to LBI as a student for the winter term, she said that she knew a little about my battle with the state to get permission. She admitted she had never considered the state regulations and bureaucracy as limiting the choices and lives of the disabled. I shared one of my pet peeves, giving a crash course on the ways the state and federal governments lump the physically and mentally disabled into one fruit basket. They always want to apply the same rules to every case. The only way to bend the rules to meet an individual's needs is to have the right person in the system on your side.

Professor Jordan seemed genuinely interested in the challenges I faced. I felt encouraged to have become acquainted with someone who might be one of my professors when I started school at LBI. I had no idea that she would become much more.

———————— • ————————

Late in the evening, when the halls of the Lutheran Bible Institute were deserted, I would often wheel myself into the magnificent chapel to pray. I prayed about my future. I also asked God to forgive me for being such a bad person and to help me control my anger, which had begun to surface during some recent confrontations with other residents of the group home.

The silence of the chapel seemed almost deafening at night—the only light an "eternal flame" hanging over the pure white altar. The place seemed so sacred that it was almost scary. I felt small and imperfect sitting before that splendid altar in my worn wheelchair, my tattered pink robe, and my scuffed-up shoes. I wondered if God in heaven sometimes looked down and turned to his Son to say, "I'm really disappointed in Carolyn. She causes so much trouble." Or did he say in understanding, "I know Carolyn really wants to please me even though she's made some terrible mistakes in her life and will make more. She's still my daughter. I love her, and I died for her."

I didn't share my problems at the group home with anyone at LBI. So I knew that the great encouragement I found in many little incidents was because God heard my prayers in the darkness of the chapel and answered them in the brilliant sunshine that smiled through the huge windows in the school halls.

I took my daily exercise walking up and down one of the big back halls with my walker. And I found encouragement in a worship banner hanging on the wall there. It boldly declared: "Fear not, for I am your God."

While wobbling down that same hall, I often encountered Lucille, an LBI professor's wife who also happened to be Pastor Jim's mother. She always had something cheerful and positive to say. Her genuine friendliness always affirmed me—saying that she saw me as someone worthy of her time and interest. We never talked much, but each time we met in the hall it was as if God poured fresh new wine into my tired and discouraged wineskin.

Each morning at LBI we had chapel. A creature of habit, I always sat in the same place. Josee Jordan, the professor I'd met at my church the previous fall, usually sat beside me and helped me turn to the hymns so that I could find them before the final verse.

We talked for a few minutes before and after chapel. Josee (she asked me to call her this) was always concerned about my dorm situation. "Are you warm enough at night? If you need the heat turned up, just ask the resident assistant. If you need anything else while on campus during the week, just ask me." She'd discovered early on that when I got cold, I stayed cold for hours. So whenever it seemed cool in chapel, she would take off her suit jacket and drape it over my shoulders. When I asked how she would stay warm, she just laughed and said that she was warm-blooded and well-insulated.

As the days and weeks rolled by, Josee asked more and more questions about me. "Where is your family? Why are you all alone here in Seattle? What is the hardest thing for you to deal with about being disabled?" I wanted to answer honestly but was afraid to say too much. What if she found out what I was really like and was disappointed? Could I really trust her?

Sometimes she stopped herself in the middle of a question and gave me an out: "If I'm being too personal and you don't want to answer, don't. I don't mean to pry."

As time passed, it seemed that Josee was always there, combing my hair, fixing my collar, putting my books in the wheelchair bag. She really seemed to care for me. I didn't think it was an act.

I decided that maybe I should ask Pastor B, one of my favorite professors at LBI, about Josee. I had no reason not to trust him. Pastor B was a bald-faced truth-teller. But before I approached him, he came to me after class to say, "I had dinner with Josee Jordan last night. You came up in our conversation, and she said she has come to love you dearly. Josee's a special person. You're a very lucky woman to have a friend like her." My question was answered without my even asking.

If she really did love me, I wanted to love her. And I began answering her questions. I also teased her by complaining, "Honestly, Josee, you ask more questions than a Tennessee lawyer!"

She would then back off and apologize, but she said, "I just want to know you and what you go through."

After a few months we began eating most of our lunches together in the school cafeteria. She later admitted that it was hard for her to eat with me at first. My lack of coordination, the need to mash all my food together, and my difficulty swallowing, often results in an unappetizing mess. "Finally the Lord had to get stern with me," she admitted.

I was honored that she felt she could be so honest with me.

Eating with Josee, I discovered that she wasn't perfect either. She was an unrepentant cookie-snatcher. A permanent sign over the cafeteria buffet always said, "ONE COOKIE APIECE." Somehow I always ended up with several in my book bag after every meal with Josee. She insisted that she was simply worried that I would blow away if I didn't put on some weight. No amount of scolding did any good.

"What if you got caught? You of all people. What kind of example would you be? Or what if I get caught? You steal them, but they always end up in my bag."

She smiled and said very innocently, "I'll just tell them you got up out of your wheelchair, walked over, and snatched a handful!" When I responded indignantly, she insisted it really was my fault—she never did anything like that until she started hanging around me.

But you had only to see Josee's office to realize she had a very broad fun-loving streak. Among all the serious artwork and texts on her huge bookcase were a number of toys and dolls. A Kermit-the-Frog phone sat on her desk. Prominently perched on the top shelf of her bookcase was a toy mouse dressed like a granny complete with a shawl and a straw hat.

One morning after chapel we were talking. I was using my communicator as usual when she looked me straight in the eye and said, "Your communicator is getting in the way of my knowing you. I want to hear your voice." I lifted my arms so that she could remove my wheelchair tray. She leaned it against the communion rail and sat down to talk—really talk, with me.

That morning we began a wonderful journey of understanding. Josee proved as good a student as she was a teacher. She quickly learned my speech patterns and my vocal idiosyncracies. When we get stuck on a word, she could often guess it if I gave her the first letter. The fact she wanted to understand me and hear my voice made me love her that much more.

I insisted that turnabout was fair play and made her tell me all about herself as well. The more I learned, the more I respected and loved her.

———————•———————

Despite the dreams I'd nurtured for years, I still wondered whether or not I could ever be a non-institutionalized person. I'd been like an undecided caterpillar, wondering whether I really wanted to shed my cocoon.

My experience at LBI was giving me new hope—not just my friendship with Josee and my positive interaction with other professors, but my exposure to fellow students. One amusing incident in particular encouraged me.

One day in Apologetics, the professor, Pastor B, asked a thorny theological questions. Dead silence filled the room as we tried to decipher the question and then consider the answer. After a few minutes, I took the risk and typed out the answer on my communicator.

Pastor B was thoroughly delighted with my answer and he let the class know it. I groaned silently inside, wondering what my classmates must be thinking about the special attention he was giving me.

I found out in the hallway right after class when a number of students ambushed me. "We've had enough of your smart answers, Carolyn," one of them said. "And we certainly know who was the teacher's pet from the beginning."

Someone else spoke up: "Take away her fancy tray and her communicator and let's see how smart she is without her words." "Good idea." Off came my tray and everyone laughed. "Hey," said the boy who now had my communicator. "I never fought like this before. It's easy. All we have to do is take her tray away and we don't have to listen to her anymore."

I finally convinced them to give back my tray so I could defend myself. "I'm not responsible for Pastor B's praise," I said. "I bet if any one of you had answered his question, he would have reacted the same way. That's just the way he is. And I'm not the teacher's pet. It's just the circumstances, and I can't control them."

In a final plea I added, "I'm twenty years older than you guys; I can't help it if I knew the right answer. But I agree with you that Pastor B does make too big a fuss over me."

With that my classmates laughed and told me they'd let it go this one time. But if it happened again they'd hide my tray.

I agreed to their terms and felt honored that they'd felt free to tease me and try to take me down a peg. They not only accepted me, but they accepted my disability as a fact of life and playfully let me know they didn't think I ought to have special treatment because of it.

That incident, as much as anything that had happened at LBI, said to me I could make it out in the real world. People could get beyond my limitations and see me for the person I was.

But did I want anyone to see the real me?

Chapter 30

Foundation of My Dreams

At school I was a new Carolyn Martin, aspiring Christian writer, recognized and respected by professors and fellow students alike for my determination to pursue worthy goals. At the group home, despite the progress I made in learning a broad variety of living skills, I was the same old Carolyn Martin—desperate for peace and privacy in the middle of a chaotic institutional system. Too often I was frustrated and angry, much of the time falling discouragingly short of being an exemplary Christian.

The biggest problem was my relationship with my new roommate. When Diedra, my first roommate, left to get married, I enjoyed a month of splendid solitude living alone. What luxury! Then came Jennifer. I knew her from my last few years back at Sea Ridge. She was about my age. A case of childhood polio had left her with a useless right arm and a severe limp. More recently she had developed diabetes. For a long time she lived at the nursing home with an older woman named Amy, who was emotionally rigid and very dependent on Jennifer to help care for her. The two had been inseparable and fed off each other's negativity. They viewed their problems as worse than everyone else's. When they weren't consumed by personal crises, it seemed they were worrying about some horrible event seen on the TV news.

I never tried to establish a friendship with either of them. But when I learned that Jennifer was moving to the group home and would be my new roommate, I vowed to give her the benefit of the doubt. It did not prove to be easy.

Jennifer seemed to want me to be another Amy—someone emotionally and physically dependent on her. When I declined her help, she thought I was a snob. I wanted to be emotionally independent and expected her to carry her own mental baggage. I listen politely when she got upset. But when I refused to get upset with her and resumed my own tasks or tried to read, she was hurt and angry. It seemed that she expected me to be available to her every waking minute.

Another issue we struggled with was privacy. I wanted privacy; she never even wanted our door shut and seemed threatened whenever I closed it.

Along with her disabilities, it seemed to me that Jennifer had an even more crippling attitude. Once in a residents' meeting she said, "Since I have diabetes, I don't think I should have to do everything everyone else does around here. You guys need to know that if you upset me, I could go into a coma and die."

When Jennifer began counseling with her minister, I hoped it would help, but I never saw any evidence that counseling did any good. She evidently spent most of her sessions telling him what a terrible person I was to get along with. After each session she would tell me, "My minister said that you need a psychiatrist, because you're so mean to me."

I got ragingly angry with Jennifer when she spent two hours on my phone, sitting in my favorite rocking chair talking to everyone in her church about what a horrible person I was. While I could do nothing about her lies, I did demand that she get her own phone and her own chair.

Time and again I went to the staff to tell them I'd reached the end of my rope with Jennifer. Most of the time they were sympathetic, but there was no place else to put her. All the rooms were full. We were stuck with each other.

One of the oddest things about Jennifer was her speech. Whenever she was telling lies or spreading gossip, she had perfect syntax and coherent pronunciation. When she said anything remotely resembling the truth, she could no more say it straight than I could thread a needle.

Believe it or not, much of the time the other group-home people depended on me to translate for her because they couldn't understand her.

I felt guilty for not being able to get along with her. I'd studied psychology, was going to a Bible institute where people treated me like an inspiring Christian example, and I couldn't even stand my own roommate.

One day I looked out the window and spotted my friend Russell from the Res in a brand-new electric wheelchair. I knew that he had waited for that chair for more than two years. I squealed with happiness for his good fortune and jumped in my own chair to race out and give him a celebratory hug. I couldn't believe Jennifer's words as I headed out the door: "There you go again, leaving me all alone."

I stopped and told her, "Come with me then and let's tell Russell what a handsome devil he is in that jazzy new wheelchair."

"I can't go rushing around," Jennifer replied, "I might go into a coma."

I retorted, "Then stay in this house and rot. I'm out of here." By the time I reached the front sidewalk I could hear the poor crippled girl wailing for sympathy. I don't suspect that anyone gave her any.

I resented the fact that everyone expected me to deal with Jennifer along with everything else in my life. I hated the feelings of anger I felt toward her. I prayed for forgiveness and even demanded that God give me the grace to get along. I wasn't helping Jennifer or pleasing God.

I felt even worse when Jennifer started telling me that she wanted to kill herself. And when she did, she wanted me to know it would be my fault because of the way I treated her. At that point I fought back, telling her, "If you think I'm buying into your little pity party, forget it. No one gets special treatment around here just because they're disabled. We all have our own problems. What makes me furious is that you won't even give yourself a chance.

"Furthermore, when and if you ever commit suicide, do it in the shower where it will be easier to hose the mess down the drain!"

I was so angry that my words were even more distorted than usual. One of the aides helped translate my tirade. Predictably, Jennifer flew into a rage of her own and declared for the umpteenth time that she was going to kill herself. I snapped back, "Then hurry up and do it! I hate hearing about something again and again and never seeing it done!"

Nothing seemed to help me with Jennifer. Not all my prayers and Bible reading. Not my Bach tape, which usually lightened my darkest spirits. I just wanted a separate space for my bed where I could curl up in private and weep until I felt better. But I didn't have that luxury.

That next weekend, while Jennifer was gone, I decided that maybe if I swept the floor and washed the dishes I could work myself into a better mood. As I put the dishes into the sudsy hot water, I noticed a butcher knife lying on the counter. I stared at it for the longest time, thinking through the movements I'd have to make and wondering if I really had the strength and coordination to kill myself with that knife. If I was going to do it, I wanted to make sure that I succeeded.

Before I made up my mind, I had another thought. I obviously deserved to be punished. But there was another way. I dumped all my writings out of my drawers and boxes and onto my bed. I stared at that pile of papers for a long time. Every word I'd ever written was an extension of myself. They were everything I lived and worked for, my personal heritage of tears and pain. Destroying them would be the most effective way possible to destroy myself.

I picked up one of the pages, ripped it to shreds, and stuffed it in a garbage bag. It seemed as painful as sawing my wrists. I cried as I reached for another page. Then I realized that this wasn't what I wanted to do. The Lord reminded me that everything I'd written had been the foundation of my dreams. They were the dreams he had given me. Here I was letting some unfortunate circumstances threaten to destroy everything I'd worked toward for almost forty years.

I carefully returned all my papers to their proper places. I retrieved the torn page from the trash. I laughed when I realized that it was a fourth draft of a draft. I marveled that I could have been despondent one moment and laughing at myself the next. I didn't understand it, but I knew that I wanted to live. I wanted to keep writing.

———————— • ————————

Pastor Jim came to visit me the next week. I told him the whole story—from my conflict with Jennifer to my thoughts of suicide and my thwarted plan to destroy my writing. He told me he thought that I'd done the right thing in calling Jennifer's bluff. "You can't allow her to ruin your life."

I knew that. "But what if she does go into a coma and dies or gets so angry at me that she kills herself?"

He straightened himself in his chair and gravely said, "What she does is her responsibility, not yours. It would be tragic, but God has given her a free will. She chooses to deal with her anger and pain in that way. You chose to stop and listen to God at your lowest point. Jennifer can, too."

I didn't know how long I could continue living with someone who kept me so emotionally worked up. Pastor Jim promised to come and see me whenever I needed him. And he advised me to keep writing through this ordeal, because he believed that my best work might come out of my tears and pain. He kept me aimed toward my dream.

Things got better with Jennifer for a few months until one weekend she invited her former roommate, Amy, for a visit. Though they talked right in front of me as if I were deaf, I tried to ignore their constant dialogue about what a terrible person I'd been for the past twenty years.

I had just about reached the breaking point as we all sat around the dining table sharing a snack when Amy said, "Oh, well. You know how Carolyn is. She's always been mean and snobbish."

Though I fought for emotional control, Jennifer seemed to sense I was seething inside. She lit the fuse with her worn-out threat, "If you get angry with me, I'm telling my minister. He says you need a psychiatrist."

I exploded and threw my heavy rubber spoon at Jennifer. Amazingly, in a fluke that shocked me even more than it surprised her, that spoon actually hit her on the hand. Usually when I try to throw something it ends up behind my chair, sailing opposite the direction I want to throw.

Jennifer retaliated by throwing hot coffee all over me and threatening to go into a diabetic coma and die. By this time Amy had gone ballistic, kicking and screaming and beating the air. To add to the horror of the moment, the other residents in the room howled in laughter at the whole sordid business.

An aide rushed in to break up the fight. While she shooed the cheering section out of the room, I fled to the back of the house, where I wept until I was too exhausted to cry anymore. *Why couldn't I be the person I wanted to be? Why couldn't I ever control my anger?*

When the aide finally came to me, she said, "Hey, sweet lady. Don't be so hard on yourself. That brawl was long overdue. And I'm going to come tomorrow on my day off and make sure you finally get a fair deal."

Arrangements were made at the beginning of the week for Jennifer to move into one of the private rooms and to move that woman into a room with me. When Pastor Jim came for his next weekly visit, I had much to tell him. He smiled at my account of the fight and said, "I told you she wouldn't die if you stood up to her." When I told him how guilty I felt about my anger, he encouraged me by saying, "Sometimes we have to break before the healing can begin." He reminded me that God understood my anger and still loved me.

A few weeks later it became clear to everyone that Jennifer needed a more structured program than the group home could offer. When she transferred out, I couldn't help feeling a little guilty. I thought, *Maybe she wouldn't have failed if I hadn't failed her and failed God by letting my anger destroy any hope for a positive relationship.*

Chapter 31

One Naked Soul

One of the men in my church decided to attend LBI the fall of my second year. We commuted together every day and I didn't have my own dorm room. The new arrangement allowed more flexibility in my course selection—I could now take five-day-a-week courses—and earn more credits. But that proved more of a drawback than an advantage. I got home every night, exhausted from the trip but with two or three hours of homework and all my daily group-home chores to do.

By the midpoint of the first quarter I had fallen behind in all my classes. Josee saw what was going on and confronted me: "I know you're exhausted. But if your grades get any worse you'll have to go on academic probation. I know you can do the work, but you are going to have to get caught up."

When I got back to the group home, I made a deal with my new aide, Robin. I told him that if I could have the next Saturday and Sunday to concentrate completely on my schoolwork, I'd catch up with my chores the following week. Thoughts of Josee and her faith in me kept me working the entire weekend.

Monday morning I was all smiles and ready to beat out a victory tune on my tray. I couldn't wait to tell Josee, "I got it all done" and receive a big wonderful bear hug from her. But as Josee walked into class and I slipped my bag off the wheelchair, the lack of weight told me that something was dreadfully wrong. I looked inside. Nothing. My homework was gone. I looked again. Except for a few used Kleenexes, the bag was empty.

I pounded my fist on my tray and began to cry. When Josee rushed over to learn what was wrong I showed her the empty bag and told her "I lost all my homework."

Josee groaned. "Oh, sweetie, no! Maybe you left it at the home. It's okay to be angry. But right now I need you to stay calm. When we're finished with class, we'll figure out what to do." She had affirmed my feelings of anger, but she stayed so calm herself that I was able to check my emotions and avoid one of my long, uncontrollable bouts of tears. I had achieved an inch of restraint, but it felt like a miracle. *I could control my emotions.*

I never did find that homework, but I was able to recopy my first drafts and had to completely redo only a few questions. So what seemed like a tragedy at the time motivated me to break my lifelong habits of sloppiness. Robin helped me get my assignments organized by purchasing a zippered notebook and tying a shoelace into a loop so that I could open and close it. Slowly I began to catch up and saw my grades begin to rise.

———— • ————

On the last weekend of October a number of group-home residents took a Saturday outing to Bainbridge Island to enjoy the woods one last time before cold weather arrived. I spent much of the day searching out lonely trails where I could park my electric wheelchair and sit alone to think as I gazed out over Puget Sound, which wore a thick coat of fog and looked magnificently mysterious. Once again I felt a kinship with the sea—knowing my own existence, at least the existence of my true self, also remained shrouded from everyone around me.

I dozed off on the long ferry and van ride back home. When it was time to unload in the group-home parking lot, I backed my wheelchair onto the lift just as I'd done hundreds of times before. But someone had misjudged or gotten distracted because the lift wasn't there yet. I toppled backward out of the van. My chair, with me strapped in it, crashed to the cement below.

The blow knocked me unconscious. When I came to, Robin was checking me for broken bones. Finding none, he picked me up in his arms, carried me gently to bed, and gave me two aspirin to dull the pain of my bruises. He asked if I remembered calling for Josee while I'd been lying on the ground. I told him, no. He said that it was a spontaneous reaction for someone in shock to call out for the one person they felt was emotionally nearest to them. I thought about his comment that evening as I tried to ignore the pain and fall asleep.

The next morning my shoulder and back hurt so much I skipped church and slept till mid-afternoon. I got up and tried to call Josee and tell her what had happened, finally reaching her early in the evening. Since this was the first time I'd ever called her, I wasn't sure she'd be able to understand me over the phone. But she did. I felt better just talking to her.

Her last bit of advice was to go back to bed. And since I insisted that I'd be coming to school the next day, she made me promise to come see her the first thing in the morning.

She was waiting in the front lobby with a pocketful of aspirin when I arrived at LBI. She told me that she didn't like the way I looked, or sounded, and questioned whether I could make it through the day. After I promised to get a nap during lunchtime, she assigned students to push me to all my classes. When I protested, she said that she was worried that I'd make my neck worse if I had to jerk it around to push my own wheelchair. So I gave up. It's useless to argue with a saint.

When we had a few minutes to talk later in the day, she quizzed me about the accident. She seemed upset that the staff hadn't been watching more attentively. I tried to defend them, but Josee angrily insisted, "They should have been more careful with you!"

The intensity of Josee's feelings surprised me. I realized how much she cared about me. I started thinking, *If she cares so much about this fall out of the van, maybe she'd still care if I told about my emotional struggles with my anger and maybe even that terrible secret that caused me to fall in my own eyes.*

I knew by now that Josee was no "cookie-cutter Christian"—she used a biblical perspective and common sense to think for herself. She'd never been anything but open and accepting toward me. Surely if I shared my anger and my pain with her, she'd be neither ashamed nor disappointed.

I made up my mind. The time had come.

Later that week I asked Josee if I could talk to her. She promised to meet me in the lobby of the dorm as soon as she checked her mailbox. We moved to a corner where no one could overhear us. I didn't know how to start until Josee said, "I can feel you're upset."

I told her, "My aide, Robin, suggested I talk to you." But Robin knew nothing about what I really needed to talk about. Seeing my struggle to compose my thoughts, Josee very calmly said, "Why don't you try to tell me what it is you're upset about?"

I tried to speak, to say what I'd been afraid to tell anyone for so long, but the words had rusted in my heart. I couldn't seem to get them up and out of my mouth.

Josee sensed my distress and took my hand. "If it takes all day, I'll sit here and listen. So take your time." I tried to talk again, but my emotions tangled my already muddled words. I resorted to gestures and pointed at the private portion of my body.

"Were you sexually abused?" Josee asked.

I nodded.

"Recently?" I shook my head.

"When you were younger?" I nodded. "By your father?"

I quickly shook my head.

"By whom?"

I pointed at myself again and then made the sign for a church from the old children's rhyme, "Here is the church, here is its steeple, . . ." by putting my hands together and making a steeple with my two index fingers.

I saw the understanding and the anger in Josee's eyes. "A minister?"

I nodded.

"Where? In Alaska?"

I nodded once more. The key had turned. My box was open and the dark truth I had hidden was exposed to the light. I could feel its hold on my soul begin to loosen, like an anchor pulling free. The words, too, began to loosen, and I could now begin to speak.

I told Josee how ashamed and disappointed I was in myself. I confessed that I sometimes worried that my anger would destroy me. And that after my bouts of anger I would cry uncontrollably for hours because I felt so guilty, so trapped, so alone.

Suddenly I began to weep with relief and exhaustion from the effort to drag all these words out of the depths of my soul. As Josee held me, my tears and spittle ran all over her black skirt and made a terrible mess. She didn't seem to care about that because she wouldn't let go. She just held me and said softly, "Oh, sweetheart. I always knew you had a lot of pain inside and I sometimes pried too deep. But I'm so glad you trusted me this far."

She told me it was okay to cry. So I did. This time I didn't feel guilty, because I knew I'd finally reached a turning point in my life.

———————— • ————————

Josee convinced me that I needed to get professional help to deal with the emotional ramifications of my abuse. But I didn't want to go through the state system and have the painful details of my case exposed to people I didn't trust. So Josee found a Christian psychologist, and Pastor Jim paid for my sessions out of his congregation's emergency fund.

I liked my counselor from the start. Vickie was a profound and wise woman with a deep faith in God. She groaned out loud as she read the letter I wrote to her describing my rape and my reactions to the experience. I admitted that I had always blamed myself for letting the minister do what he did to me.

Vickie helped me understand that I had been both physically and emotionally helpless to resist his power. She judged my emotional maturity at about that of a six-year-old at the time of the abuse. I felt ugly and unloved, and the man made me feel pretty and desirable in order to take advantage of me for his own pleasure.

At last I understood. The abuse wasn't my fault.

But this new revelation spawned new feelings of anger—at the minister for what he did to me, and toward myself for all the suffering I had put myself through, and for hiding the truth and deceiving myself and everyone else for so many years.

Vickie and I talked a lot about anger, about the rape, but also about how angry I got, feeling trapped in my own body, and how my anger had become a trap of its own. I told her how I always wanted so desperately to be loved but felt unlovable as a child because I could never control my anger. I used to plead with God to let me be a good girl. My tantrums would set my parents off into their own tantrum-like arguments. These made me feel ugly and unlovable all over again for being so bad.

I confessed to Vickie that I believed my anger was more of a handicap than my cerebral palsy. I always managed to find ways to outsmart my physical disability, but I seemed hopelessly addicted to my anger and had no tools for beating it.

Vickie slowly taught me over the next three years that I did have the tools to begin coping with both my anger and my guilt. She taught me to forgive myself and allow myself to be angry in the presence of God—to honestly show him all my pain.

God wants truth. He is truth. There is nothing he wants us to cover up. And when I've exposed everything, when I've vented all my anger, God is still there. And he still loves me just the same. I didn't have to pretend anymore.

As I learned to be honest with God about who I really am, I began to find it easier to be honest with myself and with others.

———— • ————

By the end of my second year at LBI I began to see myself in a new way. I'd never before experienced close, meaningful relationships with peers who were not disabled. At LBI those friendships grew. Just as important, I proved to myself that I could get along outside a special facility. After so many years in homes for the disabled, this fact struck me with a powerful force.

Near the end of that school year I was asked to speak to my fellow students in chapel. I was to tell them about my life and all that I'd learned through the years of my personal pilgrimage. I selected this passage for my Bible text: "But we have this treasure in jars of clay to show that this all-surpassing power is from God and not from us. We are hardpressed on every side, but not crushed; perplexed, but not in despair; struck down, but not destroyed. We always carry around in our body the death of Jesus, so that the life of Jesus may also be revealed in our body" (2 Cor. 4:7–11).

I'd written out my chapel address. Josee read it for me in her strong, clear voice as I sat beside her on the platform.

It seemed strange at first, hearing my own words spoken so well and with such strength by another voice. Then I realized that God had given me a voice at last. Through my writing I could get around the weaknesses of my own body, the jar of clay that Paul wrote about.

Now I knew for sure that my life had meaning and worth.

Chapter 32

The Sparrow Has Found Her Nest

It was a cold and windy winter day when the UCP broke ground for a small complex of apartments just off the Burke-Gilman trail in North Seattle's Hawthorne Hills community. This was the third and final stage of UCP's long-term master plan that began with the building of the Res, next the group home, and now a cluster of independent-living apartments.

The blueprints called for each apartment to contain a living room; a kitchen with lowered, wheelchair-accessible counters, sinks, and appliances; a bathroom off the front hall; and one, huge, double-sized bedroom divided by a two-sided wardrobe.

Months shuffled past. The UCP apartments were well on their way to completion. Anyone, married or single, who did not need a twenty-four-hour attendant could rent one of the new apartments. I immediately signed up for an apartment. The director of the Res, who also supervised the new Burke-Gilman project, said that I could have first pick of the units.

I spent the next few weeks planning what I needed to furnish my own apartment. My old vision of what I wanted my home to look like came back. Candles on the table, lots of baskets sitting around, plenty of bookshelves with room for my antique dolls, and Gaga's antique mirror sitting on a pink dresser scarf.

But practical considerations had to come first. I needed a bed, a table and chairs, and living-room furniture. I collected some of what I needed from things donated to the group home. Pastor Jim rounded up a kitchen table and chairs. Robin gave me a mattress and frame. Other friends gave me furniture they'd stored away for years. I couldn't believe how quickly everything came together. All my friends wanted to share my joy.

The first day of June 1982 descended like a butterfly. This was the morning I would pick out my new home. Some of the group-home staff went with me to the nearly completed project, teasing me all the way about "finally getting rid of the old lady." One of them suggested that I consider the unit in the corner of the complex. It was nestled back in the trees and had room for a small flower garden in the front. She was right. I thought it looked like it was waiting for me to move in.

Something about the entrance at the front of the apartment cluster reminded me of that tiny beach cottage Gaga and I shared so long ago. The units were all connected, each with its own front door opening onto a small, fenced courtyard. The back of the corner unit sat near the edge of a wooded ravine, a green urban oasis of trees, bushes and under-brush, which was home (I would later learn) to a wonderful variety of birds and countless thieving squirrels who would attempt to eat them-selves into oblivion while swinging on a bird feeder, and a raccoon fam-ily that occasionally waddled across the backyard.

I opened the door of the corner unit and went in. Everything looked and smelled brand-new. The layout seemed perfect for one per-son in a wheelchair. The walls were carpeted up to the baseboards. All the corners were mitered to withstand bumps from wild electric wheel-chairs. The bathroom felt roomy, the kitchen and living room appeared to be a scaled-down version of the group home, with a broom-and-coat closet added in the front hall. The huge, divided bedroom made a won-derful combination bedroom, library, and office.

I opened the living-room curtains and looked out toward the ravine. Just outside the window stood an old cottonwood tree with a large gash running diagonally across its trunk. Its bark had been torn away leaving a patch of exposed wood roughly the shape of Africa. I fell in love with that tree immediately. It was scarred but still beautiful, marred but determined to stay green and live.

My apartment decision was made. In the days that followed, Robin and I made several trips to the surrounding area to acquaint me with my new community. And of course we always stopped to check on the building progress at the apartments. Every time I saw my apartment's green roof and rough board siding, I thought I remembered seeing this same "little house" somewhere before. *But where?* I kept ransacking my memory.

Robin told me that I was probably confusing it with the beach house I lived in with Gaga in Santa Cruz. While the front of the apartments did remind me of that old cottage, it had been painted white with an outhouse behind it. But I knew I'd seen an exact replica of my UCP unit somewhere years before.

I was stumped. Robin laughed and said that it would probably dawn on me sooner or later.

The day before my scheduled move, it hit me: I had seen this apartment in a dream I had had at the nursing home almost twenty years before. I'd put Donna down for a nap on a rainy Saturday afternoon. Then I wrapped up in a blanket and sat reading a book in my rocker when I dozed off. While sleeping, I dreamed about this little house with woods around it and flowers in front. In the dream I approached the front door and heard someone telling me to go in but thought it would be rude because whoever lived there was undoubtedly working and would want privacy. But oh, how I wanted a home just like that. It was just my size and had the most wonderful old trees around it. When I awakened from that dream, it was so vivid that I knew this was the home I wanted. But, I told myself, it was just a dream, and I tried to forget it.

I told Robin about the dream. He agreed with me that life is sometimes stranger than fiction.

The next day, I entertained my first visitors, my old Res aide and friend Jeannie, who had brought along Nancy and Joe, a married couple I'd known from my days at the nursing home. They were now going to be my neighbors when they moved into the next-door apartment.

Jeannie had told me that they'd be coming, and she expected toast and coffee when they arrived. Since I didn't drink coffee, I told her that I thought she'd better fix her own. But I'd promised to see to the toast. The trouble was, the electrical outlets in my apartment were still so stiff and new that I couldn't get the toaster plugged in. I had to wait till my company arrived to ask Jeannie for help.

She launched into one of her fake tirades and complained, "Buy you books, send you off to college, and you can't even plug in the toaster." And then in mock frustration she looked toward heaven to say, "Oh, please, Jesus, come and take me home."

I laughed and felt grateful to know that as soon as the paperwork was cleared with the state, Jeannie would be my aide, coming to the apartment three days a week to spend a couple of hours fixing meals ahead and doing routine chores I needed help with. The state, of course, had an illogical system that required that I be dismissed from the group home for two weeks before I was eligible for the chore-service program. So I was going to be totally on my own the first two weeks.

Before I knew it, my birthday arrived. I told all my friends not to worry about presents. Now that God had given me the home of my dreams, I couldn't imagine needing anything else. But I received a special bonus when Josee, who'd been out of town on moving day, showed up to spend the entire day with me.

She loved my new home and made the exact same assessment other friends had made: "Your apartment is just your size!" Was I an elf who needed everything just my size? Josee laughed off my protests and told me she thought, that like an elf, I looked right at home with woods all around me.

She hung pictures on the walls for me, drove me around my new neighborhood, shared a special birthday cake with a few of my neighbors, and together we planned a big, proper party celebrating my new home. I asked Pastor Jim to preside over a special dedication service. He said that he'd be honored. I told Josee that I wanted to invite everyone I could contact who'd ever been a part of my life—from my days at Sea Ridge to my new acquaintances from the church I'd just begun attending a few blocks from my apartment.

"I sure hope it's a nice day," Josee replied. "We'll never get all your friends into your apartment!"

Sure enough, on the eve of the party we had a glorious thunderstorm. The only way I could get to sleep was to turn on so many lights I couldn't see the lightning flashes through the curtains. I felt certain that it was going to rain on my party.

But the morning dawned bright and clear, with fresh colors and scents celebrating the victory of life. The earth had taken a shower and donned her prettiest party dress. Inspired by her example, I did the same.

Josee and Pastor B's wife (from LBI) arrived to make ready for the party with punch and piles of homemade goodies. By mid-afternoon a crowd of guests had arrived loaded down with love and laughter. Iola, Ruth, and Dorothy were there along with friends from LBI and from the churches I'd attended.

When the time came, Josee began the actual service by inviting everyone to tell how their lives became intertwined with mine. John, the fun-loving man who had started the lay ministry at the Res, began by telling how we met in the hall my first day at the Res. He concluded by saying that he and his wife, Mary, "fell in love with her funny face and didn't want to let her go."

Pastor Jim grinned as he remembered, "It was Iola and Ruth who roped me in with Carolyn because they didn't know what to do with her."

When all my friends were thus introduced and understood each other's connection with me, Pastor Jim continued the service by reading Psalm 84, the same psalm I had sung at my high school graduation: "The sparrow has found her nest where she may lay her young."

Didn't Jesus say that two sparrows might be sold for a penny, but not one of them ever falls to the ground without the notice of the everlasting, all-powerful God? And we are more valuable than these tiny birds. God is not just the Lord of the powerful. He's also the Lord of the sparrow, and he provides her a home where she can nurture and bring up her dreams.

Pastor Jim concluded by offering a blessing on my new home and my continued work in it. Then we all held hands to sing "Bless This House."

I thanked everyone for coming. Then I thanked God for all my friends and prayed that I'd one day be able to give each of them a small fraction of what they'd given me.

After the party, with my friends all gone home, the apartment seemed especially quiet, but outside I could hear birds chirping a joyful chorus.

All my life I'd longed for a home where I could feel that I belonged. Now I had finally found a place of my own.

Just before I dozed off in my rocker, I remember thinking: *I still have many miles to go. But I'll get there—an inch at a time. And when I wake up, I'll type out a new list of dreams.*

Epilogue

A decade has passed since I moved into my own apartment. I still live here. And I'm working hard on that list of new dreams.

I've nearly completed all the requirements for my four-year degree from Lutheran Bible Institute. And by the time this book comes off the presses, I'll be moving full-speed-ahead on one of several more book ideas.

Of course, full-speed-ahead for me is an inch at a time. Yet I've made great progress over recent years in many areas of my life. My crusty old friend Jeannie still comes by two or three times a week to help with a few of the difficult chores. And she prepares meals ahead so that I can simply pull a plastic container out of my freezer, pop it in my microwave, and get a hot, nourishing meal when I don't have the time or energy to fix something for myself. Other people regularly volunteer transportation. Josee still frets and keeps close tabs on me. And many additional friends call or drop by from time to time to watch out for my needs. After so many years trapped in the impersonal routine of various institutions, I'm grateful every day for the measure of independence I now have to control my own life.

Physically, I'm in worse shape than ever. A lifetime of unnatural body movements—from the awkward "Carolyn wobble" to the constant bobbing of my head on my bungee-cord neck—has wreaked havoc on my spinal column. The result is even more limited mobility and constant pain that sometimes grows so excruciating that I can't sleep at night.

There seem to be more and more days when my heart and mind say, "Let's go," and my body screams, "Oh no you don't!" Those are the days I have to declare, "Majority rules!" And I tell my body, "My heart and mind are going with me, so like it or not, you're coming, too."

I'm slowly learning to be realistic. I know that I won't ever be able to thread a needle, and I'll never climb mountains. But I'm willing to try just about anything in-between.

Progress is being made in allowing disabled people like me to achieve a greater degree of self-sufficiency. The American Disabilities Act that became federal law in 1992 was a big step in the right direction. But many hurdles remain.

One of the biggest frustrations I face can never be legislated away because it's rooted deep in people's attitudes. I'm constantly frustrated, not to mention embarrassed, by the need to establish and prove my intellectual capabilities to the people I encounter in everyday life. Until I somehow evidence my intelligence, I'm treated as if I'm mentally retarded or, worse yet, deemed unworthy of attention and completely ignored. Particularly galling are people who speak to the friends or helpers with me to find out about me or to comment on my plans or activities but never directly address me. When I see these same people stop to pet and talk to stray dogs, I get a pretty good idea where I stand in their eyes.

I still get angry toward society for its ignorance and prejudice against people with disabilities. For so long I was denied my basic human rights—the opportunity to be educated to the level of my ability and the opportunity to live in freedom and dignity. To have these basic rights, the disabled are often paraded like circus animals in front of telethon cameras and those individuals inclined to support organizations committed to helping the disabled. I want to scream, "*We're* part of a free and democratic society, too! Why can't we have the same control over our lives as the nonhandicapped do? Why do there have to be so many rules and regulations limiting our freedom of choice?"

I still sometimes get angry with God. Those feelings used to frighten me and trigger bouts of shame and guilt, but God has patiently taught me that anger is just one of the emotions he gave me. He is neither shocked nor threatened by it. Unlike my human parents whose emotional reactions to my rantings and my rage often exacerbated my own insecurities and guilt, my heavenly father is not so changeable or so vulnerable that he gets upset just because I'm upset with him. He is not a fragile God.

I have at times been so angry I've told God to "Go to hell!" But those feelings are tempered now by my understanding of the third stanza of the Apostles' Creed, which says, "He descended into Hell and on the third day He rose again from the dead and ascended into Heaven and is seated at the right hand of God. . . ." God already went to hell for us! He's been there and knows what it's like, just as he's been here and is here with us still. Knowing this helps turn my anger into thankfulness and praise.

So today when I get so angry I want to curse and scream at God, I often end up praying and crying and laughing—all at the same time. I find it wonderfully freeing to be emotionally naked and vulnerable before God. He is unshakable, merciful, and patient with me. He wants us all to turn to him with our anger rather than choose bitterness, self-destruction, and death.

There are times when I direct my anger at myself—especially when I get discouraged that I'm still not the kind of gentle, mature person I've always longed to be. But I'm learning an important lesson in this area as well.

For much of my life I told myself that God couldn't possibly love me until I became a more lovable, more acceptable person. I've now begun to understand that he loves me just the way I am. I've seen how my accepting and believing that love has slowly begun to change me and has helped me become more acceptable and lovable. For too long I made the mistake of thinking that I had to earn God's love by being a better person; and I always felt like a failure. I now understand that it's only in accepting his unconditional love that I can hope to find the grace and strength to become the kind of person he and I want me to be.

———— • ————

One day, watching a television program on the Discovery channel, I saw a picture of a bear with his leg caught in a trap. As I watched him struggle and fight and lash out angrily at the steel casing that shackled him, I experienced a flash of insight. I knew just how that bear felt. For more than thirty years I felt trapped. I fought to the point of exhaustion. I struggled and lashed out so violently that my efforts to escape often hurt more than they helped. My fight was so long and futile that I lived with a constant sense of overwhelming powerlessness. And I tried to deny that—as much as I tried to deny my limitations and my failures.

What I finally learned was this: It is only when I accept and admit my powerlessness that I'm finally free to experience God's strength working in me. It's what the apostle Paul told the Corinthians when he said, "When I am weak, then I am strong."

————— • —————

Admitting weakness requires me to admit that I'm far from perfect. And that is never more evident than in my relationships with others.

Just a few years ago I was crying about the unkind way I had behaved toward a neighbor, when my pastor dropped by for a visit. He stood by my chair as I cried and very calmly told me that it was okay just to be me. When I spelled out the details of my unpleasant encounter, he listened, then calmly told me it was still okay not to get along with everyone. His calmness and acceptance was a human channel for God's grace and acceptance. It spoke volumes to me, giving a peace I'd never known before in my relationships with others.

That positive healing experience pushed me to another depth of self-acceptance. Just a few days before this incident I'd been thinking about asking an artist friend to illustrate some of my essays in hopes that we could publish something together. But after Pastor Jon assured me that it is okay for me to be me, I saw another application for that truth. I thought, *If God wants me to be the person I am, then maybe I should feel free to draw the way I draw—like a three-year-old child.*

Many years ago I abandoned my love for art because I wanted what I drew to look grown-up, sophisticated, and mature. My decision to give up on my art was influenced by a college art teacher who let me know that she didn't think that drawing is my talent. I now realize that I was in the wrong class, using the wrong tools—hard-to-grip skinny pieces of charcoal and thin pencils.

After Pastor Jon's pep talk, I went to the store and bought *my* kind of art supplies—huge sheets of paper, big thick pencils, and wonderfully fat crayons. But even those supplies stayed in a bag for weeks while the lifelong perfectionist inside me thought through the steps I'd need to take to draw and plan the "perfect" patterns of my art. Finally an idea jumped into my head—I need to be an *im*perfectionist! I need to let my art celebrate the fact that I'm imperfect. I need to praise God for his wild and wonderful mercy wherein he takes me into his all-powerful arms along with all my anger, pain, joy, tears, and everything else that I am.

I chose a sentence from an article I wrote about my Pappy's recent death: "Growing is agonizing and glorious." I took my new crayons and drew a colorful basket of flowers under which I typed the sentence. I then studied the picture. It actually looked like a basket and flowers. Amazing!

As I regretfully recalled the reasons I gave up on art so many years before, sobering thoughts flooded my mind and spirit. *How much enjoyment have I missed out on because I wanted to be someone I wasn't? How often have I done myself a disservice by wanting to pretend to be less disabled than I am? How many opportunities have I lost to become the author of my dreams because I didn't want to write about the truth of my life experience, because I didn't want to be seen as disabled? How often in my search for meaning and significance have I tried to hide and deny my own true identity?*

As I've learned to admit my imperfections to myself, to others, and to God, I've begun to realize that I'm not nearly as different from other human beings as I feared. None of us is perfect. We're all handicapped by our own imperfections.

Now I see the truth: I have been far more handicapped by my humanity than I ever was by my disability. The good news is that God chose to meet our universal spiritual needs with his own Divine Disability Act. The all-powerful Creator handicapped himself to come to earth as a human so that he could endure our suffering, spring our personal traps of sin, and enable us to live freely forever as the whole and healthy individuals he wants us to be.

Not that I don't have doubts and questions. I'd like to ask God about why I've had to go through all that I have. But I've finally reached the point where I don't feel I have to know the answers. I can simply say to God, "I am your servant, if there's any meaning or message to be found in my disability, I want you to use it."

God never intended my disability to paralyze or cripple who I am. If I allow my imperfect body to stunt and deform what's inside me, then I become the cause of my own pain. But if I refuse to be defeated by my limitations, they will actually make me a stronger person. I get valuable exercise pushing against my disabilities every day, whether I'm trying to make a pot of tea or convincing a state social worker that I have the presence of mind to make my own decisions, thank you very much.

So I do not yet fully know the role that my disability will play in my life. Maybe I'll never know. But I do know that accepting that disability as a fact of my life was the turning point in my journey toward becoming everything God wants me to be.

Another important milestone in my journey was the recent conclusion of the darkest, most painful chapter of my story. I thought I had exorcised the last of those ghosts more than six years ago when the healing effects of time and professional therapy had strengthened me to the point that I wrote and actually sent a letter to the minister who had caused me so much pain. I told him that with God's help I was finally able to forgive him.

Mailing that letter proved therapeutic in itself. After years of pain, anger, and hatred, I found a surprising sense of release and freedom in the mere expression of forgiveness. I thought that episode was finished, but I was wrong.

Some months later I received a letter from the minister's wife, telling me that her husband had just died. She also said that when my letter arrived, she was so excited to hear from me that she ignored the fact that it was addressed only to him.

She opened it and read it. When her husband came home that evening, she confronted him with my letter. He denied ever touching me in a sexual way and forbade her to respond to my letter. Now she wanted to let me know that he had died and to apologize to me on his behalf for the pain I had been through. She chose to believe my letter. That in itself was a healing realization.

We exchanged several letters over the next few months. I was never sure why she wanted to maintain contact with me. Perhaps to salve her own conscience. Maybe she hoped to protect her husband's reputation by asking me never to tell anyone else what had happened. Possibly her motives were pure and she was reaching out in compassion and concern for me.

But her letters were never healing instruments. Each one seemed to rip through a layer of tender scar tissue to expose the raw emotion of my old wound. I finally wrote to her one last time, thanking her for the concern but asking that she not write again. I needed to put this pain behind me once and for all.

I placed the packet of our correspondence on a shelf in my back closet along with a collection of other things I hoped never to deal with again. Years passed. Then one winter morning I awoke with a holy sense that I needed to get those letters out of my house and destroy them. My first thought was to simply tear them up and scatter them in the ravine behind my apartment. But when I shared my intention with Nancy, who was helping me pull together all my writings for this book, she suggested the more symbolic act of burning the letters and letting the smoke rise to heaven as a sacrifice of my pain.

Nancy also suggested that Gregg, my coauthor, should have copies of the correspondence as background documentation for this book. So she took the letters home with her to make photocopies and to be obedient to my feeling that God wanted them out of my house.

On a magnificent Sunday morning a few weeks later, Nancy, Gregg, and I visited the church that Pastor Jim now serves. After the morning service, on the patio deck of his home, Pastor Jim placed the original letters in an old coffee can and lit them on fire. As the flames twisted the paper into ash, we sang the doxology, and Pastor Jim prayed. He thanked God for the privilege of trust I had given to him so many years before. Then he thanked the Lord for all the healing that had already taken place in my life and asked him to accept this burning as an act of praise and sacrifice and a further release of my old pain and brokenness.

When the flames died down, we all took a ferry ride. Standing at the rail of that ship, with my friends supporting me, I poured my old pain into the depths of Puget Sound. The ashes hit the water and were quickly swallowed in the ferry's foam and the powerful, silent, and seemingly indifferent waves of the sea.

Something sacred occurred on that ferry. My pain was washed away by God's deep and soothing sea of love for me. The burial ceremony of my most tortured, personal memories took only a few moments, and their scars continue to slowly fade and fall away.

When I was a child and for long into my adult years, in my nighttime dreams I had a perfectly normal body. I could walk and run and jump. And every awakening was a rude one as I faced again the harsh reality of life, trapped in a body twisted and limited by cerebral palsy.

But for the past few years, whenever I dream at night, I find myself in my wheelchair, with the very same limitations I have in real life. And yet now, when I awaken and struggle to maneuver my uncooperative body out of bed, I feel a sense of peace and freedom that I never thought possible.

I used to think that I wanted to be just like everyone else. I wasted many years and much energy trying to march in step with the rest of life's great parade. It's taken me forty-six years to accept the fact that I'll never be a great marcher. And that's okay.

———————•———————

Today, with God's help I can laugh and say, "I cannot walk—*so I'll learn to dance.*"